Praise for *Your Self-Confident Baby*

"Magda Gerber shows us how to raise healthy human beings. Her voice is clear and wise. *Your Self-Confident Baby* gets to the heart of what it takes to provide quality care to infants and toddlers."

—J. Ronald Lally, Ed.D.
Director of the Center for Child and Family Studies at WestEd

"A vital resource for new and expectant parents . . . timely, practical, easy-to-read, and informative. Grounded in the traditions of Resources for Infant Educarers and principles of child development, the book leaves no doubt that respect for infants is a key ingredient to successful parenting."

—Ed Greene, Ph.D.
Senior Associate, Families and Work Institute
Board Member, National Association for the Education of Young Children

"Magda Gerber shows parents the value of slowing down, not pushing their children, but observing the true wonder of their development and uniqueness. There is good advice on all aspects of childcare. You will learn to see your child with new eyes."

—Karen Miller
author of *Ages and Stages* and *Things to Do with Toddlers and Twos*

"I wish every new parent to have Magda Gerber's *Your Self-Confident Baby*. It is a treasure. It will promote your baby's well being and your own peace of mind."

—Laura Huxley
Founder and President of Children: Our Ultimate Investment

Your Self-Confident Baby

How to Encourage Your Child's Natural Abilities—from the Very Start

Magda Gerber
and
Allison Johnson

John Wiley & Sons, Inc.

New York • Chichester • Weinheim • Brisbane • Singapore • Toronto

Photo Credits:

Photographs on pages 1, 9, 135, 155, 163, 183, and 189 © by Debra Classen.

Photograph on page 21 © by Jude Keith Rose.

Photographs on pages 43, 75, and 177 © by Allison Johnson.

Photograph on page 89 © by Annina Arthur.

This text is printed on acid-free paper.

Published by John Wiley & Sons, Inc.

Library of Congress Cataloging-in-Publication Data

Gerber, Magda
Your self-confident baby : how to encourage your child's natural abilities—from the very start /
Magda Gerber and Allison Johnson
p. cm.
Includes bibliographical references and index.
ISBN 978-1-118-15879-1 (paper : alk. paper)
1. Infants. 2. Toddlers. 3. Parent and infant. 4. Child rearing. I. Johnson, Allison. II. Title.
HQ774.G47 1998
649'.122–dc21 97-18840
CIP

Printed in the United States of America

1 2 3

To my children, Mayo, Daisy, and Bence
My grandsons, Tony and Jason
My great-granddaughter, Bailey
And to the memory of my husband, Imre

—Magda

To my husband, William, for sharing the joyous and difficult journey of parenthood, and to my daughter, Juliana, for lighting the way

—Allison

Acknowledgments

Together we would like to thank:

Carol Pinto, Ruth Money, Polly Elam-Ferraro, and Liz Memel at RIE, and Ann Davidson. We are grateful to all the RIE parents and families. A special thanks to the children.

Thanks to Alison Picard, our agent; to Judith McCarthy, our editor at John Wiley & Sons; to her assistant Elaine O'Neal; and to John Simko in Wiley's production department.

Magda would like to thank:

With gratitude I think of the late Emmi Pikler, M.D., my children's pediatrician and my friend. Her ideas influenced my approach to children.

Thanks to Tom Forrest, M.D., who cofounded RIE and who trusted me to codirect the Demonstration Infant Program at the Children's Health Council in Palo Alto, California.

I would like to thank Carol Pinto, my friend and colleague, who helped me to establish the RIE Center in Los Angeles. She is a sensitive, talented, and insightful person whom I enjoy working with on an ongoing basis. I cannot imagine the last twenty-five years without her.

Allison would like to thank:

My mother, Marlene Livingston, and my father, Herman Groves, for their love, support, and guidance over the years.

I am grateful to Barbara DeMarco Barrett for encouraging me to write this book and for supporting my "voice." Also, thanks to my Thursday writers group.

Thanks to my family and close friends. You all know who you are.

A special thanks to Magda, who showed me how to see babies with "new eyes."

Contents

Introduction

I am a great-grandparent, but I remember clearly how I felt as a young mother of two small daughters—confused, uncertain, and at times, overwhelmed. Now, having worked with young children for the last fifty years, I have come to recognize a fundamental truth: the importance of respect in caring for children. This is why I founded Resources for Infant Educarers, or RIE (pronounced "wry"), an organization that helps parents and children from birth to twenty-four months learn to treat each other with respect.

What do I mean by respect? That's what this book is about.

If you treat your child respectfully from birth, he may have a better chance of gaining confidence and developing good judgment. This plants the seeds of lifelong security. He learns how to relate to other people in a healthy way and how to realistically, rather than blindly, trust the world.

Respect is a two-way street. Equally important, you as parents have needs, too. Being a parent is the most difficult undertaking in the world, a twenty-four-hour-a-day job that requires your time, patience, and energy whether you are sick or well, in a good mood or not. And the task is no easier as your child grows into adulthood. Often parents are left with residual guilt, feeling "If only I had done this in the beginning . . ."

My respectful approach helps to make parents' lives, in these first few challenging years, easier and more predictable through implementing consistent routines. I try to help parents simplify their lives and develop the ability to recognize when they should step in to influence their child's behavior and when to save their energy for larger issues. I would like parents to use some of that energy for nurturing themselves.

In this book I use the term "educarer." It is a word I coined—combining educator and carer. "Educarer" means one who educates children in a caring manner. And I prefer to use the word carer rather than caregiver or caretaker because a carer neither gives nor takes. For clarity's sake, I use the word "caregiving" when referring to an activity such as a "caregiving task" so that it won't be confused with "caring," which might be understood to simply mean loving.

A carer puts love into action. The way you care for your baby is how he experiences your love. Everyday caregiving routines, like feeding and diapering, can be educational and loving interactions. These everyday routines form the building blocks of educaring and respect.

Allowing infants to learn on their own rather than actively stimulating or teaching them is a basic RIE tenet. Children learn all the time, from the day they are born. If we refrain from teaching them, they learn from experience. What we need to do is not interfere, step back, and allow learning to happen. What young children need to learn is how to adapt to their families.

In my early motherhood in Hungary I was fortunate to meet a pediatrician, Dr. Emmi Pikler, who had a great influence on my life. I'd like to tell you the story.

One day my older daughter, Mayo, then six, was sick with a sore throat. Our regular pediatrician was ill so Mayo suggested I call a schoolmate's mother who was a doctor. In those days physicians made house calls, so Dr. Pikler came to our home to examine Mayo. When I opened my mouth to speak, Dr. Pikler waved her hand indicating for me to be silent. Then she asked my little girl when her throat started feeling sore and how she felt now. My child answered so intelligently, so politely that I was surprised. The doctor then asked Mayo if she wanted to "look in her (the doctor's) throat," and afterward she asked permission to look in Mayo's throat. "Open your mouth wide," she told my daughter, "and I won't have to use the tongue depressor." She then told Mayo to go to her room so she could talk alone with me.

The cooperation Dr. Pikler elicited was so striking that I decided to ask her to become our pediatrician. What struck a deeper chord was the realization that she related to children in a more honest, respectful manner than I'd ever seen. After meeting Dr. Pikler, I raised my third child, a son, from birth following her ideas.

This encounter was the beginning of a long, fruitful collaboration between Dr. Pikler and me. Inspired by her, I obtained a master's degree in early childhood education in Budapest. In 1945 I began to assist Dr. Pikler at the National Methodological Institute for Infant Care and Education, popularly called "Loczy" after the street on which it was located. Loczy was founded as an orphanage for healthy babies who had lost their parents due to death or illness during World War II. Since then, Loczy has become a worldwide model for quality infant care and education.

Dr. Pikler spoke directly to her young patients and listened to their responses, always telling them what she was going to do before she proceeded. She believed in treating all human beings, no matter how young, with respect. I remained in touch with Dr. Pikler over the next twenty-eight years. She directed Loczy until her death in 1984.

When the horrors of World War II ended, there was a new spirit of optimism in Hungary. Three years later, after the Communist takeover, Hungary was in political turmoil. My charmed life with my husband and our three children was suddenly interrupted. My husband was jailed as a political prisoner. Mayo was caught by the border patrol, trying to flee the country. Even though she was a teenager, she was imprisoned for almost a year. We were expelled from our comfortable home in Budapest and exiled to a tiny village. After the 1956 Hungarian revolution, our family sought sanctuary in Austria. In Vienna I worked as an interpreter at the American embassy until 1957, when we came to the United States.

Our arrival in America was a joyous time. We were placed at Camp Kilmer, a military base in New Jersey, to await relocation. Eventually we settled in Boston, where I worked at Harvard University as an interpreter. A year later my family and I moved to Los Angeles, where I once again became a child therapist, working with children who had cerebral palsy at Children's Hospital.

I spent the next seven years at the Dubnoff School for emotionally disturbed children in North Hollywood, California, working with autistic children, especially the most difficult. I loved this work. I was somehow able to develop relationships with extremely disturbed children whom no one else had been able to reach. The director, Belle Dubnoff, called me "Madge with her magic." (Madge was my American nickname at that time.) My magic was simply observing closely and expecting of the children only what they could do. When a child is expected to do something he cannot, he is set up for failure.

In 1968 I developed and directed the Pilot Infant Program at the Dubnoff School. Four years later, with Tom Forrest, M.D., I became founder/codirector of the Demonstration Infant Program, a preventive mental health program for babies sponsored by the Children's Health Council in Palo Alto, California. In 1973 I began teaching parent/infant guidance classes in Los Angeles, the beginning of RIE. Infancy has always fascinated me—the first few years of life, before language develops. Too often children aren't taken seriously until they speak, nor are they well understood.

Over the years I have lectured on infancy, participated in national conferences, and made television appearances. I have taught early child development at the University of California, Los Angeles; California State University, Northridge; and Pacific Oaks College in Pasadena, where I currently teach. I travel the country and have traveled the world conducting RIE seminars for parents and professionals. I teach both professional training classes and RIE parent/infant guidance classes at our RIE center in Los Angeles.

My desire is to help parents and those who work with babies and young children to understand them better. I would also like to teach parents, perhaps a better word would be to *sensitize* them, to being in tune with young children. Basic patterns of life—trust, endurance, and optimism—develop at this age.

My goal is to help parents learn how to treat their children respectfully from birth. If you begin well, by trying to understand your child's point of view from infancy, there is a greater likelihood you will continue doing this throughout your life. Many misconceptions exist about babies and small children, and too little knowledge is based on observation and empathy. Observing your child carefully helps you to tune into his unique rhythm and understand his unique needs. I try to help parents learn to relax, observe more, and enjoy what they see their child doing, even if he is lying peacefully on his blanket. For babies, "being who they are" is the curriculum.

This respectful approach differs from most other childrearing theories in that it is based on the simple concept of observing your child. In our fast-paced modern culture, child development fads appear and disappear like fashions that come in and out of style. Hanging black and white mobiles over babies' beds, showing them flash cards, putting them in walkers to "help" them walk, all activities that push a child to learn, have nothing to do with the reality of a young child's day-to-day needs. The RIE approach is simple and based on common sense rather than on following the latest fads.

In our modern world, parenting issues grow more and more complex. Questions arise daily. In this book, I would like to offer you a simple framework to which you can turn in many situations. I hope this book will encourage and support you, and help you to experience more confidence and joy with your baby.

How to Use This Book

Part I of the book summarizes RIE philosophy. It examines what is meant by respecting your baby and his respecting you. I explain in detail the basic principles of my philosophy and how the RIE approach evolved from my initial work in Hungary and developed further in the United States. It has been applied to children from many backgrounds and over many decades.

Part II takes an in-depth look at how to observe your child and how to apply RIE's basic principles in everyday situations. It also examines the early developmental stages your child goes through, from the newborn period until he takes his first steps. It discusses various issues that arise, such as crying, sleeping, safety, and play, and how to use the RIE approach in handling them. In Part II RIE parents reflect on how they were raised. Part II also touches upon the benefit of RIE philosophy for children with special needs.

You may notice that the chapters are not divided according to specific ages. This is because age is not my focus. There is no "right" age for a child to achieve certain milestones. Rather, I am more concerned with developmental stages. Part II contains a chapter written especially for new parents, offering encouragement and sharing insights based on my many years of work with families. Also included is a chapter on how to choose the best child care situation.

Part III continues discussing developmental stages, ending in the early toddler phase. Recurring issues such as sleeping and eating are examined, as well as new issues that will surface: toddler behavior, discipline, and tantrums. By describing a typical evening and bedtime routine with a RIE family, I show how the RIE philosophy can be used in your home. I conclude my discussion at the stage when your child is typically walking and starting to talk. By this time you and your child will have learned to respect each other and to communicate in a healthy manner. Similarly, children "graduate" from our RIE parent/infant guidance classes when they turn two, when they are most likely walking and talking.

Every chapter contains comments from parents, stories from my work with families, and anecdotes from my RIE parent/infant guidance classes. Through observation, demonstration, and discussion, RIE classes help parents establish healthy patterns of behavior with their children.

(Note: To promote gender equity, chapters will alternate in their use of *he* and *she* when referring to a baby. The real names of some of the parents and children used in this book have been changed.)

◐ I ◑

How RIE Can Benefit Your Baby

◐ 1 ◑

Respect

The Key to Raising a Self-Confident Baby

Respect: To esteem. To honor. To refrain from interfering with.

Respect. Honor. Esteem. These words aren't usually associated with young babies. Yet it is widely agreed that these concepts are vital later in life. A child's personality is largely formed in the first three years. Her outlook on the world is being shaped. Why not engage in a respectful relationship with your child as soon as possible? The benefits will be long-lasting.

What does respect mean, in terms of parents and children? It means accepting, enjoying, and loving your child as she is and not expecting her to do what she cannot do. It means allowing your child the time, the space, and the love and support to be herself and to discover the world in her own unique way. It means trying to understand her point of view.

To respect your child is to believe in her competence and see her as dependent on you rather than helpless. It is to accept and support both her dependence and independence, based on the developmental stage she is in. It is love plus consideration, treating your child as you would treat an honored guest. To respect your child is to create a little distance so that you refrain from interfering with her experience of encountering life.

Respect means setting boundaries for your child and for yourself as a parent, and enforcing these boundaries. It is letting your child know your expectations of her behavior so that she can cooperate and, thus, respect you. Respect means taking care of your own needs as well as hers. It is nurturing and honoring yourself.

RIE's respectful approach encourages a child's authenticity, or genuineness, which means encouraging her to be honest about her feelings. It tells a child, "to thine own self be true." Be who you are. It's an ongoing life struggle. No society allows total honesty, so we must all wear masks and learn to pretend at times. People lose touch with their real selves. That's too high a price to pay to fit in.

You may wonder how to encourage the spirit of authenticity. I say simply, let your child be. Spend time sitting back and observing her. See who she is and what her needs are. Don't expect her to do what she is not ready or able to do. Let her crawl until she can, on her own, take her first steps. Don't encourage your child to smile when she doesn't feel like smiling. If she is sad, let her cry. Don't expect or demand behavior that is not genuine. Rather, value what she does.

Children are often expected to "behave" rather than be who they are. In many situations people unwittingly teach children how to be less than honest. When a child cries, she is not asked, "What happened?" but is usually told, "You're okay." We do this as a society. The message is: if you are not okay, keep it to yourself. Often, too, with children, conformity, rather than honesty, is encouraged. I would like to see children feel free to express their emotions and, as they grow, learn how to control their impulses.

Basic Principles

The following are the basic principles of my philosophy. I believe that adhering to these principles promotes a respectful approach to raising your child:

- Basic trust in the child to be an initiator, an explorer, and a self-learner
- An environment for the child that is physically safe, cognitively challenging, and emotionally nurturing
- Time for uninterrupted play
- Freedom to explore and interact with other infants
- Involvement of the child in all caregiving activities to allow the child to become an active participant rather than a passive recipient

- Sensitive observation of the child in order to understand her needs
- Consistency and clearly defined limits and expectations to develop discipline

Basic Trust

Basic trust means believing in your child's competence and supporting her authenticity. It is believing that whatever your child needs to know, she will learn. In this way she will grow to trust in herself and in you. This will promote her feelings of security and allow her to begin to develop good judgment. Basic trust also means that you as a parent will learn to trust yourself and your instincts.

The foundation of basic trust is built by observing your child in order to understand her and find out what interests her. By observing her, you will discover that she is competent, able to figure many things out on her own, and you will grow to trust her even more. Often when we are busy teaching a child to grasp a ball, for example, or to stack blocks, we don't realize what she already knows. And what she knows may surprise us.

The question is: what is your child ready to learn? Pumping information into a child not ready to receive it is to convey knowledge that is not useful to her. Your child's curiosity, interest, and readiness are what count. Observation is the key.

Erik H. Erikson, the famous psychoanalyst and Harvard professor who coined the term *basic trust,* describes it in *Identity and the Life Cycle* (International Universities Press, Inc., 1959) as an attitude toward oneself and the world formed during the first year of life based on one's experiences. He notes that "reasonable trustfulness as far as others are concerned and a simple sense of trustworthiness as far as oneself is concerned" is the basis for a healthy personality.

Environment

The environment must, first of all, be safe for your child's protection and sense of security. In an unsafe environment a parent can never relax to observe his child. At least one completely safe room, or a gated-off portion of a room if the house or apartment is small, is needed where the child can play.

A cognitively challenging environment provides simple, age-appropriate play objects to help a child grow and mature through problem solving during the course of play. For example, I recommend play objects like large cotton scarves and balls for young babies. Toddlers need different challenges such as sand, water, wheel toys, and climbing structures.

An emotionally nurturing environment, provided by an attentive parent or carer, gives a child the confidence to solve problems.

Uninterrupted Play

Children play beautifully on their own. They do not need to be taught how to play. Children work out their conflicts in play, which is connected to their readiness. Readiness refers to the ability to solve problems at each developmental stage. For example, a young infant is ready to reach for and grasp objects near her. A toddler is ready to fill a bucket with sand and dump it out. Note that problems occur naturally in an adequate play environment, where a child may need to figure out how to retrieve a ball that rolled under a chair. It isn't necessary to create problems.

A parent can observe his child's play and, based on that observation, see what she needs—maybe a new object to play with. If a parent, instead, interrupts and says to his child, "Let's roll the ball," then the play becomes therapeutic for the parent rather than for the child, and the adult's goal becomes more important than the child's interest.

Uninterrupted play promotes concentration and a long attention span. When we interrupt a child, we also stop what she is doing, whatever process she may be in the middle of, as she focuses on us. Our interruptions, no matter how well intended, become distractions.

Freedom to Explore

Play groups, where infants and children interact with each other, are desirable. Children have different agendas with adults than with their peers, and they learn from each other. When infants are freely exploring, however, there must be rules. Mainly, children should not be allowed to hurt each other. Once the rules are established and reinforced by the supervising adults, the children can be free to interact.

An Active Participant

It's fine and healthy for a child to be active, even though it's not easy to diaper a wiggling baby. Cooperation is encouraged during caregiving times. Your goal is to encourage your child's active involvement by inviting her to become part of the process. For example, during diapering you can talk to your baby and ask for her cooperation, even if she can't yet understand you. This sets up the beginning of a dialogue between you that promotes cooperation.

Sensitive Observation

It is often easier to engage in an activity with a child than to sit and simply observe her. But from our observations come the answers, though it takes time to understand one's child. Parents are so involved with their children that they sometimes lose perspective. Nobody knows for certain what a baby is thinking or feeling, but observing is the best way to tune in to your child. If, through observation, you can perceive and accept your child at her own developmental level and learn how to understand and respond to her needs, you have a better chance of preventing problems before they develop. Over time, observation skills improve with practice.

Consistency

Consistency goes hand in hand with discipline. As a parent, you set the limits. A rule is always a rule. Knowing this makes a child feel secure. For example, you may tell your child where she may or may not play ball.

Setting limits and maintaining them consistently doesn't mean that a child will always obey the rules. The important thing is that your child knows what is expected of her. Predictable routines reinforce discipline. Certain issues, such as safety, should always be enforced.

The RIE Philosophy in Action

To show how you can implement these principles in your home, let me give you a picture of how the different elements of my philosophy come together at the RIE Center.

The RIE Center, where I hold training seminars and parent/infant guidance classes, is an old, Spanish-style duplex in a quiet neighborhood of Los Angeles. I've taught there for the last twenty years. The classes, divided into groups according to the children's developmental stages, are held in a wooden-floored room that opens onto a covered outdoor deck built under the cooling branches of a large rubber tree. Many parents have told me the deck reminds them of a tree house.

In the youngest class, a maximum of six babies lie on a soft mat covered by a clean sheet. A few balls are scattered around, as well as colorful cotton scarves twisted into standing peaks for the infants to grasp. Large red, blue, and yellow wooden boxes, stacked with play objects for the use of older infants, line a wall. The play objects are things like plastic bowls, cups, colanders, and various stacking toys—all simple, functional objects. On a futon across the room are stuffed animals and dolls. A basket of balls, another of buckets, and a wooden climbing structure are available for the young toddler classes. Parents sit on cloth floor chairs, forming a circle around their children. RIE classes admit children up to the age of two, at which time I feel the children and their parents have laid the groundwork for good communication.

In the classes, as you would do at home, we observe the children playing. That's all. We enjoy them. The "curriculum" is whatever happens. The children do what they want to do, with their parents remaining nearby for support. They have free time with interference only for safety's sake. For example, we would intervene if one child was about to hurt another child or get hurt herself. My role as an educarer is to model respectful behavior.

I remember a class where two nine-month-old babies, who by this time were crawling, grabbed the same small yellow Wiffle

ball, each struggling to hold it. I watched the faces of the eager parents as they looked at their children, and then at me, as if to ask me what they should do. I smiled at them reassuringly and said, "That's the beginning of social interaction. It's a wonderful thing to allow it to go on as far as it can go without anybody being hurt. The more we allow them to interact without interfering, the better they become at it." The mothers sat back and relaxed, and allowed the children to continue playing. After a few moments one of the babies dropped the ball and picked up a cloth doll. Imagine how much needless energy would have been expended if both parents had gotten involved.

This type of environment is rare for young babies. So often they live with our expectations: Play with this. Don't touch that. What we do in class, which you can easily transfer into your home, is allow children to do what they can do. We don't prop up babies who can't yet sit or teach crawling children to walk. We let the children develop naturally and choose from among the safe play objects provided, and we support them in working out their conflicts on their own. We learn much about them in the process.

Dr. Pikler writes in *Peaceful Babies—Contented Mothers,* first published in Hungary in 1940,

> If one does not interfere, an infant will learn to turn, roll, creep on the belly, go on all fours, stand, sit, and walk with no trouble. This will not happen under pressure, but out of her own initiative—independently, with joy, and pride in her achievement—even though she may sometimes get angry, and cry impatiently.

In writing about what kinds of toys are best and how to offer them to a child, Dr. Pikler continues,

> What is essential is that the child discover as much as possible for himself. If we help him to perform all the tasks he meets, we deprive him of just this, which is of greatest importance for his intellectual development. He gains a very different kind of knowledge through experimenting independently, than from knowledge presented to him ready-made, complete. . . .
>
> Therefore, we allow a child to experience her environment in her individual way, and according to her individual development. We do not urge her. We do not encourage her to do things for which she is not ready. We do not exaggerate in praising her when she succeeds at something. We acknowledge her achievements, and this is not only through words of praise, but also in our behavior.

Your child will derive a sense of peace as well as competence if you support her in developing naturally, according to her own rhythm.

To give you another perspective, a parent from one of my classes, Peter, a telesales consultant and father of Christopher, age two, says,

> RIE is an absence of interference with a child, which almost looks like nothing. The parent is advised to simply be there, watching his child as he interacts with his world. But there's great wisdom in following the path of least resis-

> tance. I've learned to let my son figure things out on his own, that he has great resources, and that I don't need to teach him all the time. I learned to let go and allow things to happen naturally, to be more hands-off. RIE taught me that the parent is the court of last resort. It allows children to teach themselves, and they get better at it as time goes on. If you look at today's society, most of the breakdowns stem from the inability of people to get along with each other, to live and let live. RIE celebrates and enhances the child's ability to get along with others.

We at RIE are trying to put all the therapists out of business. A therapist has to undo. If we do well at the beginning of a child's life, we won't have to undo. However, RIE's philosophy is not a dogma or a set of hard and fast rules. Rather, it is a resource for parents. You don't have to agree with everything. You can incorporate into your family's life what you find useful.

Gillian, an anthropologist and mother of Jesse, age seven, says,

> RIE gave me a clarity about how I'd like things to be with my child. I learned that it's important to take care of myself, that I was important and that Jesse was important—as two separate individuals—and not to feel guilty. It gave me a clear and straightforward way to parent and made parenting more satisfying through observing, creating that little distance from where I could watch my child. RIE helped make my life easier because I always imagined I'd be an overprotective parent. Letting Jesse have freedom of movement within a safe place allowed me to relax. I found that I trusted his judgment in terms of his physical ability and didn't have to hover and worry. I followed my own feelings and instincts while using RIE as a guideline. I internalized the ideas and adapted them to suit our family. There are deep principles involved in RIE—observation, autonomy, and respect—for parents and children.

I'll let you in on a secret. This book can serve as a guide, but the real answers won't be found here. Look to your child. Observe her. She has much to teach you.

◐ 2 ◑

The Birth of RIE

In Hungary, it was said that if you went to a park or playground you could tell the "Pikler babies" from the other children. They were active yet graceful, full of confidence, and possessed a strong sense of self. They were children who were raised following the philosophy of Dr. Pikler. Her teachings have evolved into the Pikler Method, on which RIE is based.

Pikler babies have been allowed to develop at their own pace without being expected to do any more than they can do at any given stage of development. They are allowed freedom of movement within a carefully structured safe environment and allowed to choose among simple play objects offered. They interact with other infants of about the same age. By learning to trust their bodies, they have few childhood accidents. These babies are involved in all caregiving activities, and their cooperation is valued. Raised with respect for their feelings, minds, and bodies, they are confident, alert, and attentive.

Dr. Pikler believed that being receptive to a baby's efforts at communication and initiative supports his sense of competence. She writes in the journal *Acta Paediatrica Academiae Scientiarum Hungaricae* (1979) that this belief, in turn, enables parents to "bring up calmer, more balanced children . . . who would know . . . what they are interested in, their needs for food or sleep." Doing this "would eliminate the need for a number of subsequent corrective educational measures."

She held that competence leads to independence in the best sense of the word—helping children become active, self-sufficient, cooperative individuals and members of the family, and later, of society.

The First Pikler Babies

Early in her career, Dr. Pikler became fascinated with the physiology of gross motor development (the movement of the large muscles of the body that enable a child to sit, stand, or walk) in infants, particularly in those infants who had been allowed to develop without being physically restricted by such devices as infant seats and walkers. She believed that restricting a baby's movement not only impedes his motor development but also affects his cognitive growth, social skills, and personality.

Studying accident statistics in children, Dr. Pikler found that the children of wealthy families, who had been kept indoors and raised by nannies, fell victim to fractures and concussions more often than children who played in the street and who were allowed more freedom of movement. The children who played in the street and learned how to fall were apparently more aware of their physical abilities and limits. Thus, she felt it was better to allow a growing child unrestricted movement.

Dr. Pikler believed an infant who was allowed to move freely could "practice" the skills needed to progress to the next stage of development. For example, a baby who couldn't sit wouldn't be propped with pillows into a sitting position. By lying on his back, moving his arms and legs, and rolling to his side, he would naturally strengthen the muscles and develop the coordination needed to sit. A child in her care was never placed in a position he wasn't able to get into or out of on his own. He was appreciated for what he could do and not expected to do what he couldn't.

Dr. Pikler raised her daughter following these guidelines. Pleased with the results, she applied her theory to the next hundred families for whom she served as pediatrician. For the first ten days of a baby's life Dr. Pikler would visit the family every day. Afterward she made weekly house calls and spent many hours observing each child and family's mutual adaptation, making sure all was running smoothly. These were the first Pikler babies.

How Loczy Raises Healthy Children

Dr. Pikler was disturbed as she surveyed the conditions of institutionalized children worldwide. *Hospitalism,* a term coined by Dr.

René Spitz, was used to describe the syndrome of unusual behavior, caused by a lag in physical and mental development, exhibited by children raised in group care. Hospitalism usually left a devastating effect on its subjects. The children were observed to be passive and listless, developing severe personality problems later in life.

In 1945 Dr. Pikler was asked to become the executive medical director of Loczy, a state-run orphanage in Budapest. She took on the challenge, seeking to change the face of institutionalism by applying her child development beliefs to the children placed there. I assisted her in training the infant nurses.

Dr. Pikler felt that the institute could never replace a loving mother. Therefore, it was vital to provide a stable mother figure in the form of a caregiver. She also recognized that a supportive, nurturing environment was vital. To promote attachment, Loczy's seventy children were divided into groups of about nine children who had the same caregiver each day for each eight-hour shift. Each child had an assigned caregiver to bathe her and attend to her basic needs, acting as a mother figure. The same three caregivers remained, whenever possible, with the children from birth until the age of three, when the children either returned to their families or were placed in adoptive homes. As all the literature on children shows, the first three years are crucial in the formation of lifelong patterns of coping and attachment. Dr. Pikler wanted to make sure the children in her care had a healthy start.

Freedom to move and access to simple play objects invited the children to use initiative while playing. Teaching children motor skills was not allowed. The goal was to encourage self-mastery. Special attention was paid during times of feeding, diapering, and bathing in order to give each child one-on-one attention. The caregiver spoke to each child in her charge and told him what was going to happen. Cooperation was asked for and expected according to each infant's stage of development. The children developed a sense of security and attachment through the regularity and predictability of the daily routines and the continuity of having the same caregiver. After being "refueled" by loving caregiving interaction, a child would more easily accept separation from the adult to explore or play.

Dr. Pikler remained the director of Loczy for thirty-nine years, until her death in 1984, when it was renamed the Emmi

Pikler Institute. Thousands of children have been reared at the institute following the Pikler Method. Over the years, studies were conducted on hundreds of "Loczy children" who moved through each developmental stage on their own without assistance from adults. (Emmi Pikler, *The Exceptional Infant* 2:1971, Jerome Hellmuth, ed.)

An independent follow-up study funded by the World Health Organization (WHO) documented how well the Loczy children adapted to family life after adoption. They were shown to be as well adjusted as any children raised in a family environment. A further follow-up study by WHO showed that when the children had grown to adulthood, they had married, were raising their own children, and were self-supporting, law-abiding citizens of Hungary. The Pikler Institute currently cares for drug-addicted and abused children as well as orphans. The Pikler Society teaches its philosophy in Europe and in other parts of the world.

Emmi Pikler's work at Loczy sends an important message to parents. If children reared in a public institution can not only survive, but thrive, then can't children everywhere have a better start in life if parents follow this approach? This is exactly what I thought when I brought my ideas to the United States and founded RIE.

DIP: The American RIE Model

In 1972 Dr. Tom Forrest, a pediatrician and clinical assistant professor of pediatrics at Stanford University, requested a meeting with me in Los Angeles. He wanted to ask my advice on the infant program he was starting for the Children's Health Council (CHC) in Palo Alto, California. The CHC had a history of working with children with special needs and recognized how crucial the first years were in a child's development. The grant-funded program was to be one of preventive mental health, that is, to *detect* potential problems and *correct* them before they were incorporated into a child's personality and behavior. "High-risk" as well as average children were to be enrolled.

Dr. Forrest and I discovered that we shared similar views on a respectful approach to childrearing, and he invited me to be the program's codirector. I readily agreed and spent the next four years commuting to Palo Alto on a weekly basis.

The program was based on demonstration, hence called the Demonstration Infant Program, or DIP. We realized that it was one thing to present a philosophy of childrearing and quite another to apply it in a family or child care situation in everyday life. The demonstrating we did was to serve as a model for parents and carers.

Each demonstration group of four or five babies of about the same age met once a week for a two-hour session. The classes consisted of groups of five-month-olds to twenty-four-month-olds, divided according to developmental stage. Both average and high-risk infants were enrolled in the same group.

During the sessions either Dr. Forrest or I remained in a room with the babies acting as the demonstrator, while the other was in an adjacent room observing and discussing what was seen by the mothers, visitors, and trainees. The children's environment was infant-oriented, allowing them to move freely, choose their play objects, and interact with the other infants.

Selective Intervention Supports Competence

Dr. Forrest and I modeled "selective intervention," showing *when* and *how* to intervene in the children's play by remaining available without being intrusive. The demonstrator would intervene if the child's safety was involved, or if the child was too frightened or frustrated in solving a problem. The goal was to encourage the child to participate in the solution.

The DIP staff held the belief that nonintervention, or noninterruption of play, helps children develop competence in problem-solving skills. This, in turn, requires trust on the part of the parent or carer. We believed that children are very good problem solvers if given the opportunity.

The DIP philosophy maintained that in learning new tasks and finding their own solutions to situations in everyday life (fitting an object in a box, climbing onto a piece of equipment, resolving disputes over toys) children are self-rewarded, learning internal rewards as opposed to external ones. This leads to self-confidence, which carries over into later life.

Jean Piaget, the well-known Swiss biologist turned psychologist, said, "Every time we teach a child something, we keep him from inventing it himself." DIP encouraged the joy of discovery. As at Loczy, children were not taught or placed in positions they couldn't get into themselves, such as sitting, standing, or being "walked" holding an adult's hand.

I remember a baby named Beverly who was enrolled in our program. She was brought to Dr. Forrest for diagnostic evaluation. The problem? Beverly had been crying almost constantly since birth. Her parents were becoming more and more irritable, feeling helpless, frustrated, angry, and guilty. These feelings permeated their lives, their marriage, and, of course, their whole relationship with the baby. Dr. Forrest's examination showed no evidence of neurological deficit.

The first day she came to our class, Beverly, a big, strong, healthy-looking six-month-old, was "walked" in by her parents, held in an upright position, her body as stiff as a wooden board. While this might have looked like an advanced position for her age, she was completely immobilized, and when placed on the floor, she maintained a stiff posture and did not move.

Beverly joined a group of three babies ranging in age from seven to twelve months. Her mother was surprised to see them peacefully exploring their environment, and even more surprised to see their mothers say good-bye to the babies and withdraw into the adjacent observation room. The first hour Beverly spent with us at DIP she screamed for the entire hour, nearly bursting with anger.

Since our infant-oriented environment encouraged each baby to become an attentive, active, exploring person, Beverly joined the other babies in learning to become interested and self-rewarded in their mastery of new tasks. The babies were given space to move in, equipment, and appropriate objects to manipulate and other babies to watch and imitate. Although it is not widely known, we have observed that infants do a great deal of learning from each other, even at a very early age.

Beverly continued to cry for the next five visits. By Beverly's sixth visit to DIP, instead of crying constantly, she began to interact with other babies, play with toys, move about the room, and cry only briefly. It is quite possible that, had Beverly not come to

DIP, she would have continued the vicious circle of incomplete problem solving, becoming frustrated and angry, immobilized by her angry crying, so that all attempts to help would become futile, producing frustration and anger in those around her. And this can happen to a healthy, average, bright child and to well-meaning, good parents.

Children Need Limits, Too

A snack was available at a certain time during the DIP class. This was an activity with limits or rules. A small table surrounded by low stools was provided for the children. They could eat if they chose to but were not allowed to take the food away from the table. The children could either eat or play, but had to sit down to eat. The demonstrator talked to the children in a firm yet gentle voice, explaining the expectations.

Another area of limits involved safety. Children were not allowed to hit or hurt other children although they were allowed to struggle, with an attentive demonstrator sitting on the floor with the children, ready to intervene if necessary. Children struggling over a toy were told, for example, "I won't let you hit Jake. That will hurt him. What else can you do?" The children were encouraged to learn *how* to negotiate a solution to their struggle.

DIP's goal was to gently educate children and their parents in acquiring skills that would serve them well for life. They learned these skills by being allowed to explore freely and uninterruptedly within a carefully structured environment. Both elements, freedom and structure, blended together harmoniously to provide an optimal learning arena. The children came to model their own behavior after the respectful treatment they received from the carers. Reciprocity is a key element in respect.

The DIP program extended from 1972 to 1977 and involved hundreds of families. It also offered a training program for professionals as well as consultation with child care centers. DIP took the teachings of Emmi Pikler one step further by going beyond the doctor/patient relationship and beyond institutions, making them accessible to real family situations with children and parents. The results were again favorable. This respectful approach to childrearing could work as well in a Hungarian institution as in a home or play group in the United States, and also showed the promise of working well in a child care center. Children flourish where they are treated with respect.

The Beginning of RIE

RIE carried on this tradition. After the success of DIP, Dr. Forrest and I wanted to continue helping parents and professionals learn a respectful way to raise children. Our work focused on educating as well as caring, thus I coined the word *educaring*. In 1978 we founded Resources for Infant Educarers, a nonprofit organization dedicated to children and their carers. The RIE Center in Los Angeles was established in 1980.

At the RIE Center we offer professional training for those in the field of early childhood as well as conducting parent/infant guidance classes. I currently direct RIE, a membership organization that continues to grow each year and welcomes new members. Teachers, child care professionals, infant nurses, students, and parents from all over the world enroll in our certification training program. At present the parent/infant classes are based in Southern California but are reaching new areas as more RIE teachers graduate and receive accreditation. Our goal at RIE is to help raise children with the respect each person needs and deserves.

II

Your Baby at the Beginning of Life

From Birth to Your Baby's First Steps

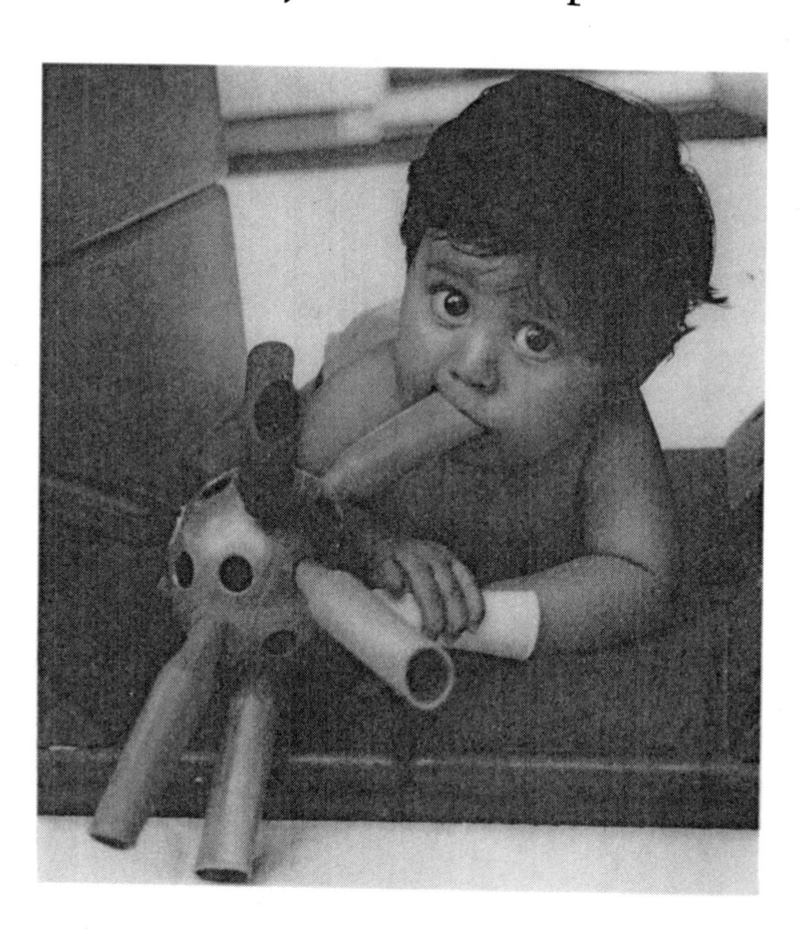

◐ 3 ◑

Your Newborn Baby

Imagine what happens when a baby is born. She emerges from a dark, cozy, cavelike place where she has lived for nine months. In those months she has heard the steady beat of her mother's heart and the whooshing of her mother's blood flowing. She enters a world of bright lights and colors, of strange noises and moving objects. This world may be frightening at times, but it is always stimulating to a young infant. She needs patience and understanding in order to adapt.

The newborn baby, up to about three months old, is between heaven and earth, not quite here yet. She uses a set of reflexes, which may appear at times abrupt or jerky, to make the adjustment from womb to world. Although there are a wide range of temperaments, new babies are extremely sensitive to the environment. They need quiet, calm handling in order to help them relax. A parent's job is to help the newborn make this transition into the world. How can this be done in a respectful manner?

There are several keys in doing this. The most important ones include observing your baby in order to understand her, helping her form attachment by talking to her and telling her what you are going to do, being slow and gentle with her, and waiting before intervening.

Observing Your Baby

My cardinal rule for showing your baby respect is to become a sensitive observer. Observation is the tool through which you will grow to understand her. You can observe your baby in any situation—as you hold her, as she lies on her blanket, in her crib or playpen, or any other safe place of your choosing.

When you spend time with your child, whether you're diapering her, holding her, or sitting quietly as she lies beside you, try to be fully with her. In this way she is refueled for the times when you're apart, whether she's napping, resting quietly, or you're away. If your child gets your undivided attention when you are together, she will feel freer to separate. This is true "quality time" (covered in more detail later in this chapter).

Unfortunately there is a tendency to not pay full attention to one's baby, but to do all kinds of other things while with her. Babies are held while a parent reads the paper, tapped on the back while a parent watches television, and bounced on a knee while her parent chats on the phone. Be fully with her, give her your focused attention when together, and you will both benefit greatly.

When you observe your baby, whatever she's doing—focusing on a pattern of light on the wall, lying peacefully on her blanket, or even sleeping—enjoy what you see. Don't worry about what you don't see, although I know parents can't be totally worry-free. When we interact with babies, we tend to project what we think they're feeling because they can't tell us. Babies have behavior—they sleep, they smile, and they cry. Adults read into this behavior whatever their background or mood permits. Close observation helps remedy this.

Some theories advocate stimulation for babies—showing them black and white pictures to promote visual alertness, shaking rattles in their faces to elicit a response, or enrolling them in baby gym classes to exercise their bodies. This is done with the idea of stimulating their intelligence or physical development, which will evolve on its own. I believe that a baby who has just come out of the womb needs a transition time with peace and quiet, devoid of artificial stimulation. Life itself will provide her with the natural stimulation she needs to develop. You may wonder, will my baby develop as quickly or as well as other babies without stimulating her? My answer is yes. Trust that she will develop in her own time, rhythm, and manner. After all, who knows better how to be a baby than a baby?

Recent American studies are starting to confirm this approach to raising infants. Dr. J. Ronald Lally, the director of Child and Family Studies at WestEd, an educational research laboratory in Sausalito, California, writes in the journal *Young Children* (November 1995) that

> traditional views of child development have suggested that infants and toddlers should be stimulated to foster their intellectual growth and development. In this view of development, adults hold the key to teaching relatively helpless infants how to receive and organize information about the world. In support of this approach, countless educational toys and materials have been designed to teach babies specific lessons. But what of the messages that this approach gives the developing self? One possible message is, "You don't know what to be interested in or how to do things. You need adults to show you how to think and what to think about."

Dr. Lally maintains that early child development experts are beginning to realize that giving infants "freedom to make learning choices and to experience the world on their own terms," rather than stimulating or teaching them, is a healthy approach. Since infants are born with an innate "urge to learn," he believes that parents can encourage their all-around growth by "providing infants and toddlers with close and responsive relationships with caregivers; by designing safe, interesting, and developmentally appropriate environments; by giving infants uninterrupted time to explore; and by interfacing with infants in ways that emotionally and intellectually support their discovery and learning."

If you sit and observe your child with interest, you won't need to entertain or stimulate her. I think it's exciting to observe children. You may notice that she's found her hands for the first time, has rolled over, or is interested in an object in the room.

A class I taught called "How to Observe" for the Education Department at California State University, Los Angeles, was the most difficult one I ever taught. The students had a hard time, too. It seems easier to busy our minds and bodies with activity than to simply sit and be aware. Since we are constantly bombarded with and essentially spoon-fed information via radio, television, and the Internet, we may have a difficult time slowing down and observing.

How to Observe Your Baby

Observation is a state of quiet and focused attention that cannot occur when the mind is in motion. The less you do, the more you observe. Start with a calm and peaceful atmosphere and let your mind tune into the present. Clear your head. Let all your senses awaken. Rid yourself of preconceived notions. To observe means to be open and detached so that you can see the situation more clearly. An observer must quiet down and let go of prejudices. The desire to become a good observer is the main prerequisite.

As you observe your baby, relax and focus on what you see and hear. Look at your child. Look at her face, her arms, her legs. What is her body language saying? See what she responds to. See what holds her interest. See what bothers her. The process becomes easier as your child grows because she gives clearer signals and you get better at reading them.

As you carefully observe your newborn, you will discover her unique personality. You will see your real child as she is rather than the "imaginary child" of your own creation. You observe her so that, in time, you will understand her likes and dislikes, moods, and abilities. And understanding these things will help you to better care for her, communicate with her, and improve your relationship.

Dr. Pikler writes in *Peaceful Babies—Contented Mothers*, "What is essential is to observe. Get to know your child. If you really recognize what your child needs, if you feel what is causing him grief, feel what she needs, then you will respond in the right way. You will guide and bring up your child well."

Forming Attachment

Your baby's first need is to form attachment to her parents. Attachment means that a child achieves a healthy dependence on a parental figure (usually the mother). She becomes secure knowing that if she cries the parent will come and if she is hungry she will be fed. The parent-child relationship develops a rhythm of its own as the child comes to realize that she can affect her environment by getting a response to her behavior. This makes her feel competent. This also promotes mutual respect as you learn to adapt to each other. The goal is to develop a predictable daily schedule that helps develop trust. Attachment is crucial to a child's feelings of security and future autonomy. She must first feel secure in order to later seek independence.

Parents can aid this process by lovingly taking care of a child's basic needs: feeding her when she is hungry, changing her diapers, keeping her warm, and letting her rest when tired. Taking care of her needs when she signals her hunger or tiredness helps her develop a sense of trust. By listening to your child's cries and getting to know them, you can respond to her appropriately. With a new baby, try to do things smoothly and peacefully because newborns are jittery. In this way you can help your child learn to relax.

Dr. Emmi Pikler writes in *Peaceful Babies—Contented Mothers,*

> Hands constitute the infant's first connection to the world (outside of nursing). Hands pick her up, lay her down, wash and dress and maybe even feed her. How different it can be, what a different picture of the world an infant receives when quiet, patient, careful yet secure and resolute hands take care of her—and how different the world seems when these hands are impatient, rough, or hasty . . . and nervous. In the beginning the hands are everything for an infant. The hands are the person, the world. The way we touch a child, lift and dress him: that is us more precisely, more characteristically than even our words, our smile, or glance.

Gentle, peaceful handling will help your baby feel secure.

Attachment is a process that develops over time as your child comes to know you and feels secure in her home. Attachment helps her grow emotional roots.

Parents have asked me if a mother or father can successfully form attachment with their child if the parent goes back to work.

I tell them not to worry, that a parent is always a parent and is the person who is with the child most of the time. Parents certainly get up with their children during the night, and working parents, in the long run, do most of the caregiving. While a child may be attached to her carer, she also senses who her mother and father are.

However, if at all possible, I urge you to rearrange your lives and careers so that one parent can stay home to raise your child, especially in these early years. I strongly believe in the importance of raising a child in the home with a parent available. In this way she can feel like the "beloved only one" and have a feeling of uniqueness that is not the same in group care. It would be ideal to stay home with your child until she has passed through the tumultuous twos, and turns three.

But there are two sides to this issue. Each parent has his or her own tolerance for being at home. If a parent is miserable remaining at home and has a passion for her career or chooses to follow her career and her child is well cared for, working can be fine. And nowadays in many homes both parents must work full-time to make a living for their families. A parent is the first choice in caregiving. Other options may be a relative, home carer, or group child care. (Chapter 6 covers child care concerns.) But I feel it is invaluable for a child to be raised and nurtured by her parents. Careers can be put on hold. Your child cannot.

Talking to Your Child

I believe in talking to your child in a genuine and loving voice. It isn't necessary to talk baby talk. Baby talk is not our language but an artificial one created for what we think children like. Why be artificial with your own child? Why not use your own voice, way of talking, and words?

Perhaps we use baby talk because we don't know *how* to relate to a young baby. I feel the earlier we are genuine with our children, the better. Show your child you believe she can understand you. It's been shown that an infant reacts to her parent's face and smell. Remember that a baby is a human being who responds to a soft and gentle human voice.

Does talking to your baby help make her smarter? Many recent studies have shown this. Psychiatrist Janellen Huttenlocher of the University of Chicago told *Newsweek* (February 19, 1996) that the more words a child hears, the faster she learns language. The brain builds up neural circuitry that it uses to absorb more words. However, the reason I believe in speaking to your baby is that that's how we human beings communicate. Why not talk to your baby as you would to your friend or your spouse? Remember that it's equally important to listen to your child.

Tell Your Child What You Are Going to Do

Tell your child what you are going to do before you do it. Before you pick up your child, say, "I'm going to pick you up now." Tell her, too, when you're going to put her down. Give her a little time for the information to sink in. Wait for her response. There will always be one, usually a subtle change of expression or movement that indicates her interest and readiness. Then proceed. She may not understand the words, but one day she will and it will pay off. Nobody knows exactly when a child understands. It's a slow process, a learning process. Even if your baby doesn't understand you now, you are forming a good habit.

If a child is not told what is going to happen to her, she is, in effect, treated like an object. Doesn't a doctor or dentist help his patient feel more secure by talking her through a procedure? Talking to your child also helps form attachment. Trust builds as she grows to anticipate what will happen to her next. Predictability brings security, at all ages. Talk to your child in simple, direct sentences. Explain to her what is happening to her. The habit will be formed for life.

This reminds me of a story which I often tell. When I was in practice as a child therapist I used to visit the families I worked with in their homes. In one home I watched as the mother quickly and silently diapered her baby, then turned to her dog and explained, "I know you're hungry, Mopsy, but if you wait just a minute I'll get your dinner." The funny thing was that she wasn't aware that she chose to communicate with her dog but not her child.

To further illustrate the point, imagine that we inhabit a world of giants, where we grown-ups are the little people. How would we feel if we were snatched up by a giant and carried off, not knowing where we were going or what was going to happen to us? This may seem like an exaggeration, but it gives you an idea of how a baby must feel in a world where she is not told what is happening to her.

Becky Hopkins, child therapist and mother of Joseph, five, and Brian, ten, teaches child development part-time at California State University, Los Angeles. She says,

> Many of my students are skeptical about RIE philosophy. They say to me, "Who talks to a baby? Why tell her you're going to pick her up?" Then they go to a home to interact with an infant they're working with. I ask them to talk to the baby, tell her what they're going to do, and wait for her response. They usually come back and tell me, "I did what you said and the baby responded. I'm amazed that it works."

Diane, stay-at-home mother of Marc, one, and Jennifer, six, adds, "I remember you telling us to talk to our babies in a normal voice and explain what we were doing and where we were going because one day they would understand us. And we wouldn't know when that day would be. If you're already in the habit of talking to your baby as you'd talk to another human being, you don't have to suddenly change how you speak to her."

William, a coin dealer and father of Juliana, two, says, "I learned to talk *to* my daughter, not at her or about her. If she's in the room and I'm speaking to someone else, I at least acknowledge her presence."

Acknowledgment makes your child feel included.

Trying to Understand Your Baby's Point of View

Carol Pinto and I have worked together for the past twenty-five years. She teaches the RIE philosophy to parents and professionals. In addition, she is a teacher of the Feldenkrais Method, a method of body/mind education that teaches, through movement, how to improve a person's ability to function in his daily activities. Her respect for the competence of infants and for how well they learn to make sense of the world through their sensory-motor development led her to develop experiential movement workshops for adults. At our annual RIE Conference, she leads a workshop that guides participants through a sequence of developmental movements.

Carol says,

> Like RIE, Feldenkrais is about self-learning and the development of judgment. Adults see infants through the lens of their own perceptions. These workshops are designed to give adults a fresh point of view, hopefully one that is closer to that of a baby.
>
> Workshop participants begin by lying on the floor on their backs, the posture in which young infants have the most security and the most freedom. They imagine what it might feel like to be a very young baby, and they experiment with sensing and moving as infants might. Students gain from this workshop an appreciation of the many skills that infants develop before they learn to stand. Learning about gravity, spatial relations, eye-hand coordination, and becoming comfortable in one's own body are some of them.
>
> I ask workshop participants to imagine how they would like to be approached by adults. Guided imagery illustrates how reassuring it is when an adult tells a baby what is going to happen before she is picked up and how startling it can feel if she is not told. If she is told first, she has time to get ready for what will happen to her.

It may help you to try to envision what your baby may feel when you are setting up her environment at home. If you were to put yourself in her place, although this is realistically impossible to do, what concerns would you have? These may be some of them: Do I feel safe here? Am I warm? Will my parent (or carer) respond to me if I cry? Do I have enough space to move in? Are my hands free for me to suck on if I need to? Are my legs free to kick and move at will? Will I be put in my bed to rest when I am tired?

Take It Slowly

Children have a much slower tempo than we do. Their thought patterns are forming, and they need time to process information in order to respond to us. Slow down with your baby and you will be helping her immensely.

You will also learn to read your child better if you take your time. I often tell parents, "Wait." So many things work out on their own. I remember in one of my classes a mother watched as her six-month-old baby, lying on the mat, began crying.

"What do you think it is?" I asked the mother.

"I'm not sure," she replied.

I knew it was best to let her learn by observing her son. "You decide what you want to do," I said.

The mother waited a few minutes as she watched her child. I noticed that she didn't hurriedly snatch him up to walk or rock him, and then try to figure out what was the matter. She took time to study him. Finally, she said, "I think he's hungry." She knelt down and spoke to her baby, saying, "I'm going to pick you up now and feed you." She took the baby into the other room.

"I liked how you took time to assess the situation," I said to her when she returned, smiling, happy she was learning to read her child's cues. I was glad, too, to see how slowly and calmly she handled him. Parents have often told me how peaceful the RIE Center feels. The attitudes of the educarers and the parents are reflected in the children's behavior.

Slowing yourself down will promote calmness in your baby. Though your baby has her own individual temperament, she also picks up on your level of peacefulness or stress.

Your Home Environment

I encourage the creation of a calm and peaceful physical environment for your new baby. Again imagine emerging from a dark cave. The world is a source of constant stimulation. Loud noises, loud people, and quick movements can be startling and unnerving, even to an adult. Soft lights, low voices, and slow movement help your baby adjust, creating an atmosphere of peace in the home. This is not always possible with older siblings and household activities, but it is a goal to strive for. Overstimulated babies can become fussy babies.

Babies don't need constant entertainment in the form of rocking, bouncing, or swinging. Children sleep well if they are allowed to sleep. If overentertained or overstimulated, they sleep less. New babies should be allowed to sleep as much as possible. They are going through continuous growth spurts. Imagine if we doubled our weight in six months! It seems to be a uniquely American attitude that one should always be busy doing something and that sleep is a waste of time. In the Europe of my day, for example, sleep was a more valued commodity and babies were expected to sleep much of the time. It seems as if we project our go-getter attitudes upon our children and expect them to lead our hectic lives. A young baby has a unique agenda, which is to eat, sleep, explore her new world, and be cared for.

If you like music and would like to have it in your baby's environment, that's fine, although I would avoid loud, jarring music. There are no harmful side effects from listening to soft music. It's best, however, not to play music constantly or else it becomes background noise.

Predictability Helps

Infants should be kept at home for the first weeks and months. Routine in the home brings security. Babies are more relaxed napping comfortably there. Ideally, errands can be run when Dad, Grandma, or another carer can watch the baby. A predictable routine evolves for a child when the same things (meals, naps, bath, bedtime) happen at the same time in the same place every day. A calm environment also promotes sleep.

As your baby learns to anticipate the next event in her daily routine, many conflicts will be minimized for her. She will need to spend less energy adjusting to new or changing situations and will have more energy to explore. In this way a mutual adaptation between her biological rhythms and your family schedule develops. You can then plan your own schedule around her eating, sleeping, and playing times. Be aware that as she progresses through developmental milestones like rolling over, emotional stages like separation anxiety, growth spurts, or stress, her routine and consequently yours, may change.

As your baby grows to anticipate her daily routine, you will learn to anticipate her needs. Anticipating your baby's needs and reactions fosters mutual understanding, acceptance, and basic trust between you and your baby. In this way anticipation becomes the forerunner of communication.

Predictability rather than novelty brings security, especially for your new baby.

Where Should My Baby Spend Her Day?

When your child is not in her crib, or you are not holding her or tending to her needs, she should ideally have an indoor and outdoor safe place to be where you can place her on her back. You may think that your new baby is more comfortable on her stomach but observe your baby when placed on her stomach. Her range of movement is limited. Her neck eventually tires from the strain. She can see only the area beneath her. On her back, she has the maximum mobility and support. She is freer to move her arms, legs, and body, and do what she can do on her own. Her breathing is easier as the front of her chest is better able to expand and contract. She can also view the entire room. When she matures so that she can turn from her back to her belly, then it is *her* choice. Placing young babies on their backs is also recommended for the prevention of SIDS (Sudden Infant Death Syndrome—discussed later in this chapter).

Choose a special or designated place, so she grows to feel comfortable there. For instance, you might want to have a playpen in your den and another outside in a shaded part of the outdoors, if possible, with the gentle breeze and sounds of nature. The outdoors is full of natural stimulation. I also recommend having a second crib outside if weather permits. Babies can learn to sleep very well outdoors. You can start this with a healthy, full-term baby at about one month of age, beginning with very brief amounts of time. Your baby should, at all times, be in a safe place under an adult's supervision.

I don't feel a baby needs to have her mother (or carer) near her at all times. I believe that there is too much emphasis on the idea of holding and touching one's baby, just for the sake of doing it. What is the value of being held or touched if it's only the skin that is in contact? I believe it is better to be with your baby while giving her your full attention whether holding her, tending to her needs, or observing her, than to carry her around with you from room to room strapped in an infant seat, or secured in a baby carrier that you wear, or held while you are busy doing other things such as talking on the phone, reading a book, or cooking. What about your minds connecting, or to become more philosophical, your souls?

Touch is, of course, essential. In 1959 Dr. Harry Harlow conducted a famous experiment with rhesus monkeys to demonstrate how baby monkeys, deprived of their mother's touch and instead given cloth or wire mothers, developed abnormally and became antisocial. This is another extreme. Babies need attention and physical contact from a caring adult. When you hold your baby or simply observe her, be fully aware and tuned in to her. Then you are both freer to separate when necessary, feeling "filled" by the other. In my mind, a few minutes of this special receptiveness is much more valuable for both of you than feeling you must remain with the baby constantly or hold her without paying attention to her.

Place her in her safe area where she can play and explore her environment. She will soon discover satisfaction and joy in her own independence. And you will have free time of your own. In this way, both your needs are met. I believe that spending time in her one or two places gives your baby more security than carrying her from room to room with you as you clean, talk on the phone, and so forth. Of course, you must attend to her basic needs and check on her at regular intervals. A baby monitor is helpful if you are not in sight or in hearing distance of her.

Then when you do go back to her, you will both be refueled and ready to interact in a calmer, more loving way. As she grows, you may encourage her to spend more time playing on her own in her safe place (more on this in chapter 5).

What about Toys?

Newborns don't need toys or what I call play objects, though they are an important part of an older baby's environment. The whole world—patterns of light, sounds, and their own bodily sensations—is new to them. Their rapidly growing awareness of, and adaptation to, the environment is all the stimulation a newborn needs.

A newborn has the grasping reflex. Placing a toy or rattle in her hand forces her to hold something she can't release at will. And the noise a rattle makes can be confusing since the baby can't see or understand what causes it. Placing a mobile over a very young infant's crib or play area can distract her from watching her hands and getting comfortable in her environment, and she can't avoid looking at it.

Will My New Baby Get Bored?

I don't believe in boredom. I think what is typically called boredom is tiredness, lack of interest in what is presented, or not agreeing to do what is presented. I don't believe that babies become "bored" in an adequate environment. Rather, it is our own projection: we think they are bored. They may, however, develop a high tolerance or need for stimulation if constantly stimulated and entertained. And at what cost? The parent must then become a better and better entertainer.

Trust your new baby. She knows what is best for herself, whether it's sucking on her fingers or watching the sunlight stream through a window. Babies do what they are able and ready to do. Nothing more, and nothing less.

Newborn babies, those in the first several months of life, need predictability, not entertainment. Predictability will help your baby fall into a routine and adapt to your family. Newborns need peaceful, quiet time and a slow transition into our busy world.

Feeding Your Baby

Whether to breast-feed or bottle-feed or a combination of both is a deeply personal choice. Each mother must decide what fits her and her lifestyle. Studies indicate that breast milk is the best food for the human infant for a variety of reasons. It is the easiest to digest, contains the perfect nutrients, and is full of protective antibodies. Further, the required sucking action can ward off ear infections. Breast-feeding is a natural and healthy choice. Much of RIE's philosophy is based on allowing a child to be in the most natural environment possible, and breast-feeding is completely natural.

Breast-feeding is also easier for the mother. Breast milk is always fresh, always available, and always at the right temperature. For working mothers, pumping breast milk is an alternative to giving formula.

How can you know when your baby is hungry or what she needs? At first, it's difficult to know what she needs each time your baby cries or expresses discomfort. Newborns should be fed on demand and may need frequent meals because their stomachs are small. Feeding is a process of synchronization in which you try to find out what your child's body rhythm is—how her pattern of hunger and satiation develops—and plan her feedings around those times. This is the beginning of a predictable schedule for you both.

You are developing a new skill: reading your baby. Observe her and be patient.

Where to Feed Your Baby

Feed your baby in a quiet, private, comfortable place, preferably the same one or two places at each feeding so it will become predictable for your baby. Focus on the present moment and the pleasurable feelings you receive during the feeding. Observe your baby's reactions.

If you bottle-feed your baby, hold her and pay full attention to her during feedings. This special time together is not just for nutrition, but also for emotional nourishment and building intimacy.

Be careful to feed the baby only when you think she's hungry. Try not to rely on feeding as a soothing device. Otherwise the habit of using the breast or bottle as a pacifier can develop.

Be respectful of yourself by getting comfortable before beginning to feed your baby. Consider wearing easy access clothing for nursing (if you have chosen to do this). Adjust the lighting, arrange the pillows, if you use them, and set a glass of water or juice nearby. Getting comfortable is a good habit to start because you will spend many hours feeding your baby.

Where Should the Baby Sleep?

Parents often wonder if their baby should sleep in a crib or with them. This is another deeply personal issue. In many cultures parents sleep with their children. In some countries the grandmother keeps the child in her bed so the mother and father can sleep. These cultures feel that children always need a warm body beside them. However, in other cultures and in times past, infant mortality rates were high. Often there was only one bed or dangerous surroundings. It's difficult to compare other cultures with ours.

The writings of Margaret Mead and other anthropologists describe how people who worked in the fields tied their children on their backs for the child's safety. They couldn't put children down because their earthen floors were cold and wet. It's different when you live in a heated home with a crib.

I feel it is important for a child to fall asleep alone in her crib, a learned behavior that will serve her well for life. Everybody should be able to sleep alone. Doing this is a way of learning togetherness and separateness, and that separateness is not the same as abandonment. A child sleeping in her own bed still knows that if she cries or if something happens, her parents will be there.

For nine months a child is carried inside her mother's body. I feel that now that she is out in the world, she should learn to live in this world and sleep in her own bed.

What does it do to a marriage to have a baby in the parents' bed? It certainly cuts down on privacy. The parents may not feel free. The question is: who should adapt? In life, learning to adapt is a vital skill. However, if a family is happy having their baby in their bed, I wouldn't advise them not to do so. Nobody has proven that those who sleep with their families will have a better life, or vice versa.

Children of all ages need boundaries. Newborns prefer small, cozy spaces. Bassinets work well at the beginning. A child can make the transition from a small sleeping space (a bassinet) to a bigger space (a crib) when she is ready. For bedtime, wrap your newborn baby loosely in a blanket. I recommend using a sleeping sack, similar to a miniature sleeping bag, which keeps your baby warm yet free to move. Swaddling is too binding and prevents a child from moving.

For a newborn, it's best to keep toys out of the bassinet or crib. The message should be to sleep rather than to play. For the older baby who will show you by clinging to a favorite teddy bear or blanket, cuddling with these things at bedtime is fine. You can also ask an older baby whether she wants to sleep with a particular comfort object.

Peaceful Days Help Your Baby Sleep at Night

There is a correlation between a baby's being overstimulated during the day by too much activity and noise, and being unable to sleep at night. The more peaceful her day, the better the chances your baby will sleep well and be able to sleep through the night. There's an old adage, "The more you sleep, the more you can sleep." Babies respond to the rhythm of a predictable schedule—one that is not arbitrarily enforced—rather, one that is synchronized to their body rhythms.

The ability of an infant to sleep through the night varies from baby to baby, depending on the maturation of her nervous system. It also depends on what her days are like. Look at your baby's schedule and see how quiet and peaceful it is. Try to make any necessary adjustments to make it even more so. If a baby has been sleeping through the night and suddenly stops, I ask her parents to examine her daily schedule to see if anything has changed. Changes in her routine or stress can overstimulate her and cause nighttime distress.

If she is still resistant to settling down for naps or bedtime, put her to bed earlier so she doesn't become overtired and fight sleep. She will learn to read her own cues and will begin to learn self-calming behavior such as sucking her fingers. When eased into a predictable routine of sleeping times, she will eventually learn to self-regulate.

Putting Your Baby to Bed

Make bedtime desirable by telling your baby earlier in the evening, "First you'll have your dinner, then Mommy will bathe you [or whatever routine you choose], and then you get to go to bed." Let your voice convey that going to bed is a positive rather than a negative event. If you believe this is true, it helps bedtime to become a natural and anticipated part of her routine. Then put your baby to bed earlier than you think she may be tired so that she doesn't become overtired and have a hard time settling down.

When bedtime comes around, talk to your baby. Tell her that it's time to rest. Let her know that she's going to rest well so she can feel refreshed in the morning.

A nighttime ritual, whether it's a bath before bed, cuddling, or a story, is important so that even a newborn begins to understand what bedtime means. Create a peaceful atmosphere before bedtime. Lullabies are soothing, and the best lullaby is a parent's gentle voice. Sing to your baby.

Start the lullaby while you are holding her, and finish it as you lay her in her bed, awake, if possible. If you nurse her or give her a bottle before bed, stop the feeding before she drops off to sleep. In this way she won't awaken in the middle of the night with no memory of how she got from your arms into the bed. This alone may cause tears. If she has fallen asleep during the feeding, put her in her crib. It's best not to awaken a sleeping baby. The next day start your routine earlier so she has less chance of falling asleep while feeding.

Your baby may cry when you put her in her crib and leave the room. Go back in briefly and talk to her. Tell her she's learning to put herself to sleep. If she continues to cry, you must decide if, and at what point, you want to pick her up and hold her. Know that learning to sleep on one's own is a gradual process. You learn to recognize your baby's signals of tiredness. At the same time she learns to give clearer and clearer signals. This requires trust and belief on your part that your baby can and will learn to self-soothe and learn to sleep on her own.

When Your New Baby Wakes Up at Night

If your baby awakens during the night, say to her, "It's nighttime. Time for you to go back to sleep." If you feed or change her, keep the lights low and make what you are doing as quiet and unexciting as possible.

Babies will eventually adapt their behavior to what we expect of them. If a baby awakens and cries at night and the parent goes in and picks her up, rocks her and walks her, or begins to play with her, she'll wake up even more often because she'll become accustomed to being stimulated in this way. Keep in mind that your baby's learning to put herself to sleep is a slow process rather than an overnight event.

What about Using a Cradle or a Rocking Chair?

I don't feel we have to use rocking to soothe babies or put them to sleep. Both rocking chairs and cradles bring about an altered state of consciousness, which is, in effect, an escape from reality. I've heard of desperate parents placing their child (strapped in a car seat) on top of a running clothes dryer and of parents driving their child around at night in a car until she fell asleep. There is a bridge in the northern California Bay Area called the Dumbarton Bridge, which shakes and rattles when you drive across it. It became a famous haunt of local parents who used to say that if their child wouldn't sleep, all they needed to do was to drive back and forth across it until she did.

Why, I wonder, are we parents driven to these extremes? Adults and children, too, are better off learning to deal with realities. In this case, the reality is that now it's bedtime and the child is learning to fall asleep. This is a skill that takes time to learn. Allow your baby the time to discover how to soothe herself. Trust that she will.

What Is Quality Time?

There is much talk these days about quality time. It seems parents are always seeking it, and always feeling guilty about not making enough of it for themselves and their children. Daily caregiving routines such as feeding and diapering provide a source of togetherness for parent and child. Consider how many times a child is diapered in her life: about six thousand. How many times is she fed? Many more. These are the times, so frequent and intimate, that promote attachment, natural opportunities for true quality time.

All these hours of interaction have a cumulative effect on your child. How will your baby look back on them? How will she feel about herself in regard to her diapering interactions? This may be a subtle point but I think that over time, the sum total of behaviors add up, either positively or negatively, to influence us.

Picture these two scenarios:

1. A mother quickly picks up her baby, saying, "Your diaper is dirty." She places him on the changing table, having forgotten the wipes. She picks up the child and goes to the cupboard to get them. The phone rings and she answers it. She engages in a brief conversation while the baby is in her arms. An older sibling yells up from downstairs, "Mom, when is dinner ready?" She yells back, "In a few minutes, honey. I want you to change your clothes and do your homework first. And please turn off the TV." She takes the wipes and sets the baby down on the changing table again. She quickly diapers him, grimacing at the dirty diaper, and says, "Now we can do something fun." She picks him up and they go downstairs.

2. A mother says to her baby, "Your diaper is dirty. I'm going to change it." She waits a moment as their gazes meet and then slowly picks up the baby and takes her to the changing table. The changing supplies have been stocked ahead of time. The phone rings and the answering machine picks up the call. An older sibling yells upstairs, "Mom, when is dinner ready?" She says, "I'll be with you in a minute. I'm changing Teresa." The mother turns to her child and says, "It'll feel nice to have a clean diaper. I'm going to take off the dirty one first. Can you lift your bottom? I'm going to clean you off and put on the new diaper. Yes, it feels soft." The baby smiles and the mother kisses her cheek. "There. We're done. We're going downstairs. I'm going to pick you up." She slowly picks up the baby and they go downstairs.

If parent and baby continually interact as in the second example, they are learning to enjoy the spirit of cooperation. The parent

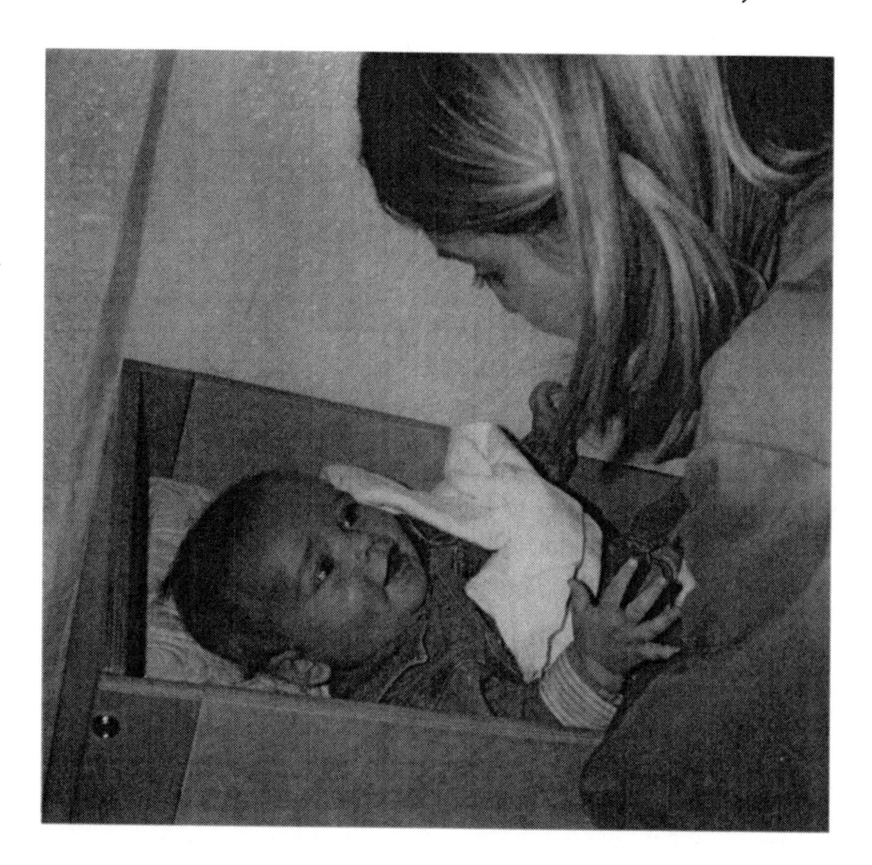

is not performing a chore on an object or manipulating the child like a doll, but involving her in a process that will come to be viewed as pleasurable and looked forward to. Importantly, bodily functions and their care are regarded as pleasant and pleasurable, not dirty or bothersome and something to be quickly gotten over.

The parent in the above scenario demonstrates respect for the infant's ability to participate, and the loving relationship is renewed each time the activity happens. Your child, no matter what age, will respond to your focused attention, although changing a toddler might require more patience. The habit you are forming will carry over into all future interactions with her. This also encourages your child to be an active participant, which sets the tone for her role in her self-care in later years.

It is not difficult to maintain this level of interaction. You can switch on the phone recorder and put other activities on hold for a few minutes. You can say to your baby, "I'm taking the phone off the hook because now I want to spend time with you." You are telling your child: "You are important. You are number one right now." The message pays off.

There is a Native American saying that, through its gentle wisdom, illustrates this idea:

Tell me and I'll forget.
Show me and I'll probably not remember.
Involve me and I'll understand.

Feeding, bathing, and dressing are other opportunities for involvement and quality time. The same steps are followed. Tell your child what is going to happen next and follow through in a slow and gentle manner. All caregiving activities promote closeness when this attitude is maintained.

"Wants Something" Quality Time

I call this type of cooperative effort "wants something" quality time. This is when you and your child have a goal to accomplish together. The goal is to elicit your child's cooperation, which is encouraged by her active involvement. Let her know what you expect her to do, even if she can't yet comply. This is the very beginning of discipline.

Diane comments, "I've learned that caregiving activities are about going slow and enjoying the process—not just about getting the clothes on. It's a way of relating to my child. Playing with my child on the floor isn't more of a quality moment than putting on his diaper. It's a process I enjoy rather than a means to an end."

Seeing caregiving tasks as quality time will give your baby the feeling that you enjoy the time you spend together, which will make her feel valued. Savor the process.

"Wants Nothing" Quality Time

"Wants nothing" quality time is when you have no goal for your child such as feeding or dressing her. You are available, watching her, listening to her, simply being with her whether she is in her crib, her playpen, or on a quilt on the floor. This is the state of sensitive observation that helps you learn about her. Rather than expecting your child to "do something," let her explore while you remain with her. Let her know by your quiet yet attentive presence that she doesn't have to perform to hold your interest.

This can be a peaceful experience for you, as many parents in our classes have told me. It is a supportive and validating experience for your child because she is allowed to be and do what she wishes (in a safe environment) as you watch. Let her be an initiator and an explorer, even if she's just studying her hands, while you stay on the sidelines.

Hank, a sales manager, and father of Haylie, two, says, "I learned to sit back and observe my daughter. I get a lot of pleasure watching her explore and play. And I feel less pressured about having to constantly entertain her."

Fully being with your child, wanting nothing, is quality time.

Crying Is Your Child's Language

Crying is a child's language. It is her way of communicating her needs to her parents. Every average, healthy child cries. It is the way a baby expresses her feelings and she should be allowed to do so. Rather than trying to stop your child from crying by distracting her, try to figure out why she is crying so that you are able to help her. Think of crying as her way of communicating with you.

I feel a baby must never be told not to cry or be distracted from crying, even if listening to it is difficult for the parent. I often say to parents that if you tell your child not to cry you better set aside lots of money to send her to Primal Scream Therapy when she grows up. People go to therapy because they no longer trust how they feel, thinking, "I feel desperate but maybe I'm not. Maybe I'm okay after all."

Parents have asked me, if crying is a child's language, isn't she telling us to *do* something? My answer is, not necessarily. It's different from when a grown-up cries. It's the baby's mode of self-expression. Since an infant cannot talk, crying is the only way she can express her feelings or discomfort. Babies also cry to discharge energy. They don't run and play as older children do.

Rather than hushing a crying baby or telling her she's okay, a better response would be to say, "I hope or I wish you would be okay," or "I hear you crying. I hope I will soon understand why so I can help," or "How can I help you? What do you need? Are you tired? Are you hungry?"

It's painful to listen to a crying baby. Grown-ups tend to overreact to a child's cry. Why? Because crying often stirs up painful memories of our own childhood, churning up issues of abandonment and fear. Perhaps as babies or young children we were not allowed to cry and were distracted or reproached when we did. Our child's tears may trigger in us these buried memories of rage, helplessness, or terror, taking us back to those early years. Our baby's message may then become muddled in our own issues. Try to listen to your baby to hear what she is saying.

In time you will build a little tolerance and figure out why she's crying. The cry slowly becomes recognizable as the hungry cry or the tired cry. After differentiating between the cries you can decide if you need to do something for her or not.

Crying is an irritant, no doubt. It is meant to be an irritant, a call to attention. Nobody enjoys it. But you still need to listen. If you tell your child not to cry, later you might say to her, "Don't talk. I'm not interested in what you're saying." The worst thing to do would be to stop a child from crying. That says to her, "Don't tell me how you feel." Think about how you would react if you were upset, had a bad day, or were depressed, and the person you relied on said, "You're okay." It's discounting.

If your child were three years older, she would be able to talk to you and say, "Mom, I'm hungry," and you would understand what she wanted. Try to understand your baby's language.

Aletha Solter, developmental psychologist and mother of two, is the author of *The Aware Baby* (Shining Star Press, 1989) and founder of the Aware Parenting Institute in Southern California. In an article published in *Educaring* (Winter 1994), RIE's newsletter, she writes,

> Crying is actually very beneficial for people of all ages. Research has shown that helpful physiological changes occur in the body during crying. Dr. William Frey, a biochemist, has analyzed human tears and found substances in them

> that are produced in the body during stress. These chemicals, no longer needed after the stressful event is over, keep the body in a needless state of tension and arousal until they are eliminated through tears. Physiologists have found a decrease in tension in people after they have had a good cry. If we can remember to think of crying as a healing mechanism, it is easier to deal with it in a loving and supportive way.

An atmosphere of healthy relating between you and your baby is the goal. Your challenge is to try to understand what your baby's cry means, a skill that develops as your relationship deepens and as you better understand your child.

How to Respond to Crying

A crying baby responds to gentleness and calmness. Respond slowly and acknowledge that she is crying by saying, "You're crying. What's the matter?"

Next, make sure that her basic needs are taken care of. Be sure your baby is fed and warm. Some babies are more sensitive to a wet diaper than others, so check that. If she is neither hungry nor tired and seems to have no other pressing need, observe her to discover the possible source of any other discomfort.

Tell her you're trying to understand what she wants. You can hold her gently or lay her down. She doesn't need to be jiggled and jostled, which can stimulate her further. Be sure the light and noise levels in the baby's environment are kept low and nonstimulating.

Quiet calms a baby. I may softly talk to her. I may hold her, although some children prefer to lie quietly. I wouldn't pat or bounce her. Patting can be intrusive. It is a mild form of hitting. I've seen patting go from gentle tapping to less and less gentle if the baby didn't stop crying. Think about what *you* like if you are upset or anxious. Would you rather be held gently and talked to softly, or bounced up and down and struck on the back? I don't believe that a child needs to be struck on the back for burping, either.

All the many forms of what we call comforting, bouncing a child on one's knee or rocking her in a rocking chair, often express our own nervous energy and frustration when confronted with a crying baby. Perhaps doing these things calms us rather than the baby. Parents do many things out of desperation under the guise of soothing the baby, and children get habituated to what parents do. Babies can learn to calm down by getting used to anything we do or don't do to them.

What should you do if your baby cries during bathing, dressing, or diapering? Try to see what helps her. Try to figure out whether she might be cold or tired. Observe her to get clues and adjust accordingly. Try to please her while hoping and expecting that she will adapt to what you are doing. Do things slowly. Slowing down automatically creates more peacefulness and cooperation.

There is a question I have been asked by new parents more than often. How long should I let the baby cry before I pick her up? There really is no answer to this, if you're looking for a specific amount of time. After her basic needs have been met, it depends on your tolerance. Even the intensity of the cry doesn't necessarily matter (unless you think she's in real, physical pain—then you must do something). Some babies can scream for a moment and in the next, drop off to sleep. Observe her, talk to her. Your presence and soft voice may calm her.

The cry cuts straight to the heart, and it's meant to. It is the baby's survival mechanism, that which summons a groggy parent from a dead sleep in the middle of the night. Respect your baby by listening to her, even when she's crying. Give yourself time to understand her.

A Word about Baby Slings, Swings, and Bouncers

Parents do many things to prevent crying, to stop crying, and to soothe a baby. There is a market glut of slings, swings, and bouncers, even electronic bouncers and baby videos. The consumer baby industry wants us to believe that we need all these things to survive. They know parents, especially anxious, new ones, are tempted to do many things to alleviate crying and to keep a baby "happy."

It can be very tempting to place children in mechanical swings and bouncers. These store-bought baby-sitters are touted to be mothers' helpers, but the quiet they produce is artificially induced, putting your baby into an altered state of consciousness similar to what a rocking chair or cradle does, what I call "zombied out." In such restraining devices, a baby cannot move freely. She is more or less a prisoner. A baby's natural inborn desire to move should not be hindered by her environment.

I will briefly review some of the equipment parents may think of using with their babies and discuss what I consider to be the drawbacks:

Baby carriers: Using a baby carrier, like a Snugli or baby sling, leaves your baby hanging from your body in a passive position, unable to move. I equate love with empathetic attention rather than simple physical closeness.

Infant seats and bouncers: These, too, keep a child from moving in a natural manner on her own.

Swings: These hypnotize children with their back and forth movement. I like for children to be aware of what they do and how they feel, even if what they feel is tired, hungry, or frustrated. Swings encourage passivity. What goal is accomplished by not letting your child face reality? A swing is fine for an older child who can get into and out of it and pump it herself. That's an active activity.

Theodore D. Wachs, in *Early Experience and Human Development* (Plenum Press, 1982), supports this idea. He cites ample evidence that "physical restrictions of the child's attempts at exploration, defined primarily in terms of lack of floor freedom and possibly in terms of physical barriers, tends to be related to lowered cognitive-intellectual development."

Walkers: The term *walker* is a misnomer. It is a piece of equipment on wheels in which a dangling baby rolls across a floor. In order to walk, a baby needs to learn how to support her weight and balance on one foot. She does neither of these in a walker. Studies have also shown that walkers are dangerous.

The February 1987 issue of *Child Health Alert* reveals that surveys in the United States and Canada have shown that walkers are used in the majority of homes with children and that although parents employ walkers to keep their children out of harm's way, as many as 40 percent of children using them suffer injuries ranging from pinched fingers to falling down stairs. Since walkers can move at about three feet per second, parents may not be able to react in time to prevent injuries. In addition, children over six months old have been found to use walkers to get into poison products (as reported in *Child Health Alert,* September 1986). Finally, the report noted that walkers may slow motor development.

I would like a child to develop naturally and do what she can do by herself. Some children move their heads from side to side or rock in their beds to self-calm. That's natural. When a child is placed in a bouncer or mechanical swing, she's strapped in. And she may become dependent on artificial devices to relax or fall asleep. Further, the more distractions a parent presents, the less she observes her child. Allow her to move freely and to feel free, without being suspended in an unnatural position.

David, a chief financial officer, father of D.J., eighteen months, says, "We used to have a walker and a bouncer, and tried to assist D.J. to move, sit, and walk. We wanted to take away all of his frustrations. We learned from you to sit back, observe, and let him be. When we did this he seemed much happier and his development took off."

If you allow your child to cry and settle herself, you encourage her to learn coping skills. She will discover what *she* needs to do to feel better. If allowed to self-soothe, an infant can learn to suck her wrist or thumb, find a comforting body position, or focus on an object in the room, as suggested by Dr. William A. H. Sammons in *The Self-Calmed Baby* (Little, Brown, 1989). The coping skills will serve her long after the swing has been put in the closet.

To Use the Pacifier or Not?

The pacifier is yet another soothing device. In fact, antique pacifiers were cloth sacks stuffed with poppy seeds—the source of the sleep-inducing drug morphine—and sedation was duly achieved. The problem with the pacifier of today is that it is an object that inconveniently falls out of the child's mouth. Worse yet, the child has no control over it. A parent decides when his child needs to suck on it and pops it into the child's mouth or pulls it out. By plugging the child's mouth the message she's getting is "Shut up." The parent also decides at what age it should be taken away.

The thumb is the perfect, built-in pacifier that your child controls. Children feel empowered by making choices. It is always best to let your child make choices in her life when it is safe and reasonable.

There seems to be an instinctual social prejudice against thumb-sucking in some cultures. A German fairy tale dated back to 1845 about the Struwwelpeter comes to mind, where the thumb-sucking child's thumbs are cut off with a big pair of scissors. Babies are natural thumb-suckers, often sucking inside the womb. Allow your child to do what comes naturally.

Helping Your Baby Learn to Self-Soothe

During her awake times out of her crib, I believe in placing a baby on her back on a blanket or a quilt, or in her playpen, indoors or out, whichever is the designated safe place. In this way she can look around and move her arms and legs. She can explore her body and her world. Quiet is calming. If needed, you can talk to her for comfort. If she isn't picked up at the slightest expression of discomfort, she will learn to calm herself. It sounds simple but it works. Children do not need to be held constantly, and may not want to be held when they cry or are upset. Parents often associate crying with pain. An infant's cry can stir in us feelings of fear or pain from our own childhoods and we may assume our baby is experiencing the same pain. With babies, this isn't necessarily so.

A child can calm herself by sucking her blanket or thumb. Some children cry to calm themselves. It's usually a steady, rhythmic cry. A child quickly adapts to what a parent does to calm her. An electronic bouncer may quiet her, if that is the goal, but it won't help her help herself. As with everything concerning babies, they need time to learn a new skill. The more time she spends on her back, the more she will adapt to it. And in this position, she can explore her environment. Eventually, she will become accustomed to spending time on her own in her safe place, which will give you more free time (more on this in chapter 5).

Placing infants on their backs also works well with colicky babies who can move their legs to relieve stomach tension. The belly is massaged by the leg movements.

If Your Baby Is Colicky

There is a time in the first few months when some babies can be colicky, until their bodies learn to get rid of the gas bubbles in their intestines. You can put a little pressure on the baby's stomach to help the bubble come out by applying a warm hand or a washcloth. If you allow a child to lie on her back, she can kick her legs to help get rid of the gas. It's sometimes less helpful to hold her. Chamomile tea, brewed very mildly and cooled, fed through a bottle, may help. Colicky babies also need a peaceful environment, as they are especially sensitive to overstimulation.

Zina, a former elementary school teacher, mother of Emily, ten, says,

> From birth Emily cried really loud and hard at anything that bothered her so it was hard to figure out what she wanted. It was difficult to get her to go to sleep and then she would burp or spit up and wake herself up. The nurse that came to our home for her two-week checkup put her hand on Emily's abdomen and said she could feel the gas bubbles. One day Emily started crying at four in the afternoon and didn't stop until eleven that night. After that, every time she started crying I had this feeling of dread that if I didn't stop it immediately she would cry endlessly. As a result, I got in the habit of nursing her or picking her up the minute she started to fuss. RIE helped me to get out of that habit. I learned to wait and try to figure out what was going on. I gave her a chance to solve the problem without immediately rushing to pick her up and rock her.

There is a mantra you can use: This, too, shall pass. Colic subsides after the first several months.

Preventing SIDS

Over the years there has been much controversy about the safest position for a new baby—stomach, side, or back. Sudden Infant Death Syndrome (SIDS) has been at the heart of the discussion. I have always been a proponent of placing young babies on their backs, for sleeping as well as awake times.

There is increasing support in the medical community for using this position over side- or stomach-lying to prevent SIDS. A recent study, the largest of its kind, encompassing more than 350,000 births over a two-year period, was conducted by Dr. Peter Fleming of the University of Bristol in England and published in the *British Medical Journal.* In it Dr. Fleming found that allowing a baby to sleep on her back rather than her side or stomach cuts the risk of SIDS by 50 percent. Following this study a Back to Sleep campaign was conducted in England. As a result of public awareness the incidence of SIDS in England has dropped by two-thirds in the last five years (*Los Angeles Times,* July 26, 1996).

In late 1996 the American Academy of Pediatrics reaffirmed its "back-to-sleep" recommendation. In the February/March 1997 issue of *Healthy Kids,* Dr. Robert Hanneman, president of the AAP, noted that the incidence of SIDS has dropped nearly 30 percent in the United States since 1992.

Note that there are other risk factors involved in SIDS, such as the parent's smoking, putting the baby in heavily wrapped bedclothes, and lack of prenatal care. In addition, certain medical conditions may require that an infant sleep on her stomach. Be sure to check with your pediatrician.

Parents have asked me, what if my baby prefers to sleep on her stomach and fusses when I put her on her back? A baby may become accustomed to certain positions she is placed in before she is old enough to turn over on her own. Or parents may interpret or misinterpret what their baby wants. In any case, stomach sleeping is the least safe, so I wouldn't advise placing a young baby on her stomach. Of course, an older baby who can turn over on her own makes her own choice and cannot be prevented from sleeping on her stomach.

Can We Spoil Our Babies?

When we think of spoiled children, we think of those who are rude or willful, who seem to be concerned only with themselves. How does this process take place, transforming a tiny baby who is newly experiencing the world into a child whom nobody wants to be around?

I think of a spoiled child as one whose ability to cope with the world has been damaged, or spoiled. Perhaps her parents worried so much that they tried to remove every obstacle or challenge from her path. Perhaps they got into the habit of being her entertainers or provided enough distractions so she lost her natural curiosity and never learned how to entertain herself. Perhaps they overdirected her play and experiences so she never felt free. Or perhaps they didn't set appropriate limits so their child never learned self-discipline.

Attending to your new baby in a loving manner is not the same as spoiling her. It demonstrates your love. While you attend to her needs, allow her the space, the time, and the support to do what she can on her own, whether it's to self-soothe, cry when she needs to cry, or explore her environment. Through observation you will learn to distinguish the fine line between her needs and yours, and learn how to help her help herself.

The effort will be well worth it as your child grows to be a confident person who respects her parents because they respected her.

◐ 4 ◑

Newborn Parents

You have just brought your baby home from the hospital. It is all you've dreamed of, welcoming this new little person into the family. It's a major adjustment, for the mother and father as well as the baby. You are newborn parents.

As a mother, your body is healing from the baby's birth and recovering from the hormonal changes. Your milk is coming in and you may be sore and tired. As a father, you're adjusting to the baby and to your wife's becoming a mother. Both parents have just ridden an emotional roller coaster and may be physically and emotionally drained, more so if there were complications at birth with either the mother or the baby, or both. It used to be that when a mother gave birth in a hospital, she rested and recuperated there for ten days at a minimum. Unfortunately, two-day stays are now the norm.

Coming home from the hospital can be a time of great anxiety as well as joy. Having a baby is a very big change in a person's life. Parenthood is a forever relationship. Take time to prepare for it.

Ask for Help in Your Home

It is vital to plan well ahead of time to have help in the home, whether it's a friend cooking meals, Grandmother watching the baby while the mother naps, or a neighbor helping out with the marketing. Newborn parents should do nothing else but focus on their child and each other. In many countries a new family employs a "doula," from the Greek word meaning "one who ministers." A doula is brought in to mother the mother—help her with household chores. Some doulas also assist in labor and childbirth.

A doula takes care of the mother, leaving the new mother and father time to spend with their baby. The new family unit is thus respected.

For newborn parents, rest and quiet are a priority in the first weeks. The longer both parents can take time off to rest and be with their baby, the better. In order to treat their new child with respect, parents must first treat themselves with respect.

Try to Do Less

Our society tells us, do, do, do. Do a lot. Do more. And if you don't do, at least pretend to do. Being busy is considered a virtue, while not being busy is considered laziness. Laziness, or what is perceived as laziness, often a slower pace, is not appreciated in our fast-paced culture.

I believe in slowing down and doing less. After giving birth, parents need time to heal physically, mentally, and emotionally. Let go of extraneous and unimportant things. For the first two and a half years, keep your child home most of the time. Have a safe playroom and an outdoor play area. Lead a simple life. Some people might call it boring. It wouldn't, however, be boring for your child. Children thrive on routine. In this way they develop inner rhythms of sleep, hunger, and satiation. Routines help them slowly settle into a schedule of mutual adaptation to the family.

I believe children need sleep, peace, and quiet. Rather than stimulate our babies, we should respect the enormous changes that occur as a child makes the transition from the womb to the world, and allow it to happen slowly. Doing less with and to your baby, in the way of scheduled activities and interruption of her play, also means doing less yourself.

Parents may be scared at the thought of staying home with their child and worry that they'll lose their drive to work or pursue other goals. I would advise you not to worry. When you have a young child, your whole being may want to stay with your child. As your child grows and becomes more independent, the pendulum usually swings the other way.

Relax and enjoy your child. Let him adjust to his new world as you adjust to him.

Take Your Time

By slowing down and taking your time, you are not only doing your child a great service, you are doing the same for yourself. By observing him, learning to read his cues, and not rushing in to try to solve every problem he encounters, you are setting up an environment of inner-focused direction in which he will thrive. You are also reserving your own energy for the times you need it. Try to build extra time into your schedule to allow for this important, unhurried time.

Geralynn, thirty-two, a child development teacher turned stay-at-home mother of Delanie, two, comments, "The most important thing I learned from RIE was to *wait*—your famous four-letter word. When in doubt, when I don't know what my daughter needs, and especially if I'm in a hurry and may misread her signals, I take a deep breath, wait, and observe her. Delanie learned what the word meant at a young age because she's so often heard me say to myself, 'Wait.'"

Abraham Lincoln once said, "Nothing valuable can be lost by taking time."

Listening to Your Child's Cries

I don't feel I can talk too much about crying. It is one of the most difficult areas new parents must learn to deal with. A story is sometimes a better teacher, so I include another one.

I remember a RIE parent/infant class that was filled with first-time parents and young babies, around five to six months old. I watched as one of the babies, lying on the covered mat, started to fuss, which escalated into a cry. The mother, looking concerned, turned to her husband. "What do you think she needs?" she asked him.

The husband thoughtfully regarded the baby. "I don't know. She's been fed, burped, and changed." They both observed their crying child for a moment, then turned to me.

"What should I do?" asked the mother.

"Maybe she's cold," I offered, noticing it was becoming breezy outside on the deck.

The mother pulled a receiving blanket out of the diaper bag and covered the baby, then looked at me. "Oops. I forgot to tell her."

I smiled and said, "It's forgivable."

The baby continued crying and the mother again looked at me. "How long should I let her cry?"

"As long as you can listen to it," I said. "If you don't think she's in any real distress. Crying is her language. It's okay for her to cry. It doesn't mean she's in pain."

I watched as the mother waited for about a minute, then told her daughter she was going to pick her up. Like the domino effect, the other babies chimed in and began crying, one by one.

"They are making a symphony," I said. The parents laughed, some I could tell, nervously. I could see that they were having a difficult time listening to their children cry.

The class ebbed and flowed. There were moments of peace when the babies gazed up at the rubber tree over the deck, watching its patterns of shadow and light. At other times they studied their hands, reached for nearby play objects, or slept. There were moments such as those I described, when all the children cried. There was a moment when a mother cried tears of frustration when she wasn't able to calm her screaming child. "It's very hard to listen to your child cry," I told her. Our support helped her through it.

As I sat watching the class, one of the fathers asked me how I was able to sit through all the crying. "You must be used to it," he said.

"I've been doing it a long time," I replied. "But I also know that crying is okay. It's part of being a baby. Allowing a child to cry is healthy for parents and children."

This may be a difficult lesson to learn—listening to your child's cries—but eventually you will understand what he's saying to you. Give it time.

The Qualities of a Good Parent

I have often been asked what qualities are desirable in a good parent. I consider optimism to be a good quality. Having trust in oneself is important, too, so when a parent fails or goofs he can say,

"Next time I'll try harder." It's helpful to be naturally optimistic without becoming a Pollyanna.

However, nobody is an ideal parent all the time. Parents get tired, upset, and frustrated. In real life, mistakes happen. People get angry, sometimes unduly so. Dealing with a parent's genuineness, whether it takes the form of a positive or negative emotion, prepares a child for life. Is life fair? At times, no. You need to make peace and go on.

Be honest with your child. It's okay to say, "I'm tired right now. I'm listening to you, but I'm tired." That teaches a child reality. You must listen to your own needs, too. In this way you will also help him learn to listen to his.

The following suggestions offer guidelines for good parenting:

1. ***Feel secure, but don't become rigid.*** A secure parent, one whose own needs are met, is more able to relax. He will feel more flexible and be better able to deal with his child. Flexibility works better than rigidity in any life situation. Your child changes a little every day. When you look back on the weeks, months, and years of parenthood, they will seem to have flown by. Children grow up fast. It is helpful if parents are flexible enough to bend, adjust, and change with each passing day.

2. ***Be accepting, but set limits.*** Be accepting of the stage and state (meaning physical state, whether sick, teething, or type of mood) your child is in. Limits are important so that your child is aware of the rules. However, always acknowledge what he wants even if you won't let him do it or have it. For example, you might say, "You want to jump out of the car right now but I won't let you do it because it's dangerous." Desires should be acknowledged and accepted, but rules enforced.

3. ***Be available, but not intrusive.*** Being available means that you are with your child without trying to dictate what he should be doing or playing with (as long as it's safe). Achieving this available, nonintrusive state is a learned process. There is, however, a great difference between an observant parent and a neglectful one. An observant parent is aware and tuned in to what his child is doing. He has made the decision to let the child explore on his own and not to intervene unless a changed situation, such as the need to go out or get ready for bed, warrants it.

4. ***Be patient, but be true to yourself.*** Your patience, as hard as it is to achieve at times, supports your child's growth and self-confidence by allowing him time to work out his inner processes. However, we all have individual strengths and weaknesses. These come into play when we interact with our children. Be as patient as you can but be aware of what behavior really bothers you or makes you anxious and feel free to act on it. Let your child know the reality of the situation (of course, first deciding what's appropriate for him to hear) by saying, "I don't want you putting your shoes on the couch. The furniture will get dirty," or "I don't want you to take your food away from the table. This is where I want you to eat." You can also explain yourself further by saying, "You have me for a mother (or father)." Respect your own vulnerabilities.

5. ***Be realistic but consistent in your expectations.*** Expect only what your child is able to deliver. If he can only crawl, don't expect him to walk or help him to walk. Consistently express what behavior you expect, whether it's his cooperation in diapering or keeping his food on the table. Education means that you have a certain goal and you consistently work with your child to achieve that goal. Please note that it's more difficult to be consistent when you are tired or angry. By meeting your own needs consistently (getting enough sleep, relaxation time, or simply time away from caring for your child), you are more likely to be consistent with your child.

6. ***Have the wisdom to resist new fads.*** When a new book or idea becomes popular, parents may feel compelled to try it out. Our "on the go" and "faster and sooner is better" society may promote this faddist mentality. Be wise enough to resist passing fads. Simplicity, observation, and unhurried time never go out of style.

7. ***Achieve a balance between giving quality time to your child and to yourself.*** If you only give, you deplete yourself. It's helpful if both parents can work together to raise their child so each parent can have time for him- or herself. You might consider hiring a carer to come in for a few hours to give you time away. Or arrange baby-sitting exchanges with other parents. Try to find ways to enjoy your child without depleting yourself.

8. ***Achieve a state of self-respect and give equal respect to your children.*** Respect your own strengths and weaknesses, likes and dislikes. Make your life as easy and comfortable as possible.

If you do this, there is a much greater likelihood you will respect your child and become better parents. If you are satisfied and happy, you are more likely to interact with your child in a healthy way. It's important to keep your sense of humor, too.

Go Out, Have Fun

Living with babies is difficult. Parents shouldn't suffer any guilt thinking or saying this. Even the most angelic baby gets on the saintliest parent's nerves from time to time. Babies can be very tiresome, although I love babies and enjoy being with them. Parenthood, however, is a twenty-four-hour, seven-day-a-week job. A parent is always on call. You don't get breaks.

We live in a time when the extended family is typically spread apart. In times past, extended families lived together and children were also taken care of by grandparents, aunts, and cousins. Mothers and fathers were not the sole carers, as they are in many households today, which puts parents under even more stress.

I suggest that you get a trusted carer and go out and have fun, once or twice a week, or as often as you can. Forget you ever had a baby. Go dancing, go to the movies. Remove yourself from the home environment. You will return to it refreshed and happy to be with your child. Raising children is not easy, and it's important to take care of yourself.

Give Your Child (and Yourself) Time Alone

One of RIE's basic principles is allowing your child time for uninterrupted play. He can do this very well in his safe place, all by himself, with occasional checking in done by you. You can put your young, not very mobile baby on a blanket in a safe, gated-off area or in a playpen, and tell him you are leaving the room for a few minutes. When he's a little older and moving about, you can place a ball or a few simple toys in with him. An older infant or toddler can play in his safe area or room. In this way, a habit is developing that will carry over as he grows. And you will be making life easier for yourself by helping him become autonomous.

Geralynn comments,

> I put Delanie in a playpen and let her play alone from the time she was three weeks old. An out-of-town guest commented once, "I've never seen such a young baby play by herself for so long." This echoed a statement you made in the early childhood education class I took in college when you said to put babies on their backs so they can explore their bodies and their world. At two months, Delanie played alone for thirty to forty-five minutes. From what I've seen, the ability to enjoy solitude starts in infancy although I'd read research that said it starts at school age.

RIE's Principles Will Help You

By following RIE's respectful approach to parenting, you will make your life easier, in the short term and in the long run. By letting your child self-calm, spend time alone, and work out his own conflicts, he will also learn to be self-sufficient. By laying the groundwork in the ways I encourage, I believe he will be a happier, more cooperative child.

Patty, an associate professor of child development at Los Angeles City College and mother of Laurel, fifteen, and Robert, twenty-three, says,

> My son was ten months old when I first encountered RIE. I had already developed certain patterns with him—I rocked and nursed him to sleep and he had the run of the house. With my daughter, I started using the RIE approach from the beginning. She had a safe, gated area to play in. I put her in her bed awake to go to sleep. I find it invaluable to have had the before and after experience because when I teach RIE my students see someone who has personally experienced both things. Laurel was quite an active little person who needed a more predictable environment and more predictable caregiving than my son. I feel like I overparented my son. I had him on the kitchen table as I cooked dinner. I never got the opportunity to see him hold out his

> arms for me to pick him up because I never waited long enough.

Becky comments,

> RIE gave me permission to be tired, to not be the perfect mom, to take care of myself. It has carried over in the way I do therapy in that I trust that my clients have the answers and I wait to see how they're going to resolve a problem.

Zina adds,

> Having taught school and having been around children all my adult life, I thought being a parent would be easy. Emily was a colicky baby who didn't take regular naps or sleep through the night until she was two. I learned to sit back and observe her, to not interfere in her play with other kids, and to trust her judgment. I learned to become a better and less nervous mother.

Iris, a part-time office manager, mother of Angelica, eighteen months, says,

> Very few books about children's self-esteem and effective parenting talk about how to interact with a baby. Most of them address reasoning with an older child. Self-esteem begins in infancy. RIE has taken this important principle and applied it to babies. Because of your many years of experience, you also put everything in a long-term perspective while we parents are focused on the immediate problem.

Elizabeth Memel, infant specialist and RIE instructor, in her master's thesis titled "RIE and Its Families: The Impact of Family Support on Parents and Their Very Young Children" (1991, Pacific Oaks College, Pasadena, Calif.), has documented the low stress level of RIE parents. The instrument used was *The Parenting Stress Index/Short Form,* published by the University of Virginia in 1990. In comparison with the eight hundred families in the standardized norm, the twenty-three families from the RIE Parent/Infant Classes revealed lower parenting stress levels by strongly disagreeing with test items such as the following:

- My child seems to cry or fuss more than most children.
- My child makes more demands on me than other children.
- My child gets upset easily over the slightest thing.
- My child's eating or sleeping schedule was much harder to establish than I imagined.

The conclusion of the unpublished thesis is "that RIE had had a very strong impact on the people included in this study."

Respect Yourself

In order to have enough energy to observe and respect your child, you must first respect yourself. Take care of yourself and your needs, without guilt. Be kind to yourself and forgive yourself. By doing this you will set an example for your child. Parenting is not a science. Rather, it is a learning process that continues throughout life.

If you work, save energy when you go home to be with your family. Find available people who will help with the baby while you rest or go out. Start a co-op of two or three mothers in which you exchange caregiving. It's okay to feel fed up and frazzled. At first the days, and especially the nights, feel eternal, but the baby grows and changes, and the next stage starts with its new challenges. With babies, there is time distortion. A day lasts forever, and the years fly by. Remember, whatever you are going through: this, too, shall pass.

After about the first three months, at the end of the newborn period for you and your baby, he is learning to adapt to you and to his home. He is getting his days and nights straightened out, and family life is falling into a somewhat predictable routine. Your baby has given you his first smiles and all the sleepless nights seem worthwhile. You are becoming seasoned parents. Congratulations.

5

The First Months with Your Baby

After the newborn stage, your baby has grown accustomed to life "outside." Her jerky reflexes have subsided and her movements are smoother. She is becoming more aware of her world. If her needs are being met and you are available and responsive to her, she feels secure.

This chapter and the following two chapters on child development discuss your child in terms of developmental stages rather than age because children develop differently, and I feel you should expect what is appropriate for your child, without making comparisons.

At the end of the newborn stage your baby is starting to move about and will roll from her back to her side. After that, she will roll to her stomach, then eventually over again to her back. If given ample space a baby will roll across an entire room. Lying on her stomach, she will learn to pull up and rest on her forearms, then eventually start to crawl. This is the usual progression of gross motor development in a young baby if she is allowed to move naturally through it. There is a wide range as to when a child achieves certain motor skills. Some babies may not move for many months, and some may learn to roll and crawl quite early.

I believe in giving your baby a safe space in which to play and letting her move freely and develop on her own without assisting her. Refrain from propping her up to sit or helping her roll over. She has an innate desire to move through these developmental sequences and has inborn knowledge of how to do it in a way that is "right" for her. She does this at her own pace and she gets pleasure from doing it.

Dr. Pikler reveals this in *Peaceful Babies—Contented Mothers.*

> What is most important . . . is not the result, but the way to do it. The learning process will play a major role in the whole later life of the human being. Through this kind of development, the infant learns his ability to do something independently, through patient and persistent effort. While learning during motor development to turn on the belly, to roll, to creep, sit, stand, and walk, he is not only learning those movements, but also *how to learn.* He learns to do something on his own, to be interested, to try out, to experiment. He learns to overcome difficulties. He comes to know the joy and satisfaction that is derived from his success, the result of his patience and persistence.

Look at the animal kingdom. A foal stands moments after birth without having to be taught how. The cat and fox, even the elephant and the giraffe move with graceful, compact ease, in a way "right" for each species. Your baby will do the same if you allow her to. Loving parents, eager to help, may hinder their baby's growth by aiding her to move in ways unnatural for her. I encourage you to sit back and simply observe your baby as she moves through each stage of physical development. In this way you will be able to relax and enjoy your baby, and she will be supported by your attentiveness and interest.

Refining Your Observation Skills

As your child grows, the same basic RIE principles and processes that we discussed for infants are applied at each stage of development. The key to respect is sensitive observation of your child. Notice what interests her. Respect is established by removing yourself a little, creating some distance between yourself and your child in order to see her with freshness and objectivity.

Don't assume that all babies like or don't like the same things. For example, not all babies like the same amount of physical contact. Some want to cuddle more than others. Some like to be covered with a blanket; others do not. Observe your baby's preferences.

Getting to know your child through observation is critical because how you perceive her affects how you will treat her. If you see your child as a competent problem solver, you will learn to trust in her abilities. If you see her as a helpless baby, you will treat her as such and may become overprotective. The less you do for her, the more you will observe her.

A sensitive observer is peaceful and calm. Children immediately pick up on anxiety and tension. Relax and observe what your child focuses on. What in the room catches her eye? How does she respond as you stroke her cheek? Does she startle at loud noises? Is she fascinated by the design in her blanket or is she content to gaze at her hands?

By observing your child, you discover her unique personality. By understanding her individuality, you learn to deal with her needs. Through sensitive observation you are laying the groundwork for good communication with your child. If you are so finely tuned in to your child at this young age, imagine how much better you will understand each other as your child grows.

If, for example, you carefully observe your crying child, you may find that she is not merely having a fussy spell, but that her hand is stuck under her body. You can learn about her frustration level by observing this. You may discover that your child is ready for bed earlier than you thought was an appropriate time by seeing her rub her eyes. You may observe your child's joyful expression when she holds a particular stuffed animal. These are all clues to discovering your child's personality.

I remember a time when my son was a baby and he was on the floor, scratching at the carpet, over and over. I sat and watched him, unable to figure out what he was doing. By observing him it finally occurred to me that he was trying to pick the red color out of the rug.

An interesting thing to observe is when your child discovers her hands. An infant's first "aha" experience is the discovery of her hands. They move back and forth, mysteriously disappearing and reappearing. Hand play is a natural occurrence in young babies and they spend many hours doing this.

Babies Become Involved in What Interests Them

It is a misconception that babies have short attention spans. I have watched many infants become involved and play with a particular toy for a long period of time. A mother once told me she watched her child run her fingers through a doll's yellow yarn hair for thirty minutes. The difference was that the child was involved with a play object of her own choice rather than the one the mother had tried to interest her in.

Children become involved in what interests them, which brings me to another story. I remember a little boy whom several adults and I observed while he was playing. He was in a room by a window and in a dreamlike manner, made grasping gestures toward the window, repeating these motions over and over. Nobody could figure out what he was doing.

For a long time I watched him play, making these slow, sweeping movements, as if trying to catch something. It finally hit me that he was trying to grasp a ray of sunlight. It was a very touching experience. This story reminds us never to judge what a child is doing at play, even if it seems silly or we don't understand it. Children, with their fresh view of life, see the world differently from us, and should be allowed and encouraged to do so.

The French philosopher Jean-Jacques Rousseau wrote in *Émile,* a book about his views on education, "Childhood has its own way of seeing, thinking, and feeling, and nothing is more foolish than to try to substitute ours for theirs."

Talk to Your Child

Your child's feelings of security can be increased by continuing to tell her what is going to happen next. *Knowing* what will happen next gives her a feeling of control over her universe. In this way she isn't continually surprised by events that occur. Rather, she has time to prepare for them. As you talk to her, predictability is reinforced verbally.

Stacy, a home products sales rep and mother of Christopher, two, says,

> I learned how important it was to talk to Christopher from the beginning. Talking to Christopher and giving him choices has been helpful because it keeps me involved and aware of him. I might have been a parent who diapers and changes her child, moves him around and feeds him without telling him what I'm doing. I've developed a pattern of telling Christopher what I'm about to do rather than surprising or shocking him. This has made him more aware of his surroundings.
>
> When I say, "I'm going to leave the room now. I'm going into the other room," it lets him know that I don't unpredictably come in and out of his life. I have as much respect for him as for somebody at work, where I say to a coworker, "I'm going to the rest room now. Will you please answer my calls?" It's an awareness of, and a respect for, the other person.

Give your child that same respect.

Ask for Cooperation

As a child grows and matures she can be asked to cooperate and participate more in caregiving activities. For example, during bathing ask your child if she wants to hold the washcloth or if she will lift her bottom. A five-month-old baby may not be able to answer the question but will become accustomed to your inflection and facial expression and will eventually respond.

It's important to explain to her what you are doing and what will be happening next, "Now I'm going to wash your tummy with the soap and washcloth. Then I'm going to dry you off with the towel." The involvement of the child changes her role from that of a passive recipient to one of an active participant. Quality time can be shared by letting your child do as much as she can according to her stage of development. Say to her, "Will you give me your foot? I want to dry it off." In time she will learn to cooperate.

Cooperation in Diapering

Cooperation in diapering is especially helpful because children go through periods where they don't like being diapered and they resist it. It can be frustrating trying to remove a dirty diaper and clean a crying child.

First, tell her you want to change her diaper. If it isn't necessary to change the diaper immediately, see if you can wait a few moments until she's ready. Ask for her cooperation. Ask if she wants to hold the clean diaper or the lotion. A slow, calm tempo on your part is beneficial. If your child still resists and you want to change the diaper, you can tell her you understand she doesn't like her diaper being changed, but you are going to do it. Follow through gently yet firmly.

Distractions, such as giving her a toy or shaking a rattle, take away from the spirit of cooperation and participation you are trying to create. If you use a distraction to "get the job done," you are telling your child that she needn't cooperate, but turn her attention elsewhere. Further, waving a toy in front of her to distract her treats your child as an object upon which a task is being performed. Take your time. Tell your child, "I'm waiting for you." Try to adjust your tempo to hers.

Try not to give your child a negative message about her dirty diaper by making faces or using negatively descriptive words like "stinky" or "smelly." It gives a young child negative feelings about her bodily functions and can embarrass an older child.

Cooperation in Getting Dressed

Even with very young babies, dressing can be a cooperative effort. Here's an example:

Mother: looks at her baby lying on the changing table. She smiles and says, "It's time for you to get out of your pajamas and get dressed."

Child: looks up and smiles, making eye contact.

Mother: "Let's take off your pajamas. Can you help me pull your arm out?"

Child: is smiling.

Mother: "I'll help you." She gently pulls the child's arm out of the sleeve.

Child: smiles.

Mother: "Pull the other arm out."

Child: pulls her other arm out.

Mother: "I'm going to pull the pajama top over your head." She gently pulls it off.

Child: starts to cry.

Mother: "I can see you didn't like my pulling it over your face." She pauses.

Child: stops crying.

Mother: "Can you pull out your foot?"

Child: smiles.

Mother: "I'll help you pull out your foot."

Child: resists.

Mother: "You don't want to take your foot out of the pajama."

Child: smiles.

Mother: smiles back. "I'll wait till you're ready."

Child: pulls his foot out of the pajama.

Mother: smiles.

Child: smiles back.

This example shows how caregiving activities can turn into moments of pleasure by allowing a slow pace and interacting with your child. Even young babies are capable of teasing and enjoy it. All children like peekaboo. However, only secure children tease, because teasing involves a child's feeling safe enough to challenge a parent or parental figure. Momentary playing or teasing by the child is all right during caregiving and should be followed by a return to the task, which is the focus. Be sure to allow time in your daily schedule for this kind of slow interaction rather than leaving dressing for the last minute and having to hurry through it.

Feeding Is Quality Time, Too

Feeding can be a great source of pleasure and satisfaction for a parent and child. During the early months a child relies solely on the breast or bottle for nourishment. As with other caregiving activities, tell your child that it is time to eat and that she will be fed. Telling your child helps her prepare for it and anticipate the feeding, which also promotes her feeling of security.

As with bathing and diapering, feeding should take place in a quiet, intimate environment. Low lights are calming. Food is better ingested and digested in tranquillity. The mother, father, or carer should also make themselves comfortable. The two-way street of respect calls for a parent's comfort and good feelings, too. Feedings should be slow, leisurely times that lay the groundwork for good eating habits.

How to Feed the New Eater

Besides recommending breast-feeding, I prefer not to take a stand on *what* to feed a child, feeling that this is a medical issue and a question better answered by a doctor or by parents themselves. What I do suggest is feeding each food item separately, for example, not mixing fruits and cereals or fruits and vegetables. This will allow your child to differentiate tastes and temperatures, like sweet and sour, warm and cold, which adds to her developing awareness.

I encourage feeding a beginning eater on your lap. In this manner the eating experience is made more intimate. A child who cannot sit up on her own can be held in a diagonal position on your lap facing you, with her back supported by your arm. After being told she will have a meal, show your child the food on the spoon and then put it to her lips. If your child indicates she wants to eat by opening her mouth, give it to her. If she gives any indication she doesn't want the food, by turning her head to the side or by tightly closing her mouth, the food should not be given to her.

A child should *never* be forced to eat. The goal is to feed your child while initiating healthy lifetime eating habits. This can only be accomplished through your child's willingness and cooperation. On the other hand, food shouldn't be needlessly wasted, even though babies can be messy eaters.

In an article in the journal *Acta Paediatrica Academiae Scientiarum Hungaricae*, Dr. Pikler writes,

> If [an infant] does not like his food, he will let it run out of his mouth and push the food away with his tongue. If he likes it he will suck and swallow actively, even from a

spoon, and may even utter a smacking sound. If people were to notice the early, subtle signs of the child, then the alarm symptoms like spitting, bringing up the food, or vomiting would appear less often. The infant, even the newborn, informs the adult quite clearly—even before beginning to cry—whether or not he enjoys his food.

Some children indicate interest in eating by making chewing motions when watching family members eat or by wanting more bottles or nursing. Some children aren't interested in solids until later. This is perfectly acceptable. If you are unsure, wait. If your child refuses food, try it at another time. There's no hurry. Children eventually learn to eat.

Teething Is Part of Life

In the first months your child may start teething. Some children don't get their first teeth until after their first birthday, but all children teethe. Teething is a different experience for each child. Some children go through the entire process with minimal pain, some have intermittent discomfort, and some endure pain the entire time, which ends when all the baby teeth come in by about age two.

Unfortunately, you can't do too much to relieve your child's pain. It's hard to see your child suffer. But can one live without suffering? Life is, at times, unfair and painful. However, your child can learn from your attitude that the pain will pass. Try to make her as comfortable as possible. Give her objects to mouth and chew on. Plastic soap holders make wonderful teething objects; they are soft and inexpensive, and can be found at a bath or a hardware shop.

Your child may be irritable or wake up at night in pain from teething and may need extra comfort during these times. She may need to be held, have her gums massaged, or be given a teething remedy. Check with your pediatrician if you wish to use an over-the-counter medication such as acetaminophen. Since medicines like this are drugs, I recommend using them very sparingly.

When Crying Becomes Specific

As your child grows, her cries become more specific. Parents learn to recognize the tired cry, the hungry cry, and the angry cry. The more you truly observe your child, the more quickly you are likely to recognize the different cries. As communication grows between you and your child, her cries become more readable. If her cries are responded to appropriately, she feels safe and comforted. Crying decreases as your child gets older and learns more sophisticated ways of communicating, such as making sounds, gesturing, and later, speaking.

It is still difficult to listen to crying. It may unnerve parents, but you can grow to tolerate listening to it. A mother once told me that when her son was a few weeks old, she wouldn't let him cry for more than a few seconds without picking him up. She said by the time he was six months old her tolerance grew, and the extreme anxiety experienced at the beginning disappeared.

Crying is an irritant and people respond to it as an irritant, wanting to make it go away. Our goal should not be to stop the crying, but to understand what the cry means and decide whether or not to intervene. Allowing a child to cry requires more knowledge, time, and energy than just picking up a child and patting her.

Remember that a crying child may be simply complaining. It may not be in her best interest to rush and pick her up. She may not want to be picked up. If a child's basic needs have been taken care of, she should be allowed to have and express her feelings through crying. Young babies use crying as a release of energy. An infant crying angrily may be winding herself down or trying to self-soothe. Crying is a good physical release. Don't we (adults) feel relaxed after a good cry?

Often crying produces strong feelings in those listening, though crying doesn't mean the same thing to a baby as to an adult. It is the child's mode of communication and expression at this age. Talk to your child, ask why she is crying, and tell her you want to understand. Then decide how much crying you feel comfortable listening to before intervening.

Josephine Klein supports this idea in *Our Needs for Others* (Tavistock Publications, 1987), saying that "accurate empathy" rather than "doing" something for a child is the first step in

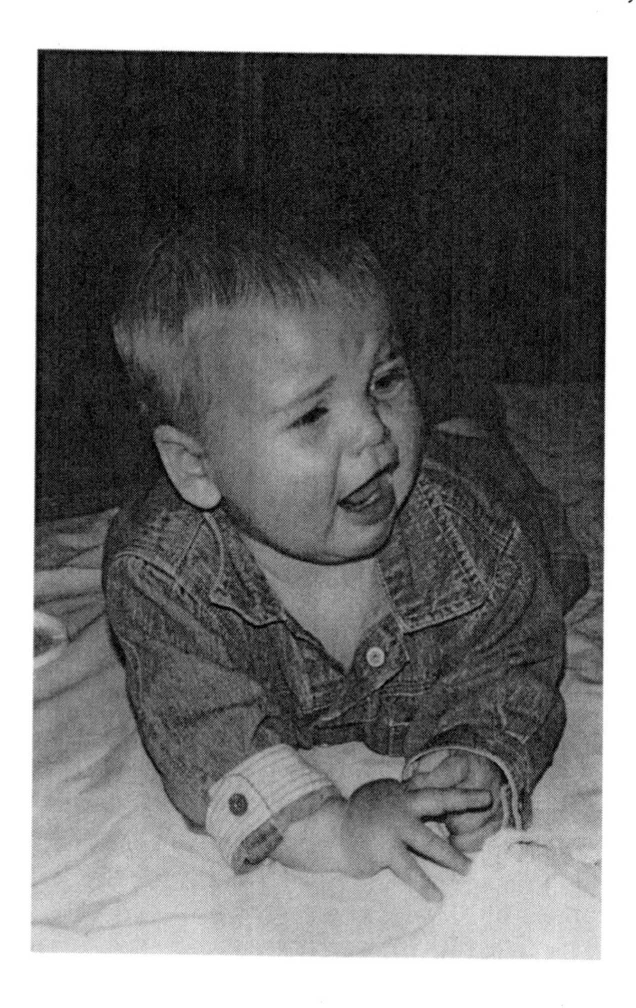

strengthening a child's sense of self. She adds, "To allow an infant to tolerate a longer interval before something is actually done about its distress . . . provides an opportunity for ego-functioning to develop in a confident, unhurried way."

Crying at Separations

Parents often ask me what to do if their child cries when they leave the room or the house. My answer is to first acknowledge the child's feelings, "You are crying, but Grandma will be with you. I'll be back soon." Then go for a short time, if possible. Parents also have asked me if they should take a crying child into the bathroom with them. I believe a child should be left in her own, natural environment. You go in. You go out. Don't take her in the bathroom with you even if she is crying loudly. Children can cry desperately. It doesn't mean that your child is as desperate as her cry would lead you to believe. And your child may still cry, no matter what you do.

There are a few unwritten, but enforced, rules at our RIE parent/infant classes. One of them is that the children must stay in the play area. Another is that if they throw a toy out of the play area, it remains there until class is over.

There are rules for parents, too. First, shoes are removed and left by the door so as not to track street dirt into the play area. Next, if a parent wants to feed her child, she takes the baby into the sitting room to give her child undivided attention. Finally, if a parent needs to use the bathroom, she goes alone, even if her child cries.

The parent tells her child, "I'm going to the bathroom now. I'll be back in a few minutes." If the baby cries after the parent leaves the room, either I or one of the assistant educarers moves near the child and says, "Your mommy [or daddy] went to the bathroom. She's coming back soon. I'm here if you need me." The child isn't pitied or told, "Poor baby." Rather, she's allowed to experience the pain of separation and the good feelings when her parent returns. This, I believe, prepares one for life.

It can be tempting to distract your child from crying, especially if you're tired or in a hurry. Iris says,

> The other day Angelica (eighteen months) and I were at our neighbor's. Angelica bumped her head and started to cry. Immediately my neighbor said, "Let's do something to distract her from crying." I said I preferred not to and held her. She stopped crying in about ten seconds. Distracting is something adults routinely do and something I would have done had I not known about RIE. We try to distract children because crying makes us feel so uncomfortable. Honoring what my child feels is an important lesson for me and different from the way I was brought up.
>
> We forget that babies are conscious beings. We tend to think that simply holding them or being with them without

> giving them our full attention is enough. RIE made me aware of this. When Angelica is clingy, I'll sit with her for fifteen minutes and focus completely on her. Then she's satisfied and lets me go. I feel this is better than holding her for an hour while I'm watching television.

It's all right and even beneficial for a child to cry, because crying is a healthy expression of feeling. If she is allowed to cry, her feelings are neither denied nor covered up. Respect your child by allowing her time to cry.

Help Your Baby Form the Sleeping Habit

In the first months, sleeping joins crying as a major issue for parents. Parents swap sleeping stories with other parents, inquiring how much each others' babies nap, how much sleep the parents get, and especially how long the babies sleep at night. Many have the mistaken notion that theirs isn't a sleepy child.

Perhaps sleeping problems in our children have deeper roots. Do we, as Americans, have a cultural bias against sleeping? Do we feel it is a waste of time? Do we feel it is time that could be better spent *doing* something? Take the phrase "falling asleep." Falling is a scary image, for children and adults. Our children's sleeping problems, or inability to sleep, may be a subtle result of our attitudes.

I remember a day in class when a father turned to me and said, "Annie doesn't want to nap. What should we do?"

As if on cue, Annie, six months, turned to look at me. I looked back at her, as she rolled a ball on the mat. "We're talking about your sleep," I told her, then turned to her father. "Grown-ups think of sleep from their point of view. Many people think it's a waste of time, time that would be better spent *doing* something. The word 'crib' has a negative connotation. People think of crib death. The crib should be a wonderful place." Annie sat up and watched as I spoke. I smiled at her. "When you want to put Annie to bed, use the word 'rest.' The word 'sleep' wakes up even the sleepiest baby. Say to her, '*I* need rest. I'll put you in your crib and I'm going to rest on the couch, or wherever.' Putting her to bed earlier than you think she's tired can't hurt. If children get overtired, they have a hard time letting go. And the less you do is better."

To have a respectful approach to your child's sleep is to help her learn good sleeping habits. You can do this by maintaining a daily routine with your child. Her body rhythms will fall in sync with the times she wakes, eats, and sleeps, and she will come to anticipate her routine. I believe in putting children to bed early. Six o'clock, seven at the latest, is an optimal time. Many parents have told me that they are surprised to find out that their children sleep longer and with fewer wakings when put to bed early. Children need to follow their own schedule rather than an adult's.

Preparing for Bed

Watch for the soft signs of tiredness in your baby before she starts rubbing her eyes, like slowing down or poor coordination. This is when you can start preparing for bed. Tell your child that bedtime is coming, "It will be time for bed in about ten minutes," so she can start preparing for it.

Good sleeping habits are formed by regularity that is reinforced. If a child learns the sequences, such as, "First you will have dinner, then you will have a bath, then you will go to bed, etc.," the routines will be expected. Speak positively to her about going to bed. Make the crib feel like a cozy, cheery place of comfort.

Children readily pick up on negative messages such as a parent saying (or thinking), "Poor baby has to go to sleep now," or, "Poor baby might be scared alone in the dark." These kinds of thoughts may reflect our own fears rather than our child's. Avoid sending negative messages, because they may turn out to be self-fulfilling prophecies. Say instead, "I see you're getting tired. I'm putting you into your crib where you can rest."

"Transitional objects" such as teddy bears or blankets can be used to help your child separate from you. It's nice to give her a choice between two objects: "Do you want your blanket or your bunny with you for bed?" When preparing your child for bed, tell the teddy bear or other transitional object what you want your child to do. Children listen when you talk to the teddy bear.

After your child has chosen a transitional object, you can say, "Bunny, it's time for you to go to sleep. I'm going to put you in the crib and put the blanket over you and Joe. You're going to have a good rest now. Good night. I'll see you in the morning." I recommend not telling your child that she is tired. Rather, tell your child that *you* are tired and want to rest, too.

A nice bedtime habit to start with your child is to recapture the day. You can say, for example, "Today we went for a walk and it rained. We came home and had lunch, etc." What we think is unimportant *is* important to a child—what she ate, where she was, and who she saw. Recapturing the day is a way of giving her security. She then carries the good feelings of the day into bed with her. You can also mention what will happen tomorrow. This reconnects the past, the present, and the future, and gives her life a connected flow. In building a bridge between today and tomorrow as you prepare for bed, you can say, "The teddy bears go on the shelf. The blocks go back in the box. Do you want to say good night to your toys? They'll be waiting for you in the morning."

Reading soothing stories and playing or singing lullabies are nice bedtime routines. I recommend a book, now a classic, called *Goodnight Moon* (HarperCollins) by Margaret Wise Brown, and first published in 1947. During the course of the simple yet lovely story the bunny's room grows darker and quieter until he is tucked in bed.

Leave your baby in bed awake and say good night. Then if she awakens at night, she will know where she is.

To form good sleeping habits, your child needs the opportunity to settle herself and go to sleep. This can be difficult for parents because some amount of crying is usually involved. Some children are better at self-soothing than others and are able to settle themselves more easily. However, all children should be put in their cribs awake and allowed to work this out.

If Your Child Needs Help Learning to Settle Down to Sleep

Some children may have a difficult time learning to settle down to sleep, especially if they are used to being rocked or "helped" to sleep. Others may go through periods when falling asleep becomes difficult.

Remember that your movements and tone of voice as well as the baby's environment should soothe rather than stimulate. Let your child know that you expect her to sleep. Rather than "walking" a crying baby or nursing her to sleep, allow her to learn to self-soothe. Remember that it is a gradual learning process; don't expect an immediate result. You are helping to establish a sleep pattern for your baby and helping her learn to adapt to the family's rhythm.

Your attitude is a key part of the process. It involves belief and trust that your baby can and will learn to sleep on her own and will eventually sleep through the night. Keep in mind the long-term goal: that your baby learn healthy sleep habits. A bedtime routine provides predictability.

It's true that at times sleep-deprived parents will do almost anything to get their bright-eyed or crying child to sleep. They might jiggle her crib, take her out for a "drive," or put her in a mechanical swing. These are temporary solutions. If your baby fusses or cries when she is put in her bed, talk to her about how she is learning to put herself to sleep. Sit in her room with her for a while without taking her out of her crib. Let her know that it is time for her to sleep. Even a young infant can understand the tone of her parent's voice. She is beginning to understand the words it conveys.

Your baby may still resist sleep. Parents in some of my classes have reported success using the ideas mentioned in a book by Dr. Richard Ferber, director of the Children's Hospital, Boston, Center for Pediatric Sleep Disorders, called *Solve Your Child's Sleep Problems* (Fireside, 1986), which gives a detailed account of the "Ferber method." If a child is not able to fall asleep alone in her bed, Dr. Ferber recommends steps for helping her to do this. A parent begins by placing the child in her bed at bedtime, and if the child cries, going in to her room at timed intervals to comfort the child without picking her up. Eventually, the child learns to self-soothe and fall asleep on her own. This is *not* the same as letting a baby "cry it out," because her parent reappears regularly and talks to his child so she doesn't feel abandoned. Dr. Ferber lends support to my belief that, if allowed to, babies can and will learn to sleep on their own.

The key is readiness. A mother, intrigued by his method, told me a story about her eight-month-old daughter. The baby was eating three meals a day and her parents were sure she wasn't hungry three times a night, which was how often she was waking up to nurse. They felt that waking for night feedings was a habit, and they were exhausted, particularly the nursing mother. A child's body rhythms get fixed on times of eating and sleeping and they become habits, either desirable or undesirable. The parents decided to try Dr. Ferber's suggestions.

I encouraged the parents to first explain to their child what they were going to do and that they wanted her cooperation, telling her that they thought she was old enough to be able to sleep through the night, and that *they* wanted more sleep. Next, they reduced the length of night nursings until she was only nursing for one minute each time she woke. This took one week. Dr. Ferber maintains that taking in nutrients alone can cause continual wakings because the digestive system is not allowed to shut down.

They decided the father should go in when the baby cried because they felt it would be difficult for her to see the mother and not be allowed to nurse. They were prepared for several weeks of nightlong crying, but were surprised when it took their daughter three nights of crying for about forty-five minutes to learn to sleep on her own.

The parents said it was painful to hear their child cry, but they knew they were helping her. They also happily commented that when their daughter learned to go to sleep on her own at night, her naps fell into place, becoming longer and more regular. She continues to sleep beautifully—happily going to her bed, hugging her favorite teddy bear, and waking in a happy mood. I use them as an example because their daughter did not naturally learn to sleep on her own. However, the parents said it was necessary to wait until they felt the time was right, for their child and for them.

Another story from Cynthia, a massage therapist and mother of Chloe, two, and Heidi, five, supports the same idea.

> At night when I was nursing my six-month-old daughter, Heidi, and thought she'd finished, I'd put her in her crib.

She'd immediately start crying so I thought she must still be hungry and I'd nurse her again. I wound up nursing her to sleep. Then she'd wake up and we'd do it again. The bedtime feeding stretched to an hour and a half. What I found out from RIE was that my daughter needed comfort, not food. She needed to learn how to put herself to sleep without my help. That was also a positive step for me, learning to separate from her, to not do everything for her, and to let her learn.

Heidi was very upset the first night I put her awake in her bed. I said to her, "I know it's hard for you but I'm not going to nurse you to sleep tonight." I let her cry for a few minutes, then went back in and said, "I know you're having a hard time." But I didn't take her out of her crib. It took four or five nights before she figured out how to comfort herself and put herself to sleep. She learned to stroke her blanket and suck her fingers. It was a blessing for both of us. Children learn their sleep skills when they're babies. If we rock and nurse them to sleep, we deprive them of the opportunity to fall asleep on their own and they may have later sleeping problems.

Night Wakings

Night wakings are a common occurrence with babies and children and must be responded to. First, wait a few minutes to give your baby a chance to settle down on her own. If you choose to go in, it is helpful to handle night wakings in a subdued, yet honest, manner. If you are tired and groggy, it's fine to go into your child's room this way. You can ask her, "What is it?" or "It's nighttime. You woke up. What happened?" Sometimes your presence alone will calm her. Sometimes children are frightened by nightmares, unable to separate their dreams from reality.

I recommend, as in all situations, responding *minimally.* One of my mottoes is: Do the minimum. Start by talking to your child. If she is still upset, you can stroke her. She may need to be held. But if a parent rushes in and does the maximum—picks up the child, rocks her, and walks her—he takes away the child's opportunity to respond to the situation by settling back down to sleep.

Naptime Sleeping

Approach naptime in the same manner as bedtime. Tell your child in advance that soon it will be naptime. After a few minutes, place her in her bed. Crying at naptime can be handled the same way as crying at bedtime. Remember that some children need to fuss or cry a little before they can settle down and go to sleep.

Repeating the same routine at about the same time every day gives your child's life a predictable rhythm. She will grow to anticipate daily events and feel secure in knowing what to expect.

Make Your Life Easier

At the end of RIE class I often ask parents, "What can you do this week to make your life easier?" Making parents' lives easier is an important part of the RIE philosophy. Parents' needs should be respected, too.

Practicing the RIE philosophy makes your life easier because a child who is raised with respect is learning to be cooperative. Daily interactions will be more pleasurable, and problems will be more easily resolved. Maintaining a respectful attitude is the key.

Let's review the definition of respect: "To esteem; to honor; to refrain from interfering with." If you treat your child with esteem and honor from the beginning, you will assist her in forming a lifelong pattern of healthy independence. How can you refrain from interfering with your child while still being helpful?

As I mentioned before, respond minimally. If she bumps her head and cries, go to her in a slow, calm manner. Your agitation will agitate your child and may give her the message that something *is* seriously wrong. A parent should be an available base of security. If she wakes at night, respond with your calm presence. If she wants to be held and you're busy preparing lunch, it's fine to tell her you will pick her up in a few minutes. If she is hungry and wants to be fed, make yourself comfortable for the feeding while telling her her food is coming soon. If her basic needs have been met and she is still crying, ask her why she's crying and observe her to discover why.

My golden rule is, observe more, do less.

Human beings tend to project their own feelings upon other people, including their children. For instance, if a parent is hungry, he may project or assume that his crying child is also hungry. This is where observation is important. Instead of projecting or assuming, why not observe your child for the answer? Over time you will understand her needs.

Your life can be made easier by using RIE's cooperative approach in caregiving tasks. Ask for and expect your child's cooperation. After a while she will know what is expected of her and will cooperate. Children naturally want to please their parents.

When asking for your child's cooperation, use a firm but gentle voice. Be clear. Children are keen observers and pick up any hesitation or doubt in a parent's voice. Use simple statements such as, "It's time for your bath" or "I don't want you to climb on the table." Compare these statements to questions such as "Let's take a bath, okay?" and "Can you get off the table?"

Tell your child what you want (what behavior you expect) rather than asking her, which may turn to pleading and is much less direct. If you use a firm tone of voice and mean what you say, your child will get the message. Waffling doesn't help anyone. When a child senses doubt, she'll work on her parents. Whining and nagging may ensue.

In talking to your child in a respectful manner, don't offer her a choice where she truly has none, as in saying, "Do you want to get dressed?" or "Do you want to go to Grandma's?" Be honest. If there is no choice involved for the child, tell her what is going to happen, "I'm going to dress you now" or "We're going to Grandma's now." If she has a choice, offer it to her, saying, "Do you want the red cup or the blue one?"

Establishing a good daily routine with your child, including good eating and sleeping patterns, will make your life easier. The day should be arranged around a child's eating and sleeping schedule, which will add predictability to your life and your child's. For instance, you can plan to take care of household chores, read a book, or even do your home business during your child's regular naptime or while she is playing quietly in her room. Your child will thrive on the predictable rhythm of her daily routine. A daily routine is not always easy to maintain with more than one child, but the benefits are great.

A Child's Life

A child should have a child's life and not be an appendage of an adult's life. Children should have their own age-appropriate experiences. Few adults adapt to a child's life—her size, temperament, and timing. Many expect children to adapt to adult life. This is very difficult for children to do. Children *can* adapt to anything, but it isn't in their best interest.

Sadly, children hang on to their parents' lifestyles. The mother needs to shop, so the baby shops. The mother needs to run errands, so the baby runs errands. Everybody survives this, though it's not ideal for your child. A child's life should be boringly the same—boring for the adult rather than for the child. In this way she develops an inner rhythm. Children aren't happy spending hours in car seats or shopping. Malls are not for children. They are overstimulating. Children need a life of their own.

Allowing your child a child's life means letting her play peacefully at home, indoors or out, with her play interrupted only by daily caregiving necessities and occasional errands. In earlier times children had more of a chance to do this. In modern culture, life is more urban and less rural, and it takes effort to provide a child with this kind of environment.

David Elkind, professor of child study at Tufts University in Medford, Massachusetts, supports RIE's belief in letting a child have a child's life. He writes in *The Hurried Child: Growing Up Too Fast Too Soon* (Addison-Wesley, 1987) that

> the trend toward obscuring the divisions between children and adults is part of a broad egalitarian movement in this country that seeks to overcome the barriers separating the sexes, ethnic and racial groups, and the handicapped. . . . From this perspective, the contemporary pressure for children to grow up fast is only one symptom of a much larger social phenomenon in this country—a movement toward true equality, toward the ideal expressed in our Declaration of Independence. . . . Its unthinking extension to children is unfortunate. Children need time to grow, to learn, and to develop. To treat them differently from adults is not to discriminate against them but rather to recognize their special

> estate. . . . Recognizing special needs is not discriminatory; on the contrary, it is the only way that true equality can be attained.

Make Clothing Comfortable

I recommend dressing your child in loose, comfortable play clothes that don't bind or interfere with her movement. Respecting a child means respecting her level of comfort. Dresses may look pretty but are impractical for a creeping baby. She will catch her knees and feet on the hem of her dress as she moves.

It's important to dress children in simple, unsophisticated clothes. This is part of allowing a child to have a child's life. Some parents may inadvertently dress their child like a little adult instead of age-appropriately, and a parent treats a child the way he perceives her. Perhaps a child dressed like a grown-up will subtly cause a parent to treat her as a little adult instead of a child. A little girl in a frilly dress, hat, and stiff shoes adorned as a princess receives the message: Don't get dirty. Don't act like a child.

I suggest leaving your child in bare feet as much as possible. She will be able to achieve better balance by gripping with her toes for support. Parents may feel that little shoes look adorable, but small babies have no use for shoes. For warmth, use soft, flexible shoes, moccasins, or socks with nonskid soles. I also recommend letting your baby be naked, weather permitting, for part of the day. This gives your baby a sense of freedom and also helps prevent diaper rash by letting her bottom dry.

Safety Always Comes First

The number-one rule in your child's play environment, or any environment, is safety. A parent never knows when his baby will be able to roll off a bed, so it's better to put her on a quilt on the floor or in her safe play area. Safety becomes a more important issue as your child is able to get herself into new positions and move. The rolling baby may roll over, onto, or off of something. She will soon learn to crawl and can maneuver herself to many new places. Parents need to be one step ahead of their child.

It is never too soon to adequately safeproof your home. However, I recommend safeproofing one room, or part of a room, completely. The room should so completely safeproofed that if you were locked out of the house for hours, you would feel confident that your child would not be in danger (though this is *not* recommended). This is another way to make your life easier. You can relax while letting your child play with her toys in this safe room. (Safeproofing your home is covered in chapter 7.)

The Play Environment

Your child's play environment should be as natural as possible. Stimulation changes the way a baby feels. Natural stimulation is fine. Our goal is to accept and acknowledge a child's feelings, though not always the behavior, and allow her to express them. Stimulation brought about by strong artificial lighting, loud noise, overwhelming decor, and complicated toys only serves to distract a child from her feelings and from her process of discovery.

Outdoor play, supervised, in a safe place, is the best choice, weather permitting. Stroller walks are fine for a nonmobile child if pleasurable for the parents. If your child can't yet sit on her own, use a stroller that flattens down so she can lie in it comfortably, or use a pram.

Indoor play should be in a simple, age-appropriate space. For a nonmobile child this may be in a large playpen or on a blanket on the floor in a safe, gated-off area. For a mobile child, a small, safeproofed room or part of a room, gated off, is appropriate. In order to develop her mind and body, your child needs an optimal size area to practice her budding skills. A too-large area may overwhelm a child, while a too-small space may limit her. The play environment should be neatly arranged so a child will know where to find her things. This also demonstrates neatness so she will learn to be neat.

Dr. David A. Caruso, child development professor and director of Child Development Laboratories at Purdue University, writes in the journal *Young Children* (September 1988) that several studies "strongly suggest that a rearing environment that is sensitive and responsive to infants' behavior can influence their exploratory play." He relates that these studies also found that "the environment's social and physical responsiveness are the most important factors in the qualitative dimensions of the exploratory play of infants."

Play Objects

What kinds of play objects are appropriate for the child who is beginning to move and explore her environment?

The best choices are a variety of sturdy, simple objects that allow your infant to explore their properties through her touching and mouthing. After looking at a toy, your baby wants to discover how it feels and tastes. In this way she uncovers the similarities and differences between things and begins to form a mental record, like a computer's memory, of how things work. Her intellect develops as she stores these experiences in her memory.

I'd rather see a busy child actively manipulating a simple toy in a variety of creative ways to see how it works than see a passive child playing with a busy toy that encourages her passivity. A simple toy that allows a child to discover its many possibilities is a good choice—for example, a box that can be opened and shut or a ball that rolls and bounces.

David A. Caruso notes in the journal *Young Children* (September 1988) that research shows that play objects that best enhance exploratory play and learning are those that a baby can manipulate in a variety of ways while understanding how they work. He writes, "For example, toys that make sounds when moved are better when the sound-making parts are visible, as in a bell whose clapper children can see and touch. . . . Simple, attractive, homemade playthings are as effective as commercially made products if they allow infants to create an outcome that is a natural result of their actions." However, I prefer that a child play with a clean, empty frozen orange juice container that she can bang on the floor to any type of rattle.

Recommended play objects at this age are large, sturdy cotton scarves (through which a child can breathe and big enough that they can't be swallowed if balled up), soft balls, soft plastic teething toys, large beads, plastic bottles and containers, soap holders, plastic colanders, stacking toys, and plastic hair rollers.

Wiffle balls are nice because a baby can grasp them through the holes. Semi-inflated beach balls can also be easily grasped. Inflated plastic pool inner tubes can be grasped and climbed over and through. Babies are attracted to shiny objects, so lightweight stainless steel pots and pans can be fun. Board books are great. So are lifelike baby dolls. Any object that is simple, safe, cleanable, and easy to manipulate is a good play object.

Let your baby initiate her play using simple objects. This means less work for you. You can relax knowing her mind is at work and that you don't need to entertain her.

Babies are stimulated by all the sights and sounds of life. They don't need toys with flashing lights and moving parts. The simpler the toy, the more a child must use her imagination and resources to play with it. Simple objects help children discover how things work. Noisy, windup, or battery-operated toys don't make sense to a child. They only excite her, and a child can be easily overstimulated or scared. Bombarding children with flashy toys also encourages passivity and diminishes a child's capacity for figuring things out.

David Elkind underscores the importance of providing simple toys such as blocks, crayons, and clay, which allow a child to use her creativity and imagination. He advocates using toys that allow for "personal expression" rather than complicated toys whose novelty quickly fades. Toys should, of course, be age-appropriate. Crayons and clay are fine for an older toddler rather than for a baby, who might eat them.

The media, representing toy stores and the consumer baby products industry, bombard parents and children with ads for fancy, flashy toys and baby paraphernalia. Parents are made to feel guilty if they don't cave in and buy the latest item on the market. Parents' insecurity is fed by the media-promoted idea that happiness and good feelings can be found through external sources, and that the more you have, the happier you'll be. I want to liberate parents from this thinking. Help your child focus inward through simplicity in toys.

Another Look at "Wants Nothing" Quality Time

You can respect your child and yourself (and make life easier) by *not* "teaching your child to play" or showing her what to play with. Enter your child's world rather than expecting her to enter yours by allowing for "wants nothing" quality time. You are simply available to your child without inflicting on her your desires in regard to what she should be doing or how she should be doing it. Let her find out what she can do in her environment rather than showing her how a toy operates or "should be" played with. If she finds joy in banging her plastic bowl on the ground to hear how it sounds and experience what it feels like, then why not?

I am reminded of what Piaget said—that teaching a child something "keeps him from inventing it himself." Teaching a young child takes away her joy of discovery. From my many thousands of hours of observing children, this is sadly true. Over the years, I've seen many adults show an uninterested child how to play with a particular toy. It is not respectful to expect or demand that a child play with a toy not of her choosing, for example, the "new toy" she has just been given. And how many times have parents said that their child spent more time playing with the box the new toy came in? I encourage you to let your child play with that cardboard box. It is a simple, safe object that your child can understand by exploring it.

David A. Caruso writes in *Young Children* (September 1988) that findings from follow-up studies confirmed the importance of infants' spontaneous play in relation to cognitive growth as measured by later IQ tests. The studies measured episodes of play that were structured by the investigator who encouraged the babies to play against episodes of free play where the investigator only observed. When tested later, the babies allowed to play freely had higher IQ scores.

Respect your child by letting her discover the world on her own. It is more satisfying for her to finally figure out how to pull apart two cups that are stuck together than to have an adult show her how to do it. If you do it for her, you also take from her a valuable learning opportunity. Let her develop tolerance for frustration by discovering how the cups come apart and fit together. She will fare better in life by developing problem-solving skills.

Playing: What Children Do Naturally

Play is an opportunity to help strengthen your child's self-respect and her sense of self-reliance. Two of the building blocks of self-confidence are security and mastery of tasks. Security is reinforced by a child's attachment to her parents. Mastery of tasks begins as a young infant is successful in picking up a toy she wants.

Allow your child to freely explore her environment, which must be safeproofed. It is vital to provide a safe play environment so that your child can be safe and feel secure, not fearful that, for example, she will bump her head again on a sharp table corner. Security helps promote confidence. She should have access to an assortment of simple play objects (as mentioned previously) that invite initiative. You, the parents, originally choose the play objects so her choices are already preapproved and acceptable. Avoid a "circus atmosphere" in which your baby becomes conditioned to being constantly entertained.

You can remain with your child but try not to influence what she does during playtime. It's all right if she momentarily engages you in play. For instance, your child may give you a toy and take it back. An older baby may bring you a book to read. The goal is for your child to be the initiator of the play and for it to be her experience. If you take over or get too involved, she loses her sense of self-exploration.

In a 1973 study published in the *Merrill-Palmer Quarterly*, Sybille Escalona, studying infants older than five and a half months, concluded that the more a young toddler was intruded upon, the more his behavior would seem to be reactive rather than self-initiated, at least in the social realm.

It can be difficult to step back and let your child take the lead, but in this way you will observe and learn from her. You will discover with delight that your child has many inherent abilities that might have been missed if she had not been allowed to explore in her own way. With practice, this relaxed sitting back becomes easier. Part of RIE's "do less" philosophy, it also takes the pressure off you to feel as though you must entertain her. Support what your child chooses to do as long as it's safe.

Play and Problem Solving

If your child gets herself into a difficult situation, first give her the opportunity to figure a way out of it. When adults provide "magical" solutions to problems, they not only rob a child of the satisfaction of discovering a solution, they get her accustomed to a quick and easy fix. Taken to the extreme, isn't this the type of thinking that leads to chemical and other types of dependency in later life?

Here's an example:

> Gabriela is playing with a ball. It rolls under the folds of a blanket, and she cries when it disappears. She has not yet grasped the concept of "object permanence," the realization that when an object disappears behind or under something it is not gone, just out of view, which happens at about eight months. Her father observes this.

Father: "The ball rolled away and you look unhappy about it. Where do you think the ball is, Gabriela?"

Gabriela: continues crying.

Father: "Did you see where the ball went?"

Gabriela: looks at the blanket, then begins crawling toward it. She stops and looks around, still crying.

Father: "Where do you think the ball went? (Pauses as Gabriela looks around.) Did the ball roll under the blanket?"

Gabriela: lifts the blanket and gleefully retrieves the ball, experiencing the joy of discovery.

Father: smiles, appreciating her initiative and joy.

Look at an alternative intervention:

> Gabriela is playing with her ball and it rolls under a blanket. She cries when it disappears. Her father observes this.

Father: "Don't cry, Gabriela. I'll get the ball. Here it is." (He lifts up the blanket and hands her the ball.)

Gabriela: smiles and takes it.

Father: smiles because Gabriela is happy.

The result may look the same in both cases. Gabriela loses her ball and smiles when she gets it back. The subtle difference is the *process.* The process of allowing her to do it herself is the crucial, competence- and confidence-building factor. This builds your child's trust in her ability to solve her own problems. It happens when you respect your child enough not to interfere with her process of encountering life and its many obstacles.

Many people view struggle as a negative. Life is full of struggles, but they can be made positive or negative. The more people learn to appreciate the results of struggle, the better off they are.

Again, start with the minimum. If your child has her hand stuck in a cup, can't get it out, and is upset, it's all right to help. Ask her if she can pull it out. If she isn't able to, help her unwedge her hand. If she has rolled into a corner and can't move, you can help turn her around. But start with less. Most people do the maximum (retrieve the ball) and take care of the situation. This doesn't prepare your child for life. Life consists of ongoing problems and learning how to respond to them. A good strategy for life is to let your child figure out what to do.

If your child is playing and you want to hold her, ask her if she wants to be picked up. Allow her to indicate her preference. If she wants to continue playing, let her. Respect her by making her desires (when reasonable) as important as yours. When she makes a choice, respect it. If you need to pick her up to go, first tell her, "You're not ready, but I must pick you up now." Let your words register—wait for the penny to drop—then follow through.

Encouraging Your Child to Play on Her Own

From the beginning, your baby can learn to play or explore on her own in a safe environment. You can set up a gated play area in her room or another place of your choice and place in it balls, cotton scarves, teething objects, stuffed animals, and a few other play objects. A playpen is fine for a child until she starts to roll, and needs more space.

Tell her you are going to let her play in her play area for a while and that you will be in the next room, listening. If she cries, you have learned to read the cries and can respond appropriately so she doesn't feel abandoned. A habit will be formed in the process. When she's older you can safeproof her entire room, gate the door, and let her play there.

Start leaving her for a few minutes at a time and then for longer and longer periods. She should always be placed on her back until she can get into other positions on her own. Even a young baby can be left to play alone. However, supervision is always necessary by intermittent checking-in on the parent or carer's part. The younger the child, the more frequent check-ins are necessary.

Privacy is good for children and parents. There is benefit in not only playing alone, but in simply being alone. Solitude is healthy at times. A child can learn to do this very early and is happy when left in this type of environment, although it takes time to build her aptitude for being on her own. Remain within hearing distance. If your child protests, she will find comfort in hearing your voice from the next room, which reassures her of your availability. Say, "I hear you. I'm in the bedroom. I'll come to see you in a few minutes." By learning the skill of self-entertainment, your child will learn to busy herself with her own activities while she's in the room with you, too.

The key to her playing happily alone is being *fully* with her when you're with her. Mirta, a retired tax professional, mother of D. J., eighteen months, says,

> By our following the RIE approach, D. J. has gained the self-confidence to play on his own. I've learned to give him one hundred percent of my attention, even if for a short time, when we're together. He knows he can get what he needs from me when he needs it. This hit me the other day when I was in the kitchen, cooking. D. J. kept crying and fussing. I finally went to him and spent one minute talking to him, face to face. I said, "I know you want me to hold you. I'm cooking dinner and I'll hold you when I'm done." After that he was fine until I could go back to him.

Learning to play on her own is an aptitude that will serve your child well for life.

A Word about Mirrors

I smile when asked about children and mirrors. This is because most everyone assumes that a mirror is a prerequisite in a child's play environment. I believe mirrors are too complex for a very young child. Simplicity and honesty should be consistently maintained in all aspects of childrearing. A mirror is a deceptive reflection of reality and is confusing to a young child who does not understand that it is a reflection, not a real person.

I remember mirror tests done at a university where a large standing mirror was placed in a room. Each child who entered the room looked at the mirror and appeared puzzled, then went behind the mirror to look for the child she saw.

Reality is complex. A mirror is not reality, rather a reflection of it. A child reaches to touch the person in the mirror and instead touches hard, cold glass or can't find the child behind it. Or she may run straight into it, thinking she is approaching another child. A mirror is fine for an older child who understands what it is.

Praise: Do Children Need It?

Children at play don't need praise for their actions. Let your child's inner joy be self-motivating. You can smile and express your genuine feelings but should refrain from giving excessive compliments, clapping your hands, and making a big fuss. If you do this, your child starts seeking satisfaction from external sources. She can get hooked on praise, becoming a performer seeking applause instead of an explorer. Praise also disrupts and interrupts a child's learning process. She stops what she's doing and focuses on you, sometimes not returning to the activity.

If you say "good girl," "good boy," or "good job" to your child, what happens if she can't perform a certain task? Doesn't this subtly tell her she's bad? The words "good" and "bad" connote a moral judgment. They also encourage a performer mentality. Try not to comment on her merit as a person. Instead, enjoy what she can do.

When your child does something truly difficult, like wait a few moments for her meal while you are busy, thank her rather than praise her. Say, "Thank you for being patient. I know it's hard for you to wait when you're hungry." Positive reinforcement is always helpful.

You may wonder whether a child needs her parents' support to feel good about herself. Yes, you can acknowledge her through reflecting.

Reflecting Is Support

Reflecting, similar to "sports announcing," comments on your child's actions. In doing this, you "reflect," or mirror, your child's point of view. Reflecting affirms the process of self-discovery, taking the form of a smile or a simple statement, "You pulled those two plastic beads apart. That looked really hard." Your child can then focus on her own good feelings instead of yours. This is different from projection in that you observe your child closely in order to do it. It helps to be descriptive in your comments, which will help your child feel understood, as in saying, "You've been trying to pick up that ball for a long time. You did it," or "It was hard to climb up that step."

Reflecting describes what a child is engaged in, as in, "You're pulling the blanket over your head." It also acknowledges and clarifies her feelings and desires, as in "You seem sad. Daddy just left," or "You want to go outside." When your child looks at you in pride after she has caught a rolling ball, you can smile to reflect your appreciation.

Take a look at the following example. The mother, sitting quietly on a couch, is watching her six-month-old baby, lying on a blanket on the floor, reach for a large, cloth doll:

Mother: "You're reaching toward the doll again."
Baby: on his tummy, is stretching to get it.
Mother: "You're really reaching for it."
Baby: picks up a nearby ball and rolls on his back.
Mother: (smiles) "You'd rather hold the ball."
Baby: Plays with the ball for a few minutes, then drops it and rolls back over onto his stomach. He stretches for the doll and moves an inch toward it.
Mother: "Can you get the doll?"
Baby: moves another inch and grasps the doll.
Mother: (smiles) "You picked up the doll."
Baby: smiles back.

Reflecting entails neither praise nor criticism, rather it acknowledges, informs, and illuminates. This is how a child learns, by starting to understand connections between things. Reflections are simple phrases and expressions of feeling. Reflecting does not teach or preach. It is a statement of support that allows your child to learn.

Selective Intervention Means Learning to Wait

I recommend using selective intervention during your child's play whether she's alone or with other children (as mentioned in chapter 2). Selective intervention means carefully choosing when and how to aid your child in problem solving. When she is playing alone and encounters a problem, assess the difficulty of her struggle and use your knowledge of her capabilities. In this way you can decide whether to help her or stay out of it. Perhaps given more time, your child could figure out how to get the block she's reaching for. If you help, decide how much help is needed. Perhaps you can encourage your child by saying, "You really want that block. Can you get it? How can you get it?"

You can learn how to selectively intervene in your child's play through careful observation. Observation will make you familiar with her abilities, strengths, and weaknesses. Over time you will learn when your child needs assistance and when to leave her alone. When in doubt, wait. Many things work out by themselves.

I am reminded of a story from class. The children in the class were beginning to roll over and move. Some were crawling across the floor. The big hurdle each tried to master was the door stoop between the indoor playroom and the deck. Though only a few inches high, it was a challenge for the babies to crawl over. A baby named Dion rolled onto the stoop and got stuck. He rolled back toward his mother, pulling a cotton bandanna over his face. I said, "Let's see what happens."

Dion lay there motionless, trying to figure out what happened, as his mother, looking anxious, watched. Dion started to tug on the scarf, then started to cry. Though she looked a little unsettled by his struggle, his mother moved near and spoke to him, reflecting, "You pulled the scarf over your face." He fussed a little and then calmed. After a few tries he yanked the scarf off with one big tug. Dion beamed at his mother. "You pulled it off," she said, looking relieved, smiling back.

I smiled and said, "That was lovely how you handled the situation. Most people jump in when they see children struggle. Many times you may think your child needs help but if you wait long enough, you find out he doesn't. It's called having basic trust."

This is a telling incident. Given time and his mother's trust and support, Dion solved his own problem, however small or insignificant it may have seemed. The important lesson was, and is, to wait.

Try to avoid rescuing. It is a normal parental feeling to want to protect your child and remove all obstacles from her path, but it isn't beneficial. Overcoming obstacles in life makes her stronger. Do the minimum. Rather than overreacting or overdoing, try to find the best possible response. If you overreact, it's hard to do less after. If you separate two arguing children and take away the toy, this doesn't prepare them for life. Don't, however, let children hurt each other.

It is frustrating to a child when an adult constantly intervenes in her play. This not only interrupts her learning process but also presents a mistrust in her ability. Let her actively experience her conflicts. Give her only the tiniest bit of assistance, what I call the smallest facilitating step. If she is trying to pull off her sock and gets frustrated, ease the sock off a little and let her finish the job. Avoid solving her problem by pulling the sock off yourself. Respect entails trusting your child's competence. Allow her to be competent.

Patty adds,

> I remember an incident from one of my son, Robert's (now twenty-three), early RIE classes. I was holding his hand, assisting him to walk down a few steps. You said you preferred that I allow him to crawl in a way that was comfortable for him or that I carry him. That incident had a big impact on me and brought to mind the authenticity you talk about. The message is: you may either go up and down this space on your own or I deem it unsafe and I'm going to carry you.

Modeling Behavior

Model behaviors that you desire in your child. If you want your child to be gentle, demonstrate gentleness and kindness to him and others. Reinforce only desired behaviors. If you are aggressive with a child, this only reinforces aggression.

If your child tries to bite your hand, you can say, "I don't want you to bite my hand. Biting hurts me." Redirect his biting by saying, "Here, you can bite this rubber toy or the teething ring." Teething children need to chew on things.

Don't preach. Who likes to be preached to? Children learn by modeling and imitate what their parents do, positive or negative.

Be careful not to give your child mixed messages when you speak to her. Be honest. It's all right to be sad or angry or joyful.

There is a French saying *"C'est le tone qui fait la musique."* The tone makes the music. The *way* you say something conveys the message. If you are angry while smiling at your child she will be confused because what she sees and what you are saying are contradictory. This will then make her unsure of her own feelings. Our goal is to allow, clarify, and support her expression of her feelings.

Reflections on Our Families and Childhoods: RIE Parents Speak

I believe in the universality of an infant's needs. People of different backgrounds can move beyond these differences by becoming sensitive to babies and their needs. It is important, however, to remember that the parent/child relationship is critical and should be respected, because it is within this relationship that a child forms her identity. I believe the RIE approach can, through observation of your child and the knowledge and understanding you will gain by this, enhance your relationship with your child.

Over the years parents, children, and grandparents of various family backgrounds have attended our classes. I've spoken to some of the parents and a grandparent, curious to find out if RIE was difficult or easy for them to use, how it was different from the way they were raised, and how it affected their families. The following is what they said.

Kathy, forty-one, mother of Michael, two, and Justin, four, says,

> I'm from a big Irish family, the second of seven children. We lived in a very authoritarian household where I was in dread of my actions and didn't feel free to talk to my parents. My feelings were not acknowledged growing up. My mother used to get angry when I cried so I learned to cry in private. I often heard, "I'll give you something to cry about." Spankings were common and automatic.
>
> Because of what I learned from RIE, I can accept my anger and I acknowledge my children's feelings by saying, for instance, "You look like you're mad." Since the time Justin was small and he did something he knew I didn't want him to do, he'd come and tell me. He feels safe enough to be honest. I feel that my children are self-confident and self-reliant. They know they are loved. I believe they feel safe and secure knowing we are there to support them. At times my old family patterns like the impatience and the anger resurface, but the RIE approach has made a huge difference in the way I relate to my children.

Iris says,

> RIE is the complete opposite of how I was raised. In my family of origin, if a child does something a parent doesn't deem correct, the parent will say, "That's a shameful thing to do," or "People will laugh at you if you do that." Parents tend to use such expressions to discipline. At RIE I learned to use nonjudgmental terms.
>
> In my family, if an older person asks a child to do something, like give him a kiss, she does it. I don't force Angelica to give kisses. In my family a parent is never seen as wrong and never needs to apologize to a child. Parents aren't required to thank their children for anything and are believed to be infallible and above question. In contrast, RIE honors the child's spirit.
>
> My mother notices that I don't interact with Angelica the way she would. She notices I have a different approach to crying and feeding, and that I don't manipulate Angelica into doing what I want her to do. However, my mother began talking directly to Angelica instead of talking to me about her when she saw it made sense.

Becky Hopkins, editor of the RIE newsletter, *Educaring,* is the mother of two sons, Joseph, five, and Brian, ten, with whom she attended RIE parent/infant classes when they were babies. Becky says,

> My using the RIE philosophy was a struggle for my mother to accept because I gave my sons more choices than she was comfortable with. My mother is very traditionally Mexican. In our culture, you *do* for your children rather than let them do on their own. She thought I was giving my sons too many choices and that I should decide more things for them, like, for example, what they were going to eat for breakfast. I had to explain to her that I understood that these ideas were typically upheld in our culture but that I wanted to raise my sons to be able to decide and know what they wanted. I still, however, impose

limits as to what they wear when they go out, what they do, etc.

Because of following RIE, I take care of myself more than what is typical of mothers in my culture. RIE gave me permission to do this. Giving my sons choices, allowing them to explore and not to "hover" over them was different from how I was raised. Certain individuals of my culture will not allow their children to get messy or dirty. I allow my boys to explore with my supervision. For me, how dirty they get is a gauge of how much fun they've had playing.

In my culture a child is infantilized or kept a baby as long as possible. Independence in children is not fostered. In the beginning it was hard for my parents to watch my sons' level of physical activity because they worried the children would get hurt. My older son, who is now an excellent athlete, says, "The ground is my friend." Both my sons have the ability to fall and not hurt themselves. They know how to relax and roll. Being allowed to figure things out with their hands and their feet and their toes in their own way has made a tremendous difference in their ability to know where their bodies begin and end. Although my sons have totally different personalities, they can each go into situations and may not feel one hundred percent confident, but they know they can handle things. They trust in their own judgment. They know their limits. As a result, I worry about them less.

My older son, Brian, is very direct and likes to verbalize his feelings and opinions. In my culture this type of honesty in children is interpreted as being too bold or "not nice." Children who speak up and say what they feel are thought to be disrespecting their elders, even if their elders are at the same time disrespecting them. At times I need to remind my son to save his feelings until he comes home so we can talk about them but I'm glad that he developed the capacity to do this.

It takes time to implement the good habits RIE espouses, like allowing your child time alone, but later on it makes things much easier. Laying the foundation and being consistent may be difficult but once you and your child get in sync, it makes a world of difference.

Brad is the father of Matthew, three, and Raquel, eight. He says,

> I feel my mother and father respected me to the extent they could, and I respect my children to the extent I can. However, this level of respect has been enhanced by my experience with RIE. I remember attending a RIE class one day when Raquel was about six or eight months old. When class was over, I picked her up and playfully held her up over my head, wagging her around. She smiled, probably because she was used it, and maybe because I liked doing it so much. I remember you saying, "Would you like someone to do that to you?" I had never thought she might not like what I did to her. I figured all parents did that. Fathers throw their children into the air. That moment changed the way I parent. I became much more conscious of what I did to, or with, my children.

Barbara, a grandmother who introduced her grandchild, Hunter, to RIE after hearing about it in a college course I taught, says this:

> I think of myself as having been raised in a mainstream United States family. However, I found that the RIE philosophy of respect for infants is far from mainstream. Although I was raised in a home which was comfortable, and by parents who treated me in what they considered a kind and loving manner, I was not thought of as a separate person. My behavior was considered a reflection of my family, and I had to wear pretty dresses, stay clean, and have good manners. I was never allowed to express my feelings unless they were sunny and cheerful. When I was sad and started to cry, my father teasingly got a bottle and tried to get me to put my tears in it. My parents' expectations of me seemed to be based on an ideal of what they hoped I would be as a

child rather than recognition and acceptance of me as a separate person. My daughter's family and I are trying to treat Hunter in the authentic way that the RIE philosophy advocates.

Children with Special Needs

RIE's respectful approach can be used with all children, including those with special needs. This topic brings back memories of when I worked with what I call "special children," some of whom were emotionally disturbed.

To understand any human being is difficult, especially a child who has special needs, one who is physically, mentally, or emotionally at risk. It simply takes more time and patience. My guideline, no matter whom I work with, is to try to pay attention to the other person or child, and try to understand their way of thinking. The more different the other person is, the more difficult the task becomes. I try not to use preconceived ideas about who he or she might be.

I am reminded of a very bright little girl I worked with who called herself the Crocodile. As long as she was addressed as Crocodile, she was fine. If she was called a girl, she went out of control. To understand what makes another person tick, to discover what they are almost allergic to, takes time, patience, and observation.

Interaction with a child with special needs must be individualized to fit the particular child. Work with your child slowly. The goal is for her to trust you as much as she can. An emotionally disturbed child may have more difficulty doing this. She lives in a different world. Physically and mentally at risk children are also affected emotionally by their condition.

A sensitive parent or carer who listens and reacts to the child is best. The less you do, the more you observe. Try to understand where she is in her development and what she is capable of doing and willing to do. When I observed the families of the children with whom I worked in their homes, I learned more from each visit than from all the books I read or classes I took.

Don't have too many goals for your child. Observe her to discover when and under what conditions she functions her best.

The question is, what is your child capable of doing under the best circumstances? What are the possibilities? Then provide those circumstances. Some children, for example, function better after they have eaten or slept.

The following is a review of the RIE guidelines as they apply to a child with special needs.

Basic trust: The same ideas apply. Trust in your child to be the best she can be. Allow her to develop trust in you and in herself.

Environment: The same approach applies. Provide a safe and appropriately challenging environment in which to play.

Uninterrupted play: Give her time. Uninterrupted play promotes a longer attention span.

Active participant: Let her do the best she can do to participate in caregiving routines and in all aspects of her life. This builds confidence.

Observation: Be especially observant and wait. See who she is and what she can do on her own.

Consistency: It's harder for a child with special needs to organize the world. Be consistent to help her understand your expectations so you can support her capabilities.

RIE's respectful approach will help your child develop confidence in herself. It will help you focus on and appreciate what she can do. As much as possible, relax and enjoy who your special child is.

Kristi, a former elementary school teacher, is a stay-at-home mother of Cole, two, and a daughter who is four. Kristi began attending a RIE class with Cole when he was eighteen months old. She says,

> Cole was born seven weeks prematurely and he wasn't able to breathe on his own. He was pretty sick the first year. He had pneumonia, asthma, and various allergies he inherited from his father and me. He was born severely anemic because my placenta had abrupted. All these things contributed to his poor muscle tone and some developmental delays. He was lethargic and didn't crawl until he was one.

His problems were physical rather than cognitive so he received physical and occupational therapy, which he's now done with.

RIE benefited both Cole and me. Practicing it allowed me to just sit back and observe his behavior. I was able to notice things he did that were really "normal" and was shown aspects of his behavior I hadn't understood. Cole went through a period when he'd lie on the floor at RIE class and twist his body into these unusual positions. I felt self-conscious because what he was doing was so different from what the other children were doing. I found out that he was just exploring what he could do with his body and his muscles. As someone who had all these restrictions imposed on him due to his health and his muscle weakness, he was finding out what he was capable of. I started to feel more comfortable letting him experiment and started not to care how he appeared to other people because I understood why he was doing it.

During part of his physical therapy, the therapist tried to get Cole to go up and down a step by bending and forcing his legs. Cole screamed the whole time. He hated the therapy, and anytime I tried to encourage him to practice at home, he resisted. One day at RIE class he walked up a small step [provided for the children to climb on], then began stepping up and down over and over again. He was so excited that he finally did it. Every time he went up and down without falling, he would give a little cheer, run around in a circle, and go right back to it. Before RIE, I might have thought what he was doing was a little strange, but I came to accept that this was his way of mastering what he was doing. I learned to accept his behavior and be more patient. When he was engaged in these repetitive movements, even though *I* may have been ready to move on to the next thing, I gave him time.

What we learned at RIE complemented his occupational therapy. The occupational therapist suggested he do certain activities to improve his muscle tone, like find his way around by going up and down stairs, go down slides to strengthen his stomach muscles, and for us to let him walk rather than carry him around. Since the occupational therapist didn't force him and because I learned to not push him, Cole began initiating certain activities himself. He started to thrive. He's made incredible strides in the last six months. Some of these things would have happened naturally because many premature babies start to catch up at two, but RIE helped me to see the benefit of not hurrying him or forcing him. I gave him the space and the opportunity to grow. At home I just sit on the floor with him and let him choose what he wants to play with. He seems happier and more comfortable than before and I find our time together more rewarding.

RIE helps me in dealing with both my children. I now realize how important it is to let them show me what they're interested in and to let them make choices. I believe this will help them develop as individuals. I've heard psychologists say that children don't get self-esteem from being told how great they are; they develop self-esteem from the mastery of challenges. I see this with my kids. When my daughter, who's four, does something on her own, she says, "Look, Mom. I did it myself."

I'm learning to respect my kids. I don't think this comes naturally to most people because it wasn't the way most of us were raised. Children of my generation were told what to do and scolded if they didn't conform. Parents didn't want their kids to be different. I see my four-year-old really coming out of her shell and starting to express herself. Had I not gone to RIE with Cole, I might not have felt comfortable with some of the feelings she now expresses so well. I want her to be able to say what she's feeling as long as she's not acting out in some dangerous or unacceptable way. I want to teach her to behave appropriately, but I don't think that always means she has to conform to what's right for everybody else.

RIE paved the way for Cole to be authentic. I appreciate Cole and feel more comfortable about where he is in his development. I now let him interact with other kids, which I didn't before our RIE class because I was afraid he'd get hurt. Plus I used to feel self-conscious about Cole being so

> visibly behind other kids and embarrassed when people asked questions like "Why isn't he walking?" or "Why is he so little?" or "What's wrong with him?" My involvement with RIE gave me the knowledge and confidence to be a better advocate for Cole. I don't let doctors or physical therapists scare me with their concerns or their predictions about his physical development. RIE helped me become aware of the obvious but often overlooked aspects of my son. I believe everything is going to be okay with Cole.

Support Your Child's Authenticity

All children, no matter what their background or abilities, thrive on respect. It will help them become the people they are meant to be. I think back to a RIE class where a baby crawled up to my feet and sat, gazing up at me. "Hello, Sara," I said, looking back at her. Then I spoke to the parents in class. "When I watch babies I always have this feeling that this is who we really are. Then we put on all kinds of layers of behavior and expectations. They look at us with so much honesty."

I was touched by this child, and by all the other children. These tiny human beings were learning about life. They were discovering their bodies, minds, emotions, and abilities, while learning to relate to their peers. Their direct and honest actions were a lesson to us adults. If a baby was hungry, she cried loudly until fed. If she wanted a particular ball, she went after it with a directness of purpose that was amazing. If a leaf fell from the rubber tree above, she moved it between her fingers, studying it with all her senses. We were seeing the children encounter life with authenticity.

RIE's goal is to encourage children to hold on to that authenticity and to be true to themselves. Our children begin life by looking directly and openly into our eyes without looking away. At times they appear to look through us, seeing into our souls. We can learn from them.

◐ 6 ◑

Selecting the Right Child Care

I urge parents, if possible, to arrange for one of them to be at home to raise their children. Sacrifices might need to be made, whether financial or of one's own personal career goals. I believe there is no substitute for a good parent in the home, whether both parents work part- or full-time and split the child's care, or one parent remains at home full-time. However, with the increase in single-parent households and other economic pressures, it is not always possible to remain at home with one's child.

For those parents who work, good child care becomes necessary. I have been asked if there's a "best" child care situation, whether it's better to have a relative care for your baby, to employ a nanny or home carer, or to send your child to group child care.

It depends entirely on the individual situation. It's not the type, but the quality, of child care that counts. The basic rule for selection is that you should choose the right person and the right situation. Let's take a look at the three choices.

If a Relative Cares for Your Child

A family member can be, though isn't automatically, the best person to care for your child. The advantages are that a reliable grandmother, grandfather, or aunt is likely to give your child "tender, loving care." Plus, the familiarity of the family can provide security for your child. In addition, a relative may not charge you for her services.

The drawback is that a parent's own relationship with the carer is involved. How do *you* get along with the person you have in mind? This can be a touchy issue, depending on your relationship. I have often heard grandmothers say about their daughters, "Who is she to tell me how to raise a child? I raised her. I diapered her." In families there are different ideas about childrearing. Is the relative you are thinking of flexible and open to new ideas or rigid and set in her ways? Is she patient and slow? Will she willingly sacrifice her time? Whether you pay her or not, will she respect your wishes in regard to your child?

The vital question is: How is *your* relationship with your mother, father, sister, or aunt? Is this something that will add stress to your, and your child's, life? If not, the situation can be satisfactory. If so, there are other alternatives.

If you choose a relative for a carer, discuss with him or her parenting issues such as how she will respond to crying, how she will put the baby to bed and feed her, how she will arrange the baby's play during the day and discipline her. If these types of issues aren't discussed beforehand, problems may arise later as you discover that your relative and you, no matter how close or loving your relationship, have very different ideas about raising children. If your relative is agreeable, suggest that she get to know and observe your baby, and observe you as you interact with the baby. Ask her to read this book.

What to Look For in a Nanny

I recommend choosing a peaceful, reliable person. A good nanny would be a person who is a good observer, who pays attention to your child without interfering in his play. Many nannies find it difficult to simply observe a child, feeling that because they are being paid it is their job to entertain or *do* something with one's child. It's harder to observe than to entertain. Finding a balance between overinvolvement and neglect is like walking a tightrope. Try to find a carer who is observant, is there when needed, and gives your child lots of time to be himself. A peaceful, gentle, accepting person is best. Practicing RIE's philosophy is also easier for your carer, knowing she doesn't need to artificially stimulate and entertain your child.

Cynthia says this about her home carer, "Our part-time nanny, who has been with us for five years, attended most of the RIE classes with me. If she couldn't attend, I brought home reading materials for her. She is as loving and respectful of the children as we are. She tells me that RIE's influence has rubbed off on her family life with her children, too."

Diane adds, "We have a nanny who comes in during the day. I talked to her about how we interact with the children. She's a gentle, quiet person whose instinct is to sit back. She's a slower person than I am and because of her basic personality, had less to learn than I did. I taught her the basics and left the rest up to her."

Richard, an artist, husband of Diane and father of Jennifer and Marc, adds, "We talk about RIE with our nanny. Not many parents say, 'Here's what we want you to do with our children: stand back and observe them.' It flies in the face of what most parents say to a caregiver, which is, 'Make sure my child has a good time.' We sometimes need to tell her things like, 'Please don't tickle our kids.' There's a difference between a child feeling happy and being hysterical with laughter. But when our nanny sees how RIE philosophy works, she says, 'Wow!' "

Finding that special person that fits with your family, and especially with your child, is the challenge. Be aware, however, that nobody will interact with your child the way you do.

When interviewing a prospective nanny, ask her what her duties were at her previous places of employment and how she dealt with various issues such as sleeping, crying, feeding, and discipline. This can open a discussion of how you would like her to interact with your child. Ask her to observe your child and to observe you as you interact with your child. Encourage your nanny to read this book. There is also available from the RIE Center a "RIE for Parents and Caregivers" audiotape listed in the References section.

What to Look For in Group Child Care

I have witnessed many changes in group child care in the United States in the last forty years. In the 1950s it was practically unheard of. Most women who could afford to stayed at home to raise their children and were often appalled at the suggestion that children might successfully be cared for outside of the home. (Of course I knew from my experience at Loczy that this was possible.) We seem to have come full circle. Group child care is almost the norm.

Most children whose parents work go to group child care, whether it's a family-run child care or a larger center. Child care cannot replicate a family environment. But good child care can offer a secure, predictable environment. I suggest observing several centers you are interested in before making your choice.

A center, whether a family or larger group child care, should have an identity or philosophy to provide continuity and security for the children. This philosophy should be written down and given to the parents so they know what takes place during the course of the day and how various issues such as feeding, crying, sleeping, and discipline are dealt with. Be sure to ask for this when you visit child care centers.

How Many Children?/How Many Carers?

My first consideration is that the people who work at a child care center be patient and kind. My second is the number of children in each group. Fewer is better. I would like to see no more than four. When there are many children, there is less chance that their needs are being met. A good compromise in group child care is a place that provides for each child's individual needs within the group situation. In good group care, each child's individuality is respected, even talked about: "Today we're having pears for lunch. Who likes pears? Carla?" If children are treated as individuals and talked to in a positive way, they feel appreciated.

There was a time when mixed-age groups were considered preferable in group care, but I don't believe this is the best arrangement for infants and toddlers. I would look for a situation where your infant is with other children of the same age and stage of readiness so that the environment and the routines fit most of the children. It's also more difficult for the carer to adequately meet the needs of a mixed-age group.

Consider the number of carers. Again, fewer is better. A child needs a secure base from which he can feel free to explore. Ideally, he should have one primary carer so he is able to develop attachment to an adult. Having the same carer as a child grows from infancy to toddlerhood also promotes security. When many carers are present, they tend to relax and rely on each other to help, perhaps feeling less obligated to pay attention to the children. If more than two people are interacting with the group of children, their roles should be well defined.

Dr. J. Ronald Lally, who directs the Program for Infant/Toddler Caregivers in Sausalito, California, a video-based training program, concurs. He notes in *Young Children* (November 1995) that a child's identity is formed during the first years, part of which may be spent in child care. Among the policies he feels contribute to healthy identity formation for a child in child care are: the assignment of a primary carer to each baby; the same carer for as long a period as possible; a small number of infants in each group to promote intimacy; and a responsive learning environment rather than a rigid program of intellectual stimulation.

Are the Children Free to Play?

Another thing to consider is whether the children are pushed to learn or free to play. Many centers have an agenda to teach children, to be cognitively stimulating. If you think of the wide range of things children have to figure out on a daily basis, it's apparent that their learning is ongoing. A child learns from everything around him. It's more important for a young child to be accepted and loved for who he is rather than expected to do things he cannot do.

There is no good reason for an infant or toddler to be placed in an environment where he is intellectually "stimulated" by being asked to memorize flash cards, taught how to work a puzzle, or given the task of building a tower out of blocks. Rather, he needs a sensitive, human environment—a few familiar people who are responsive to him and react to him when he expresses a need. The play environment should be set up based on what the child is ready for and interested in doing. The environment should be safe and geared to his developmental level so he can play freely using simple objects, without constantly hearing the word "no."

This reminds me of a story. On one occasion I visited the family of a child with special needs in their home. The mother was overjoyed when I came to the door, telling me how she was finally able to get her child to look at a ball she held out to him. I sat down and observed the child. The mother held the ball in front of the child who, ignoring the ball, had his eyes fixed on the ceiling. The mother tried and tried to get the boy's attention with the ball, but her efforts proved fruitless. After observing the boy for a while, I noticed the source of his interest. He was intently watching a fly that was buzzing around the ceiling. I was happy to see that the observant child had focused on the fly and that it held his attention. For me, that was real learning.

In *Young Children,* David A. Caruso notes that "caregivers should plan many opportunities for each baby to generate responses to his or her own exploratory play rather than simply be stimulated by others." This, combined with an attentive carer who provides this optimal environment for the child, promotes his security, trust, and all-around development.

Ask yourself whether what the carers demand of your child is appropriate. Can your child deliver? At this age it's more important for a child to learn how to interact with his family and his peers, and to figure out his world, a process that never ends. The goal for your child at this age should be to feel good about himself.

Look for a situation that has a dependable, yet flexible, schedule for the children rather than a set curriculum. Meals and naptimes should occur at the same times and in the same place each day, promoting predictability. Children depend on this reliable schedule for security, especially when away from home. However, carers need to be flexible with, and adaptable to, a child's individual moods and needs.

Stimulating children's minds through planned activities or academic programs doesn't promote security. A predictable routine does. If, for example, you are an adult who drinks coffee in the morning, you wake up and want your coffee. It's the same way with children. There is a spark you see in their eyes when at the expected time you say, "Now we're going outside," or "Now it's lunchtime." They know what to expect and look forward to it.

The Physical Environment

The number-one rule should be safety. The child's environment at the center must be absolutely safe. If the carer by mistake locked herself out of the facility for three hours, the children inside should remain safe, barring a few scratches or bruises they might inflict on each other. For safety's sake and because they have different needs, babies and toddlers should be separated. The center should be clean and tidy.

I believe an outdoor play area is a must. The more that children play outdoors, the better they eat, sleep, and feel. There is plenty of natural stimulation outdoors with the sky, clouds, and earth. Even the youngest baby may watch the changing patterns of shade and light.

Rest time is important. Young children need ample rest and should be provided a comfortable, quiet place for this. It's helpful for the carer to keep a log about each child (his meals, naps, and mood) that she can share with the parents. Since each infant may be on a different schedule of feeding and sleep, each activity can be recorded on a convenient form following the activity. With toddlers it can be done during the rest time as toddlers tend to nap at the same time. A carer may also want to record an anecdote that happened with the child during the week to further detail for his parents his time spent at the center. This log gives the parent a reliable way to understand her child's activities.

Questions a Parent Might Ask about Group Care

As you consider a child care center, ask yourself:

- Would my child like to be here? If yes, why? If no, why not?
- Is it too dark or too light? Too big or too small?
- Will he have many people taking care of him or one or two special people who know him well?
- Is he allowed to move freely and do what he can do?
- If he is tired, is he allowed to sleep?
- Can he move around if he wants, or is he carried?
- If he moves around, is it safe?

- If he is a young baby, are there toddlers around who might step on his head?
- Does the environment help him to be able to do what he naturally can do?
- Are the toys simple or complicated?

How Many Hours?

In an ideal world I'd ease a child into child care, letting him spend a few hours there at a time. Four hours a day is all right. I would not like to see him spend more than six hours a day, five days a week there. It may be difficult for him to be away from his parents and his family for a long stretch of time. This may be a difficult recommendation to follow, considering parents' work schedules and busy lives, but it's what might be best for your child.

Parents have often asked me whether it's detrimental for a child brought up following the RIE philosophy to be in a child care situation that doesn't follow it. Not necessarily. I strongly believe that good is good. Finding a kind, gentle person who pays attention to your child is the important thing. Honesty is a good quality, too. It isn't necessary to sugarcoat everything.

Parents have also asked me if child care prepares a child for having siblings. The answer is no. In group care, a child is there for a number of hours and then goes home. A sibling is at home to stay.

How a RIE Child Care Center Works

There are two RIE-accredited child care centers in Southern California. One of them is the employer-sponsored Cottage Hospital Infant/Toddler Center in Santa Barbara, California. Polly Elam-Ferraro, a RIE associate and early childhood professional, served as a consultant and mentor to the Cottage Center staff. She says,

> Even prior to opening the center, Zoe Iverson, program administrator, made a commitment to have the center be RIE-influenced. The staff received RIE training and is actively involved in problem-solving issues as they arise.

> One of the most challenging problems when going through the accreditation process was how to provide continuity of care as the children's parents (the nursing staff) have inconsistent work schedules. To compensate for this, the staff tried to plan as much consistency as possible within the program. For example, primary caregiving is a critical part of their program. Another is to plan consistency within the environment, i.e., making sure children sleep in the same place when they are at the center. They also plan predictability for the children within their daily schedules.
>
> Parent education is another important component to provide continuity when the children go home. This respectful RIE approach begins with the hospital administration. They have a respectful, supportive attitude toward their employees. This, is turn, contributes to a respectful attitude toward the children. It's an ongoing process of observing the children, trying to create an environment where they feel safe, have the freedom to explore, where caregivers are committed to allowing them to be who they are. Even on a limited budget, a center can still provide quality, respectful programs for their children. This doesn't require more staff, rather staff who are well informed, who train, and who have a commitment to this philosophy which comes from understanding infants.

The other RIE-accredited center is the private, nonprofit South Bay Infant Center, founded in 1988, in Redondo Beach, California. There are also many RIE-influenced centers around the United States and abroad. Even though you may not have a RIE child care center in your area, I'd like to tell you about how they are run, using the South Bay Infant Center as an example, and point out similar things to look for when you seek a center for your child.

The South Bay Infant Center's founder, Ruth Money, says,

> I set up the center so that parents and professionals could see a child care center operating on RIE principles. Our center has a homelike atmosphere where each group of four children, divided by developmental ability, has an area

of their own for sleeping, eating, diapering, and indoor and outdoor play. Each group is cared for by a team of two primary caregivers—one in the morning and another in the afternoon—who stay with "their" infants to develop a relationship with them as they move through the three different rooms. To ensure this, we ask that each staff member make a two-year commitment. Each of the three rooms gets progressively larger to accommodate the growing needs and abilities of the four children as they get older. The center accepts babies at about three months, and the groups rotate to the next room every eight months. The four toddlers leave the center at about twenty-seven months for preschool, and we are then free to accept a new group of four babies.

We offer a six-week series of parent/infant guidance classes to parents of young babies entering the center. These classes are also open to the community. In addition to learning to observe their babies and respond to their cues, and learning about infant development and care, the parents also have an opportunity to form friendships with other parents. During the classes both the parents and the infants are able to become comfortable in the new surroundings and with the carers before it is time for the parents to leave their babies for the day.

The center is operated so that each child has his individual needs met while the other three infants are either sleeping or playing. The children are put to bed when they are sleepy, waking up when they are rested. We don't rock children to sleep so they will grow to depend on this manner of falling asleep. Each infant is on an individual schedule of eating and is fed on the carer's lap, receiving her personal attention, and is fed when he is hungry. Food is never forced on a baby since we look for the signs he gives us that show us he is no longer hungry. During caregiving times such as diapering, the carer gives her full attention to the infant she is involved with, and elicits his cooperation. The atmosphere typically remains peaceful and undisturbed, as one baby is either being fed or diapered, and the other three are either sleeping or playing safely on the floor on a

> rug covered by a clean sheet. In the toddler room, although individual schedules continue to be respected, the toddlers themselves start to become hungry at the same time and sleepy at the same time.
>
> If an infant cries for attention when the carer is occupied with another child, she responds to him by saying, "I hear you telling me you are hungry (or whatever need she thinks the infant may be expressing). I'll be with you just as soon as I finish feeding Johnny."
>
> When an infant receives full attention during caregiving times, and has his needs for eating, sleeping, diapering, and security attentively met, then he seems to like to be free to explore his body and his world. The children are allowed to move and play, and attain the milestones of motor development at their own pace. Babies are not propped to sit or "helped" to walk. We have no rocking chairs, high chairs, or mechanical swings. When the carer is not occupied with caregiving activities with one of her four children, she sits on the rug and watches them play, noting their long attention spans when they pursue play of their own choosing, sensitive to their need for aware attention while watching for signs of hunger, sleeplessness, or need to be changed. The babies seem refueled by the adult's full attention and by her comments on what each is doing.

Deborah Harris, director of the center from 1992 through 1996, explains how people hear about it:

> We have a lot of visitors. All the RIE students come to observe and we're on the visitation list for six local colleges, the American Nanny Institute, and three vocational training centers. We're on referral lists through resource and referral agencies. Employers also provide this information to their employees. We advertise in the local newspaper, but the best reference is word of mouth. That's how we get most of our families. Most parents are impressed by the simplicity and uniqueness of the program. RIE philosophy is not something new, rather something that was in us all along. Maybe we just overlooked it because we were moving

> too fast, never taking the time to settle down and observe babies. Most people are surprised and eager to learn more about the philosophy, wanting to bond with their child while not wanting to overwhelm him with their own needs and desires. They learn to sit back and observe their child and pick up on his cues. They learn to appreciate the little things.

At the South Bay Infant Center staff and visitors remove their shoes at the door and are offered a pair of paper slippers. Safety gates are in place to separate age groups. Babies are held by the carers during feedings, and the toddlers eat at a little table and chairs. They use many of the same simple toys we use at the RIE Center.

There are no required activities for the children. The ratio of carer to child is one to four. The children have a team of two primary carers, one for morning and one for afternoon, rather than an assortment. All carers are trained in the RIE philosophy in order to interact with the children in the same manner. By contrast, in most other centers carers may have different backgrounds and ways of responding to the children.

The children are respectfully addressed, not treated condescendingly, ordered around, or manipulated. The carers speak in honest, direct, and loving voices. The children are given time to respond and cooperate. Crying is dealt with by listening to it to determine the individual child's need. Children are not hushed, put in swings or bouncers, or given pacifiers. Rather, they are asked why they are crying and responded to appropriately, even if that means allowing them to cry. Safety measures are evident. The prevailing feeling in the center, though full of busy children, is one of peace.

Ruth Money notes how parents who come to the South Bay Infant Center want to learn how to implement a respectful approach to parenting.

> The working parents that enroll in our center are from many different backgrounds. They are alike in that they are trying to be thoughtful about the way they raise their children. In addition, they are the first generation of parents where such a large percentage of mothers are employed. Since our society is changing and evolving, these parents

> seem to realize that their children will have to be raised for a different world. The RIE approach is helpful in that the parents learn to observe their baby's cues and try to figure out what he needs rather than discuss whose family's ideas should take precedence.
>
> Many parents, like Alex's, are raising their children differently from the way they were raised. Alex's mother described her family as very loving. They adored babies and liked to cuddle them so much that when Alex was six months old and she was visiting family out of town, she set aside a special time for him in the morning and the afternoon when he was allowed independent playtime. She laid Alex on a quilt on the floor where he could explore freely as she sat with him. Her relatives were amazed that Alex was happy to move on his own and had such a long attention span when playing with the simple toys his mother placed on his quilt.
>
> A young parent once told me, "You showed me how good a family can be." As the United States childrearing culture changes, RIE ideas are being incorporated by thoughtful parents and professionals. Modern research is also reinforcing the effectiveness of the RIE approach.

I go to the South Bay Infant Center once a year as part of the RIE reaccreditation process. There are certain criteria the center must meet, relating to how much freedom, discipline, and predictability are in the children's daily lives. I make sure the center is within those guidelines. As part of the process, I observe and interview each carer. I discuss with them the children in their care and answer their questions. I return to talk to the parents in an information session. RIE associates are available to the center and will go out to evaluate a child with special needs. The South Bay Infant Center also serves as a demonstration center to show how RIE works in a child care setting.

A Typical Morning at the South Bay Infant Center

Let's take a tour of the South Bay Infant Center, as if you were a prospective parent, to see how it runs.

The center is an older, converted house with a neatly mowed front lawn. There are front- and back-yard play areas. Upon entering the front patio area, Bert Cripps, the assistant director, greets us. Bert has been with the center since it opened in 1988. She asks us to remove our shoes and put on the paper slippers in order to keep the floor where the infants play clean.

We step inside, into a large room containing various play objects scattered around the floor—stacking cups, teethers, blocks, stuffed animals, a low ramp, and a large, plastic green turtle full of plastic hair rollers. The center follows RIE's philosophy by having passive toys that encourage active infants. The cupboards, placed high on the walls, are neatly stocked with supplies and toys. Four twelve- to eighteen-month-old infants play on the floor in the front room.

A daily ritual helps babies transition from the parent to the carer. The parent takes her baby out of his disposable diaper and puts on a cloth diaper and diaper wrap, which the center uses, so the child is given a signal that it is transition time. After a leisurely exchange with the mother or father during diapering, the baby is then taken to his primary carer. This is different from some child care centers where a child may be given to whomever is available when he arrives. Having been refueled by his parent, he may be put gently in his play space, ready to explore.

As we enter, the carer is feeding a twelve-month-old child who is sitting at a small chair and table. The carer greets us, announcing our appearance to the babies in her care. This promotes the children's feelings of security in the presence of strangers.

Carer: (smiling) "We have visitors. Hello."

In an adjacent, smaller room, is a group of babies ranging in age from five to nine months. One lies sleeping on a blanket on the floor. A carer spoon-feeds another baby on her lap. A third baby lies on a blanket on the floor, gazing out one of many windows. The play objects in this room are cotton scarves, balls, teethers, stuffed animals, semi-inflated beach balls, and small plastic swim rings. The connecting rooms are separated by safety gates. The baby room opens onto a large redwood deck.

Carer: (feeding baby) "I've got carrots for you. Are you ready to take a bite?"

Bert invites us into the toddler room. We pass through another safety gate into a large, window-lined room. In it is a small plastic climbing structure with a slide that empties onto a mattress, large cardboard boxes, dress-up hats and accessories, balls, wheel toys for the outdoor patio, and many boxes and baskets of assorted playthings, all neatly arranged.

The room opens onto a patio with a large playhouse connected to a grassy extension yard with a geodome. There are outdoor sand and water play areas. In a quiet corner of the room an enclosed area contains cribs and sleeping mats. Noticeably absent from the center are mechanical swings, bouncers, walkers, high chairs, and television.

Three toddlers, twenty to twenty-one months old, are eating breakfast in a gated corner of the room. They share a small table and are eating cereal, bagels, and milk. Bert sits with them.

Bert: "We have visitors. Colin, I don't want you to dunk your bagel in your cup. Would you like me to pour some milk into your bowl to dunk? Okay. (Pause) You're dumping milk into your bowl. I have yogurt. Do you want some yogurt? In the same bowl with your cereal?"

Colin: "Yes."

Bert: "Okay. Henry, if you're playing with your food, then I'm taking it away from you. You act like you're not hungry. Are you ready to get up and play?"

One child takes another's cereal bowl.

Bert: "Amy, I'm not going to let you take Henry's bowl away. He's not finished. If you're finished, I'll wipe you off."

Amy gives her bib to Bert.

Bert: "Thanks, Amy. It looks like Colin's finished. Colin, are your finished?"

Colin: "Yes."

Bert: "Amy, I need to wipe your other hand. Thank you for helping me wipe off the table, Henry. Now it's time for Colin. Okay, you're all finished. I don't want you to eat food off the floor.

It's time for you to go play. No, you can't play in here. This is not an area for play."

The children walk through the opened gate into the playroom. They pick up cardboard bricks and push plastic carts around. All three start to climb on the climbing structure. Henry cries out.

Bert: "Yes, you were up on the slide and Amy came close to you. You're really close to each other."

The children slide down the slide and pick up the cardboard bricks.

Bert: "Look at Amy. She's picking up a whole lot of them. Now they're falling over. Yes, you're dumping them. Colin, I don't want you to push on Henry. Henry, I don't want you to run into Amy. There's lots of space. Henry, see if you can find another space to move your cart."

Amy throws a cardboard brick at Colin. Bert's voice changes to a louder and firmer tone.

Bert: "Amy, *I don't like that.* I don't want you to throw toys at your friends. You hit Colin. That hurts." (More softly) "You can throw toys in the box. I don't want you to throw them around people."

Bert explains that the staff lounge, a guest house behind the center, is a comfortable retreat where the center holds staff and parent meetings. It has a kitchen, living room, and patio where the carers can take breaks from the children, part of RIE's philosophy of mutual respect.

Bert: "RIE also takes care of *you*, the parent or caregiver."

A few minutes later Henry crawls out of one of the large cardboard boxes. Colin crawls in. Henry goes back in.

Bert: "Now Colin's in the box. Henry, can your find another box? We need to start getting diapers changed. I'm going to open the gate. Amy, are you coming in to get your diaper changed? Okay."

Bert walks ahead of Amy to the diaper-changing station, a low, padded bench.

Bert: "I'd like you to climb up on the diapering table, please. There you go."

As Bert changes Amy's diapers, Colin walks in and grabs Bert's arm.

Bert: (softly) "Please be gentle. I don't like it when you're rough with my arm. That hurts."

After diapers are changed, the children start to climb on the climbing structure. Colin begins to cry.

Bert: "What's going on? What's wrong, Colin? You want to go up there? You might have to wait. It's pretty crowded up there right now. Did you get your finger pinched?"

Henry screams.

Bert: "Colin, listen to Henry. He doesn't want you to touch him right now. He needs his own space."

Colin is crying.

Bert: "Henry, you can tell Colin to move. I'm not going to move him for you."

Henry screeches.

Bert: "Yes, Henry needs his own space today."

Henry climbs down and picks up some blocks. Colin and Amy go down the slide.

Though full of activity, you might notice how peaceful the center is. The carers help promote this through their calm, slow movements and soft voices. The children are told what is happening, "We have a visitor," and what will happen to them next, "It's time to change diapers," so they know what to expect. The carers speak directly to the children. Bert raises her voice with the toddlers only when a child risks getting hurt. Note that she doesn't unnecessarily intervene in their play. She assists them in solving disputes, giving them a little direction. She reflects what they are doing and what they might be feeling.

The South Bay Infant Center demonstrates that by spending unhurried, focused time with children, we are rewarded with their cooperation and have the opportunity to see their special talents. Treating children with respect works equally well one-on-one and with groups. Respect helps children feel good about themselves.

When you are deciding on a child care provider, whether it's your child's grandparent or aunt, family child care provider, or group child care, keep the RIE philosophy guidelines in mind. I believe finding a person who or a place that adheres as closely as possible to these principles will give your child the security and gentle encouragement he needs to help him grow in the best way. People and institutions are never perfect. Try to find a happy solution, one you feel comfortable with. Ask yourself: when I am away from my child at work, do I feel confident that his needs are consistently being met by kind people?

7

Your Baby Becomes Mobile

The typical child learns to crawl first, then she learns to creep on all fours and climb. After this, she moves onto her side and eventually into a sitting position. From there she moves into a standing position, then "cruises" or takes steps holding on to furniture. She tries out each new position until she feels comfortable in it, then progresses to the next. Eventually she takes her first steps alone and learns to walk.

Learning these skills takes place over many months, and all average, healthy children master them, though there are variations in method and timing. For example, some children creep backward as well as forward. Some children sit before they creep. Some progress early and slowly through each stage while others move very little, then quickly crawl, sit, and stand. During this time children may also utter their first words, although many do not.

How Important Are Milestones?

Many parents I talk with are very concerned about their child's progress through this stage. Some parents may unwittingly pressure their child to achieve certain milestones before she is ready. A parent might push her child to stand by saying, "Come on, stand up," or to walk: "Come to Mommy. Give me your hand," or to talk: "Can you say bye-bye? Say bye-bye."

Why do we care so much how soon our children achieve developmental milestones? Why do many of us want our children to achieve them as early as possible? Is it because we, as parents, feel success or failure through our connection to our children? Are we projecting our egos and sense of achievement on our children? Pressure damages a child's delicate self-confidence by telling her, "Be other than what you are."

We live in an achievement-oriented and competitive society. We want our children to be successful. What about helping them to be happy? Expecting a child to do what she cannot do devalues her. Why not allow her to learn at her own pace and feel joy in what she *can* do? Why not acknowledge your child when she turns herself onto her side (which requires strength and coordination) instead of propping her into a sitting position with pillows? If she doesn't yet have the strength to hold herself up to sit, she will be cramped, have poor posture, and be unsteady. She will feel unsure rather than confident. Accept and appreciate what she does. Focus on the *how* rather than the *when*. This will build her self-confidence.

Parents may push their children out of fear, wanting their child to be "normal." They may become anxious about their child's rate of development. When they go to the pediatrician's office for a checkup they are presented with a list of "normal" skills a child should be performing. If their child is slower than average, parents may worry or even panic.

Parents may push their child's development because of their own competitive feelings with other children and other parents. They may feel pride in sensing that their child is "smarter" than their neighbor's "because she walked sooner." In some cases parents want to re-create or relive a happier childhood through their children, wanting their children to achieve what they failed to achieve. It is important to be aware of these issues and not have unrealistic expectations of your child.

Every average, healthy child learns to sit and stand and walk. It is unimportant *when* a child reaches these developmental milestones. They don't influence later life. Before getting married, did your husband or wife ask you when you took your first steps or at what age you learned to read? Milestones are not a gauge of a child's intelligence. I always think of Albert Einstein. His biography, *Albert Einstein, Scientist of the 20th Century* (Dillon Press,

1991), by Katherine Reef, states that he didn't speak until he was three years old.

Out of a person's seventy- or eighty- or ninety-year life span, a child learns all the basics—walking, talking, eating—in the first two to three years. Why do we want to hurry that process? The consequence of hurrying a child may be that the child feels that she's not living up to expectations. The most important person in her life, the parent, wants something the child cannot deliver. This is good for therapists because it breeds people who need therapy. They grow up and say, "I don't know what I want," or "I don't feel good enough."

Zina says,

> RIE helped me to feel less nervous that I was doing something wrong or that I wasn't doing enough for Emily. I learned that children develop at their own pace and if we stay out of their way, they know when they're ready to sit up, crawl, and walk. We don't have to constantly be doing something to them or for them. Nature will take its course. I learned to trust my daughter and allow her to develop on her own rather than try to manipulate her physical development. I learned to relax and enjoy Emily more, to listen to her, and to allow her to make choices, which I continue to do. RIE helped sensitize me to my child, and to other people, too.

Liz, a property manager, mother of Ezra, five, adds,

> I've always let Ezra know what's going to be happening to him. I learned to let him do things on his own. I let him pick out his toys to play with. Ezra had a rocking horse we put in his room. It sat there until he was ready to climb up on it. Letting him do things in his own time and in his own way has given him confidence about his ability to handle situations on his own. It's interesting, too, because I notice how different I feel when I'm around babies. In the past whenever I saw a friend with a new baby, I couldn't wait to hold him. Now I think about the question I've heard you

pose, "Do you think the baby wants to be held by you?" I'm content looking at the baby and talking to him.

Enjoy the present. Enjoy your child's actions and get to know her. Children at play are efficient and graceful. They do what they can do and don't withhold skills. They learn to trust their bodies and minds when allowed to develop confidence in them through trial and error.

It's important to see your child as a whole person and to help the whole person develop. Motor development and cognitive growth are only parts of the whole. There is also your child's unique personality to consider. Help your child reach her potential by seeing her as a competent, problem-solving person.

If you are anxious about your child's lack of development to the next stage, observe the quality of her movement. If the quality of her movement is good, even though she may be delayed in doing what you consider appropriate, I wouldn't worry. If you sense that there may be a problem, consult your pediatrician or a neurologist.

Making Your Home Safe for Your Child

A mobile child needs a safe environment. It's very difficult to safeproof your entire home, but you can gate off or make inaccessible certain areas that are not safe. These are the kitchen, bathrooms, and stairs. A kitchen is a dangerous place for your child because of the possibility of accidents. Children will grab pot handles, dishes, and knives on countertops, and will open drawers. The dishwasher and the refrigerator are also enticing to a small child. An oven door can be pulled open onto a child's head. Putting locks on appliances is not enough. I feel this entire problem is best alleviated by keeping your young child out of the kitchen. Many parents put safety gates at the kitchen entrance.

Bathrooms are another unsafe area. Faucets and bathtub or shower nozzles with hot water can scald. Young children can also drown in just inches of water, so toilets are especially dangerous. I advise closing the door.

Stairs are not safe until a child has completely learned to navigate them. I would gate off stairs at the top and bottom. You can let your child practice (with supervision) going up and coming down one or two steps at a time, adding a few more until she learns how.

What about the rest of your home? Is it child-friendly? To be respectful of your child you should make it safe. Move dangerous objects such as vases, knickknacks, sharp-edged tables, and floor lamps. Put socket guards on your electrical outlets. Put cabinet locks on cupboards or drawers your child might pull open. You might, however, leave one drawer available to her that she knows she can get into, leaving in it toys or books.

Move all unnecessary clutter. Keep your floor or carpet clean. Remember, the floor you walk on is where the baby spends part of her day. In RIE classes parents remove their shoes when they come in. Some have told me they carry this habit over into their homes. You might want to gate off certain areas of your house, like the living room or the dining room, leaving designated safe places where your child may play, such as the den and patio.

People have asked me why I believe so strongly in safeproofing, and why children can't just learn not to touch things. They do learn this gradually, as they develop judgment. But at a certain age, they cannot learn. We, as parents, have to be aware of what their minds can understand and learn, and at what age. Danger isn't part of a young child's thinking. Household accidents involving children happen all the time. This is not just a theoretical issue.

Sadly, many people don't respect danger, thinking, "Nothing ever happened in this room, with this appliance, or in this yard, therefore nothing will happen." I always respond, "That's true. Nothing happened until the first time it happens." When parents tell me that they watch their child every moment, I feel it's an impossibility. Parents use the bathroom and answer the phone.

You may wonder whether if you use safety gates, your child will want access to your entire house and feel imprisoned without being able to have it. I believe a child won't want the run of the house if she starts without it. Habits have a strong hold. You can develop good habits as easily as bad habits. We are not born with habits. They are societal, a mixture of what we are allowed to do, what we want to do, and what we can do. It doesn't require more energy to develop good habits. The best idea is to reasonably safeproof your home, and also to safeproof one room, or section of a room, completely.

Safeproofing Your Child's Room

When you safeproof one room one hundred percent, you are being respectful of your child and of yourself. In this way you can both relax. Your child can explore with no danger of being hurt and you can feel comfortable about leaving her there. Pick a room—her own room, the den, or a playroom—and take steps to create a safe and child-friendly environment. The following are suggestions for a completely safeproofed room:

- Plug all electrical sockets with socket guards or seal them off completely.
- Set all lamps and other dangerous objects in an unreachable place, such as on top of a high shelf (making sure that the cords are still out of reach). Better yet, remove them. Climbing children can reach almost anything.
- Bolt or attach heavy furniture to the wall.
- Put drawer latches on dresser drawers so a child cannot pull a drawer and its contents onto herself.
- Be sure windows are securely closed or have locking devices if left open.
- Remove or tie up any drapery or blind cords.
- Remove houseplants.
- Secure hanging pictures to the wall. Remove their glass plates and replace them with plastic ones.
- Remove any potentially dangerous furniture, such as rocking chairs, which can pinch toes or tip over, and lightweight changing tables, which can also be turned over.
- Install locking door stops (that hold a door in the open position) so they can't pinch fingers when closed.
- Attach a gate to the doorway. (Spring-lock gates are convenient because they can be easily removed.)
- Leave no small objects on which a child can choke in the room. (Children can ball up small pieces of cloth or doll clothes. These can be choking hazards.)

- Remove any crayons or markers. (A child can choke on them. In addition, she may color on your walls.)
- Make sure the floor or carpet is clean.
- Put a baby monitor in the room if you aren't within hearing distance.

You may need to add your own safety precautions to this list in order to safeproof the room. You may also hire a professional safeproofer. Be alert for possible safeproofing improvements as your child grows. A family told me when their daughter could stand and walk, she began to chew on the low windowsills. They solved this problem by attaching clear plastic wallpaper corner guards to the sills.

Safeproofing means considering what your child may do next, and making your home ready for it *sooner* than you think you need to. Don't wait until your child shows you what trouble she can get into.

Crying at This Stage

As a child grows and moves about, she finds alternative ways to express herself. She gestures and makes sounds, perhaps even says a few simple syllables. Crying lessens and becomes even more specific and direct. At this point you have usually become an expert at understanding the reasons for her cries. You may observe your tired child rub her eyes and break into a steady, rhythmic cry, or may notice that she hurt herself by hearing her loud wail. At this stage children clearly begin to realize that their crying is attention getting.

Screaming becomes common as a child discovers her voice and its power. It's best to ignore this type of screaming unless your child is really in distress. Undue attention reinforces the behavior. It is a normal development and will pass in time. Through observation you will be able to tell if the scream was initiated in play or indicates something more serious.

Older babies still cry to express their feelings. Crying is their language. Our goal remains the same: to listen to the cry, to try to figure out what the cry means, and to respond appropriately. This helps a child feel loved and understood. Imagine how a child would feel if consistently responded to in an inappropriate way. For example, how would she feel if she cried because she was hungry and her parent gave her a pacifier? Or if she cried because she was kept awake past her optimal naptime and was offered a bottle for comfort? It's a challenge for a parent to really understand his child's needs and desires.

I also sympathize with parents. It's very difficult to live with a small child. They are very demanding. You are always on the job. You don't get time off. Observe. Try to see who your child is and what she needs.

Geralynn comments,

> Because of RIE, I have a different attitude about crying. I care about my daughter and I'm concerned when she's upset, but I'm not *afraid* of her crying. Crying can be healing and healthy. If she falls and gets hurt, I don't rush over to pick her up. I come close to her and say, "You fell. Your hurt your knee [or whatever part of her body she's holding]." If she's scared I move near her in case she reaches out for me to hold her. From the time she was very young she's always given me some indication that she wants comfort, by holding out her arms or leaning toward me. If she's crying about something she wants that I won't let her have, and it's usually because it's not safe, then I won't compromise. For instance, if she wants to come into the kitchen with me while I'm cooking and starts crying when I won't let her, I go into the kitchen anyway. I listen to her cry and tell her, "I hear you crying. I can tell you're upset." That validation really helps.

Your child has a right to cry. Listening to her cry validates her feelings.

Communicating with Your Child

Communication, like respect, is a two-way street. Successful communication means listening carefully, trying to understand what the other person is saying, and responding. It is give-and-

take. Being a good communicator is part of being a good parent. Most parents find it easy to communicate their wishes to their child. The hard part is to truly hear your child and *understand* what she needs. Children are learning to express themselves. We can help them by modeling good communication skills—observing and listening with patience, and relating feelings and wishes in a clear, simple, honest manner.

Tell Your Child What You Expect

Talk *to* your child, not at her, over her, or about her. Tell her what you expect. "Expectations" is a word I use a lot. The expectations I would like parents to avoid are those that your young child is not ready for.

Let your child know what you expect her to do. This allows her to anticipate what will happen next: "We're going to start picking up your toys in five minutes. It's time for you to go to bed after that." It is important for your child to hear your expectations so she can prepare to do what you wish—in turn, respecting you.

Learning is repetition. Give your child time to learn your expectations and respond to them.

Allow your child transition time. Children's rhythms are slower than ours, and when absorbed in an activity, they need time to switch gears. Building a little extra time in your schedule is helpful. You will have time to wait a few minutes if your child isn't immediately ready to do what you ask her.

Geralynn adds,

> For me, respect means trying to figure out what my daughter wants and, in the process, building a relationship between us. It means both of us trying to understand and accept things as they are. If Delanie wants to do something I won't allow, she may protest at the top of her lungs. A simple validation from me like "Yes, I know you want to do that" is all it takes. On occasion when I'm sick and not able to attend to her as much as usual, she backs off and becomes even more autonomous. I respect her wants and needs and she is learning to respect mine, too.

Lucia says this:

> I remember a time when Jeremy was about eighteen months old and we had some friends over. Our male friend had a watch on that Jeremy liked so he let Jeremy play with it. A few minutes later my friend began dangling a toy in front of Jeremy with one hand and tugging at his watch, which Jeremy was holding, with the other. When I asked him what he was doing he told me he was trying to get his watch back. I said, "Just ask him for it."
>
> My friend looked at me with this puzzled expression on his face and said, "Ask him?" Then he turned to Jeremy and said, "Can I please have my watch back?" Jeremy handed him the watch.

Be Honest in Your Communication

Be sure your tone of voice reflects your feelings. Avoid mixed messages that come from trying to cover up your feelings. Don't tell a child nothing's the matter if you are crying. Don't smile sweetly when you're angry. Don't pretend to feel something that you don't. Children then become confused about the difference between what they see and perceive and what they are told.

It's all right to use a firm and serious tone with a child who has just thrown her spoonful of strained carrots: "I'm upset that you threw your food and made a mess. It looks like you're finished eating. I'll take the food away now."

Try not to overuse "no" or else it loses its weight. Save it for situations of urgency or imminent danger: "No. Don't touch the glass," or "No. Do not step into the street." When there is no danger, use a calm voice. Say what you want or don't want your child to do, "I don't want you to throw the ball in the house because you might break something." Or say, "I won't let you throw the ball in the house because . . ."

"I won't let you because" is a simple statement of fact that explains the reason behind your position to your child. Even if she doesn't grasp what you are saying at first, she will eventually learn to make the connection between what she did and why she shouldn't do it the next time. By taking the time to explain things to your child, you are showing that you respect her. In contrast, children raised in authoritarian households where they are simply made to follow orders may have greater difficulty reasoning for themselves and making decisions as adults. Being able to make positive choices is a valuable skill for life.

It's not necessary to repeat yourself over and over to reinforce a message. A message can be stated simply in a calm voice. Remember to *wait* until you have your child's attention. You can do this by saying her name and noticing when she is listening. It isn't necessary to talk continuously to your baby. Talk to her about what concerns *her.* Avoid talking about her when she's in the room. If you do, let her know you are discussing her with Grandma, or whomever. Acknowledge her presence or include her in your conversation.

David Elkind, in *The Hurried Child,* outlines the importance of politeness in speaking to and dealing with children and how it supports their feelings of self-worth, teaches them to be thoughtful, and eases the stress in their lives. Saying "please" and "thank you" to your child demonstrates consideration.

Tell Your Child When You Are Leaving

Be honest with your child. Tell her when you are leaving the house or leaving the room, even if you know tears will follow. Why do this, you may wonder, when it might be so much easier to slip out quietly? Because you want your child to trust you. Disappearing undermines basic trust. Some parents sneak out, often when a child is asleep, exchanging momentary peace for an atmosphere of mistrust. I would tell your child, "I'm putting you to bed and Grandpa will be here, then I'm going to the movies, and then I'll be home."

Over the years I've observed many children in child care centers. I am always able to tell the children whose parents tell them when they are leaving from those who aren't told. Children who are told may not react when their parent leaves, or they may cry or have a tantrum. But it's over quickly and they go on to play peacefully. Children who aren't told have anxious facial expressions and may keep looking around for their absent parent for hours.

It's a sign of healthy attachment if your child cries when you leave her. However, if she cries for hours when left at child care, take a closer look at the center for any possible problem. You may also need to evaluate whether your child is ready for it or is spending too many hours there.

Be respectful of your child by telling her you are leaving, "I'm going out now" or "I'm going to the bathroom," and when you'll be back, "I'll be back in about fifteen minutes." If you're going out, tell her who will be watching her: "Uncle Steven will be here with you while I'm gone. I'll be home before your dinner." Be honest so she can base her expectations on and anticipate what will happen (she will see Mommy before dinner) rather than anxiously wait for you to come back. Be consistently dependable to help your child feel secure. You want her to trust you. If you say you will return at a certain time, plan to be there.

Allow your child her feelings and her right to express them. Babies shouldn't need to continually smile and be happy to make a parent feel better. They should also be allowed to be sad, angry, or uncomfortable. Observe your baby to see how she feels. Separations are part of life. Your child is learning that when you leave, you do come back.

Avoid Labels

Try not to use labels, either positive or negative, when talking to or about your child, as in saying, "Rebecca is short-tempered," "Josh is shy," "Susan, you're grouchy in the morning," or even "Dani is an early walker" or "Kim, you're such a good talker." I feel labels are disrespectful because they are judgments about a child's character. They can also become self-fulfilling prophecies. A child who is told (or hears) she is shy may come to accept herself as shy. If a child is continually told how smart or brave she is, perhaps she'll feel she has no room to be slow or fearful.

Your child is a unique individual whose uniqueness you will see more and more as you observe her special talents. As you carry this style of free and honest relating into later years, you will discover that it's easy to talk to your child and she with you. By opening this valuable channel of communication, you are investing in your relationship, now and for the future.

Offer Your Child Choices

Good communication means establishing a comfortable level of relating so that both parties feel understood. As your child grows and struggles for her independence, offering her choices, no matter how small or insignificant they may seem, is a positive step in supporting her autonomy. It's also a good habit to engage in early in your child's life because it will offer special help to your toddler, whose main goal is to separate from you. In this way she will feel more understood.

You may start by offering a baby two blankets to choose from. If you are offering juice, ask her if she wants apple juice or pear juice. The blue bib or the red? The green or yellow bucket to take to the park? By letting her choose she will also get into the habit of making her own decisions. This is a good skill to develop in life.

David adds, "Communicating with D. J. has always meant giving him choices. I say things like, 'Do you want to walk upstairs to your bath or do you want me to carry you up?' I see him as a capable person with a will and an ability to make good choices."

You may incorporate choices that steer your child toward your goal: "We need to go pick up Daddy. Do you want to put on your blue sweater or your yellow one?" or "It's time for bed. Would you like me to read this story to you or that one?" Choices offer a child a sense of freedom and control over her life.

Supporting Your Child's Language Development

In the first year of life, children comprehend much more than they are able to express. They understand language before they are able to speak. They need to hear language in order to learn how to speak. This happens slowly and naturally in a social environment.

By the end of the first year your child may say her first words, such as "Mama," "Dada," or "baba." Or like Einstein, she may not speak until later. By observing and listening carefully, you will discover the meaning of her words, often single-syllable sounds. You may encourage her by repeating back to her (reflecting) what she is trying to say. For example, if she says "ba" while looking at a ball, you can say "ball" or "You see the blue ball." If she says "pe" while eating peas, you can say, "Peas. You're eating peas."

Children learn language skills by listening and repeating what they hear. All children living in a household where people talk to one another learn to speak in time, and there should be no hurry or pressure. Be respectful of your child by enjoying what she is learning and saying. If she shows interest in a particular object, you can tell her what it is: "Lamp," or "You're looking at the lamp," or "These are my shoes."

Most children like books—turning the pages and looking at the pictures. Enjoying books together is a wonderful activity. Keep in mind the goal of letting your child lead, and avoid teaching. Allow your child the time to develop language at her own pace (more on supporting language development in chapter 8).

Refining Your Observation/Intervention Skills

You can better understand your child through continued observation. As she grows older, you will notice she is becoming more expressive and communicative. Watch her at play. In observing your child you will become accustomed to her body movements, motor skills, and frustration level. This will help you relax as you begin to trust her competence in facing challenges. Let her discover what she finds stimulating and choose her learning experiences.

Allow her to struggle. Help her see herself as a problem solver. It is frustrating for a child if a parent constantly interrupts or directs her play. We interrupt children because we don't respect them, perhaps feeling what they're doing is not important or that we know better. Solving her problems or rescuing her also gives her the message that the world is a dangerous place that she is not competent enough to handle. Children are wonderful problem solvers, but they are much slower than we are.

Geralynn says,

> Delanie's learned she can be comfortable being herself and knows she doesn't need to perform. If she's apprehensive or uncomfortable about something, she doesn't hesitate to let us know. She's learned to trust herself. At RIE class when children are climbing on equipment, we often hear you tell them, "The edge is here. You're close to the edge." When she's climbing, Delanie will look down and feel the edge. She's aware of her body and the space that it's in.

Melissa says, "I currently work as a student-teacher at a children's center with two- to five-year-olds. I encourage the children to do things on their own—to use their hands. It helps them think on their own."

Learning to Fall Is Important

If your child falls down and cries, say to her, "You fell. What happened? Does it hurt?" You can move near her or hold out your hands. Be available. Give her a chance to handle the situation as best she can. Give her options rather than rescue her. A good strategy for life is to let your child figure out what to do.

Falling is not a bad thing. You fall, you get up. Falling is losing balance, which is a natural occurrence. Not allowing a baby to fall will prevent her from learning *how* to fall, an important skill. Balance cannot be taught, anyway. Reflecting on what happened shows that you empathize with your child while not making her feel like a victim. Her feelings are acknowledged while her actions are noted.

Don't reinforce a victim mentality by saying, "Poor baby. Let me help you. I'll kiss it and make it better." Not only do you rob your child of comforting herself, you also provide a magical solution of which she is not a part. You may think, what's the harm? I think all behaviors add up over time, and the sum total either helps or hinders a child.

I don't believe in saying "You're okay" to a child who has fallen down and is crying. If a child is crying, she doesn't feel okay, and saying this negates her feelings. It is a mixed message, telling her one thing while she feels the opposite. If your child is frightened by a siren's scream, for example, it's better to say, "That's a loud siren. Did it scare you?" than, "Don't be scared. It's only a siren." It's healthier to *accept* what your child is feeling (even if it seems silly to you) than to tell her how she should feel. In this way she gains security from being understood and accepted.

Iris adds, "You always say it's okay for children to cry. So often negative emotions, like hurt or anger, make adults feel uncomfortable so we try to distract kids from feeling them. I learned to let my daughter fully experience her emotions but, as she grows up, learn to express them in a socially acceptable way."

If your child wants to do something you don't like (such as bang a toy on a table or throw a toy at you), offer an alternative: "I don't want you to bang the lion on the table or throw the lion at me. You can throw the lion into this basket or that one." Offer a choice (two baskets) when possible. This gives her some power and control over the situation rather than leaving her feeling helpless. Let her use her power while aiming it in a positive direction.

Gaining Confidence

In our RIE classes, it's a beautiful thing to watch the children blossom and grow, not only in their physical development but also in confidence. When they are ready, new climbing toys are brought out to offer them stage-appropriate choices. They like to scale our low wooden ramp and our large wooden cube, which can be climbed in and out of. In time they begin climbing the large wooden boxes that border the room.

At first, the children explore these new items cautiously, testing out their properties to see if they move or tip over. They're also testing their own abilities to pull up, cruise, and climb. They carry dolls and exchange toys. They tote plastic pails, engage in disputes over toys, laugh, and sometimes cry during two hours of almost total freedom.

At this stage I notice how the parents relax as the months go by. The anxious, fledgling parents have, by this time, turned into a seasoned group, no longer panicking if their child stumbles or cries. Looking back, it's hard to believe that these same parents were in tears during some of the classes. Not that the tears go away. At every age and through every stage of parenting, new issues arise that tug at our hearts. But I see that their confidence level is higher.

The children, too, sense their parents' confident composure and revel in a growing sense of independence. The trust on their parents' faces encourages them to explore.

An Example of Selective Intervention

I remember an incident in class when a child called her mother from the indoor play area. Some of us were sitting just outside in the outdoor play area. The mother and I got up to see what was going on. One of the large wooden boxes has a child-size hole in it into which the children like to deposit toys, and climb into and out of. It appeared the child was stuck in the box, sticking out of it from the waist up. Her mother knelt down close to her and asked her what was the matter, trying to figure it out, aware her child wouldn't be able to tell her as she wasn't yet talking. Yet, the mother asked the question. As we looked at the child we noticed she had a ball in her hand, which was inside the box. The child, looking upset, repeated, "Mama."

Her mother looked at her and said, "You're trying to pull the ball out of the box and you can't fit the ball and your hand out of the hole." The child smiled. Instead of lifting the child out of the box, the mother helped her ease the ball out. The child happily took the ball, pulled her legs out of the box, and got down.

I looked at the mother and said, "I liked the way you assessed the situation before you acted." I was happy to see how she waited, observed, and minimally intervened. Waiting allowed the mother to better understand her child and to give her the appropriate assistance.

You can do the same in your home or at the park or playground, with your own child. Observe and wait. Be available and let your child struggle through her process for the answer.

Simplicity in the Play Environment

A simple play environment that contains child-size objects helps your child feel competent. Remember *Alice in Wonderland* when Alice shrinks and is overwhelmed by all the large furniture and surroundings? A child can feel small and incompetent in an adult-size environment. Child-size tables and chairs help her feel comfortable. Small, safe pieces of climbing equipment can be introduced, such as low ramps, step stools, and small, smooth, sturdy wooden boxes.

Play objects such as (safe) kitchen utensils, containers for depositing toys, push and pull toys, open and close toys, toy cars and trucks, and toy phones can be brought in. Large lifelike dolls are nice additions. Board books, especially those that show a child involved in different activities such as eating, bathing, and playing, are excellent choices. Children at this stage also like sand and water for digging and dumping.

I strongly recommend removing the television from the play area. Television not only robs children of initiative, but also affects their health. Childhood obesity is on the rise as video games and countless TV programs are molding a passive generation. Children, like adults, get accustomed to being entertained.

This situation can be avoided by encouraging your child's inner stimulation. A child who is inner-directed will not need or rely on television for entertainment. You can support this by not making a television available to your young child. Let your child create her own activities. She knows what is best for her.

Children can learn to play beautifully by themselves, but you have to trust and believe that it will happen. Parents too often expect something of themselves that they cannot deliver—twenty-four hours of totally being with their child. You will be a better parent and a fuller person if you have your own life, too. I often tell parents, "You are not your child's slave." Trust in your child's potential for creating her own play while making your life easier.

What about Horseplay?

I believe horseplay, in which a child is thrown into the air, usually the domain of daddies, treats her like an object. This type of play may come about because it's difficult being around a young baby. They don't tell us how to behave with them. For daddies, horseplay is an inherited belief system. Somehow it seems the manly thing to do. Like it or not, we also repeat what was done to or with us. Unconscious habits, learned in childhood, appear. How many times have we thought, in saying something to our child, "I sound just like my mother (or father)?" Playfulness is fine as long as it isn't forced on your child or doesn't scare her.

I don't believe in tickling children. Tickling is invasive, almost an assault. It changes the way a child feels by *making* her "laugh." Laughter should come from the soul and be a sign of happiness, contentment, and joy. When a child is tickled, she laughs hysterically, and behind the laughter, there may be fear. I believe that this laughter is a nervous reaction on the child's part, and makes the parent feel like he or she is in control. It gives one a feeling of power, almost hypnotic, when you can make another person laugh. There are gentler ways to be with children. Take a walk, look at picture books together, or simply observe her as she plays.

Parents have asked me if playing games such as peekaboo, where a child may start to laugh hysterically on her own, is disrespectful. You cannot prevent a child from laughing hysterically on her own, so this is perfectly fine. Peekaboo, by the way, is an important game for a child to engage in because it plays upon her feeling of "Are you here?" When the parent reappears, the child feels secure that her parent is still there.

Children in Group Play

Children raised with respect and inner direction tend to play well in groups, at times quite peacefully, each involved in her own project or involved with the other children. However, disputes between children are inevitable. Most adults immediately intervene when observing children struggling over a toy and attempt to solve the problem. This is usually done with the good intention of teaching young children the desired lesson, such as sharing or giving the disputed toy to "whoever had it first." Constant intervening will not resolve the issue, which is to help your child *want* to share.

Children Learn Sharing by Example

Sharing is a complex issue. Young children want everything they see simply because they want it. No child wants to share a toy, which she also views as an extension of herself. Young children don't understand the concept of sharing. A parent who models sharing can be a good example.

To better explain how children view sharing, I often cite an example from the book *Siblings without Rivalry* (Norton, 1987), by Adele Faber and Elaine Mazlish, where a beautiful woman shows up at a family's doorstep with a suitcase and tells the wife that she is coming to live there and says she's not interested in taking away the husband, but in sharing him. This is how children feel when confronted with a new sibling or are told to share a toy. I believe sharing cannot be taught to young children. They learn to do it through loving behaviors modeled by their parents. Young children learn from what they see, not from teaching.

If not by teaching, how does a child develop a conscience? Through consistency. She needs many yeses and a few consistent nos. Consistency means a no is a no whether the parent is in a good mood or a bad mood. For example, a young child knows she is not allowed to go into the bathroom alone. This helps her feel secure. It helps her learn the "house rules." It also lets her assimilate and internalize the behavior the parent wishes to reinforce, including sharing. (More on sharing is covered in chapter 8.)

Be Available As You Let Your Child Negotiate a Solution

An adult's unnecessary intervention in children's disputes tells them that they cannot negotiate solutions. I believe that allowing children to work out their problems (without anybody being hurt) is healthy. When children fight over a toy, they usually end up throwing the toy down afterward, losing interest in it. The more we intervene, the more we complicate issues. Fighting over a toy is preparation for life. Later in life you may fight for a job or for an idea about which you feel strongly.

Give your child the message "I think you can handle this. I'm here if you can't." If a child isn't given the opportunity to solve her own problems, she grows up either to overly depend on or to defy her parent.

Look at the following example:

> Anna and Rikki, both ten months old, are playing on the patio while Rikki's mother watches them. Each child is pulling on an arm of the same baby doll.

Mother: (Kneels down next to them) "You both want the doll. Rikki took the doll from you, Anna, and you didn't like it."

Anna tugs on the doll even harder. Rikki grips the doll's arm with both of her hands.

Mother: "Yes, Rikki, you want the doll, too." (She waits a moment, giving both children the opportunity to figure out a solution. She then offers an option.) "There are two other dolls on the shelf. Rikki, would you like to choose another doll?"

The children both hang on to the doll. Rikki begins to cry.

Mother: "Rikki, it looks like you really want that doll."

Anna pulls on the doll. Anna raises a hand to hit Rikki.

Mother: (Puts her hand on Anna's) "I won't let you hit Rikki."

Rikki pulls the doll away from Anna.

Mother: "Rikki has the doll now. Anna, would you like one of the other dolls? There are two you can choose from."

Anna looks at Rikki, holding the doll.

Rikki offers the baby doll to Anna. Anna takes the doll.

Mother: "Now Rikki's giving you the doll."

Anna and Rikki smile. Anna drops the doll and they both chase a butterfly flitting on the patio.

Many different outcomes could have resulted from the above scenario. Anna could have taken the doll. They both could have dropped it. Or they could have held on longer. The point is that by following the path of least resistance, Rikki's mother gave the children the opportunity to resolve the problem on their own. She remained neutral but stayed near them, letting them know that she was available and that they wouldn't be abandoned as they struggled. There may be those who feel children this age can actually be "taught" to share by forcing them to take turns or by taking the toy away. I feel children cannot be taught or forced. It is a slowly learned process.

Sometimes children need assistance. After acknowledging feelings through reflecting, I suggest offering acceptable alternatives in disputes between children. In the above example, the mother offered another doll to Anna. While commenting on what is happening or saying what a child may not do (hit the other child, as in the above example), tell her what she *can* do. Reflect. Be gentle and empathetic, yet firm. Remember to give children time. You will find that they often quickly resolve their disputes and go on to the next experience.

Patty says, "RIE gave me confidence as a parent that children can work out many conflicts with our assistance. This style of parenting has been woven into my life, especially in the area of letting children problem-solve and resolve conflicts."

Melissa adds, "My son (now five) has a friend who comes over to play. Sometimes they fight. I let them work it out themselves unless they're hurting each other. If that happens, I'll intervene and say, 'Robert, tell him what you don't like.' I encourage them to talk to each other but I try to back off because I've noticed that one minute kids will fight and the next minute they're friends again. I know it's healthy. If I keep intervening, it's not."

Help Your Child Learn to Be Gentle

It's healthy to allow children to explore and touch each other. A carer must watch closely to make sure neither child is scared nor hurt by the touching. Children can eventually learn to be gentle with each other through a parent's modeling. You can say, "Gentle, gentle. You're touching Jamie's face. We touch faces gently." If the child being touched is frightened, the other child can be discouraged from touching her. Again, the less we do, the better.

Children should never be allowed to hit or hurt parents, carers, or other children. You can say, "I won't let you hit Joe. That will hurt him. What else can you do?" You can also gently stroke the children's faces, saying, "Gently, slowly." This alone may defuse the situation. Your gentle modeling helps. Remain close to the action, on the floor if necessary, to prevent children from hurting each other, though you may allow them to struggle.

If a child hits or hurts another child during play, say to the child who did the hitting, "You hit Rebecca. That hurt her. Please be gentle with her." If the child who was hurt seems upset, offer her comfort without overdoing it or glamorizing the idea of being a victim by saying to her, "Michelle hit you. Did that hurt?" Hold her if she indicates she wants to be held. RIE philosophy discourages both bully *and* victim mentalities.

Lessons will generally stick better if children work out their own disputes, but sometimes they do need help. If your child is never able to keep other children from taking a toy she's holding, you can encourage her by reflecting, "If you want the toy it's okay to hold on to it. Hold on tight." Encouragement is more helpful than sympathy, which only reinforces a victim attitude.

If your child is doing something you don't feel is safe, you can say, "I don't want you to climb on that table. It's not safe for you up there. If you want to climb, you can climb onto the couch or on this ramp."

Aggression is a normal human impulse. It's what a child *does* when aggressive that may need to be discouraged or stopped. So if your child wants to throw something that might hurt another child, instead offer her a beanbag and give the child a choice as to where she can throw it.

Children will set their own limits. Carol tells the story of her daughter, Rachel (now twenty-seven), who at six months was the youngest child in my first parent/infant class at the Dubnoff school in 1969.

> If Rachel wanted a toy she would cry for it but make no attempt to get it because being in the habit of anticipating her every need, I usually handed her toys. I remember you

asked me to wait while she went through her crying so she could learn to solve her own problems and get what she wanted. There was another baby in the class—Melody—who came from a family of older brothers and big dogs. Melody usually overpowered Rachel and was in the habit of lying on top of her. I remember one day during snack time, Melody tried to take Rachel's banana. Something inside of Rachel must have snapped because she grabbed the banana back from Melody. This was another RIE lesson, for her and for me.

Are There Differences between the Sexes at This Age?

I don't believe in treating infant and toddler boys differently from girls. During the first few years there is no great difference between the sexes. Try to understand your child and figure out why she does what she does. The beauty of young children is that everything—problems, crises, disputes—lasts briefly. The basic idea is to be available to your child and let her know that she can count on you, not to solve every problem, but to be available for support.

Separation Anxiety Is Healthy

Separation anxiety occurs even in securely grounded children. When a child discovers that she is a separate person from her parents, she may feel scared. This is part of the normal separation process and comes and goes at different times during early childhood. During these periods a child becomes clingy toward the person(s) she's attached to. This may be a source of excessive crying or night waking. Separation anxiety is a good sign that a child is healthfully attached to her parents.

When you are with your child, be totally with her. When you leave and she cries, say, "I can see you don't want me to go, but I'll be in the next room." At first, don't go far. She will learn that not seeing you or not being touched by you doesn't mean she is being abandoned.

I reiterate my belief in honesty with your child as a basic rule, with regard to separation anxiety. It can be tempting to sneak out of a room or out of the house, especially if you know tears will follow. Sometimes it isn't even a matter of sneaking. You may drop off your child at the sitter's or at child care, wait until she is involved in an activity, then leave.

Instead, tell your child you are leaving, acknowledge her sadness, tell her when you will return, and go. If she is in a particularly vulnerable stage, don't leave for long periods of time. Separating is a part of life and should be experienced. Build her trust in you by letting her know what to expect, even if it's momentarily painful for her.

I sympathize with parents. It's hard to be with a child who is clingy. If your child is going through a clingy stage, try not to separate for too long. Reappear as often as you can. And again repeat this mantra: this, too, will pass. Think of the future, when your child will want to leave you and you'll cry, saying, "Do you have to go? It's so early," and she'll answer, "'Bye, Mom."

I realize that parents get separation anxiety, too. This can intensify a child's sad feelings. You need to be aware of this and guard against adding to your child's struggle. You can still be honest. It's okay to say, "It's hard to leave but I'll be back." Try not to overdramatize. Remain her firm base of support.

Examples of Separation Anxiety

Separation anxiety surfaces at different times in your young child's life. During our classes, at times children choose to remain on a parent's lap, sometimes for the entire class. They are never told to join the others or to stop being "shy." They are allowed to do what they feel comfortable doing. The children often move back and forth, from the indoor to the outdoor play area, as their parents sit and watch. "Poor abandoned parents," I say to the adults, sensing their anxiety or sadness. "Now it is you who are left."

At one class a mother brought up an issue. "Lately when I leave Erin in her room to play, she just stands at the gate and screams for me."

"Timing is so important at this age," I said. "I would say, 'I will be back,' and make the separation short, two or three minutes, then come back and talk to her."

A father chimed in. "When Billy and I go on our daily walks, he wants me to carry him the whole way."

I smiled and nodded at Billy, who looked in my direction. "Yes, we're talking about you. Your daddy's telling me about your walks."

Another mother spoke. "Michael's been doing that, too."

I continued, knowing these were all instances of separation anxiety. "That's very legitimate. They feel that soon they will no longer be carried. They start to sense the human condition." At that moment, Michael walked outdoors and playfully tumbled into his mother's lap.

"See how he reowns you," I said, smiling.

His mother said, "He falls right into my arms. I guess he likes the feeling."

"That's called basic trust," I said.

Separation anxiety. Basic trust. Two important pieces that fit together to spell healthy attachment. Accept your child's separation anxiety, knowing it's the proof of her need for you. Know, too, that this will pass.

Stranger Anxiety

Stranger anxiety is another common fear in young children. It's a predictable and healthy emotional development that passes with time. To respectfully deal with your child's fear of strangers, never force her to be held by or to kiss a person she is afraid of, including a relative or friend. Stranger anxiety is a self-protective mechanism that a child may use to screen new people. This discomfort will eventually pass. However, maintaining a certain amount of stranger wariness is important.

Weaning Slowly and Lovingly

The time comes when your child loses interest in the breast or bottle, typically in the last quarter of the first year. This is the best time for weaning. At this time your child can learn to use a cup. The bottle is a convenience but can become a love or security object. Children can learn to drink from a cup and can suck on their blanket or their fingers if they need to suck.

The opportune time to wean is when children are busy exploring the world around them. This usually happens when they learn to sit, crawl, and walk. I feel a child's need to suck is overemphasized. A child used to self-comforting will suck on her fingers, her blanket, or an available toy. Teething and mouthing objects should be made available.

A breast-feeding mother may unintentionally sabotage the weaning process because she also enjoys it and panics before the door closes. Be respectful of your child by letting her lead the weaning process. Observe her to see how she feels about it.

At the first signs of disinterest, start to taper off the feedings. Leave out one feeding at a time. In the evening mothers are tired and children may be fearful. Since the evening feeding is the hardest to let go of for a child, it shouldn't be the last to go. The last feeding left should be in the morning. The process of weaning should happen slowly, taking place over several weeks or many months, depending on your child.

Try a Table and a Chair

As your child nurses or bottle-feeds less, she will typically want to eat more solids. When she is able to get in a sitting position on her own, I recommend that you introduce a small table and chair instead of a high chair. At RIE classes we use small plastic molded chairs and a low, rounded table. If a child can creep or walk, she can climb into one of the chairs.

I feel that a child-size table and chair promote respect because children see the world from their own perspective. Why should a child sit at a dining room table in a high chair or a booster chair? A high chair is a convenience for the parent, but it's a little prison. Why not have a little chair and table your child's size, where she can sit down and get up on her own?

By using a child-size table and chair you adjust to your child's level, which makes her feel more comfortable. Picking her up and fastening her into a restraining device may underscore her helplessness. The table and chair encourage competence by letting her walk to the table herself. She chooses whether to sit and eat and decides when she wants to get up and leave. She also knows that it is her special eating place.

Giving a child appropriate choices is important. Having choices gives children power and promotes self-confidence. The little table and chair aid in doing this. The child knows that her meal will always be served there. At the child's mealtime the food is presented and the child chooses whether or not to eat. She then sits at her table. If she comes and goes, showing minimal interest in the food, it can be taken away and offered later. Eventually a child will choose to eat at the times the food is presented because children with scheduled mealtimes fall in sync with their eating routine.

Snack at RIE Class

Halfway through each parent/infant class, when the children are old enough to sit on small stools or small chairs and hold a cup, we provide a snack. The educarer gets up and announces it's time for snack, then goes into the kitchen to prepare it. A few minutes later she appears with a plastic bin of bananas, apple juice, bibs, a small pitcher and cups, damp washcloths, and dry towels. She takes out a small table and places low stools or molded chairs around it. Each child, one by one, makes his or her way to the table. There are disputes over chairs, but eventually the children sit around the table. Each child is given a choice between several bibs of different colors. If a child has a strong objection to wearing a bib, she can choose not to wear one (unless her parent overrules it). The children help clean their hands with wet washcloths.

When all the children who want to eat are seated, the educarer takes out the bananas. If some children want to continue playing and not eat, that's fine. The educarer peels a banana as the children watch and some help pull down the peels. Sometimes a chant breaks out, "Nana, nana, nana" as the children await their snack. A banana naturally splits down the center from the top into three sections. The educarer breaks it off and serves it this way.

"See how civilized they are," I say to parents. "This is waiting time. No child likes to wait. And yet they do."

Parents often ask me why we have snack, if it's to feed the children in class. I tell them that snack time is for learning rules. It has new and different expectations from what goes on during the rest of the class. During class there are very few rules and the kids figure them out quickly. Snack prepares them for social life. It's cause/consequence: If they leave the table, they cannot have food. They cannot walk away with a banana. And they are allowed to eat as much as *they* want to.

I remember a father's asking me, "Here or at home, how do we get our children to stay in their chairs?"

I smiled and answered, "The rules here aren't maintained with force or anger. Children are not made to sit. Rather, they choose to sit. That's the secret to good upbringing—establish a continuing habit for whatever you want your child to learn for life. Spell out the consequence of your child's action: 'If you get up from the table, that tells me you're not hungry, so I'll put the food away.' And do it. It's hard for parents to do because they feel their child won't eat enough or get the proper nourishment. Remember that a child's role is to challenge us. That they feel comfortable enough to challenge us is a good sign because only children who feel safe challenge. Fearful children may do things behind their parents' backs."

The father continued, "Is it peer pressure that makes them get along so well sitting at the table?"

Watching the children, intent on eating and watching each other, looking rather peaceful, I smiled. "There's no pressure here."

Another mother broke into the discussion. "I use a high chair at home because I want my daughter to be on the same level with us for meals."

"Many people feel that way," I replied. "I feel the little table and chair are more respectful."

Snack is handled, as all meals should be, slowly and leisurely. After the children have their fill of banana, the educarer brings out the pitcher and cups. Each child is given a choice of cups. Some leave the table. Each waits her turn until the educarer pours a small amount of juice into her cup. Older children are given small pitchers and pour their own juice. Some want refills. After they finish the juice, they use washcloths to wipe their faces and hands. Some children like to help clean the table and floor, or help put the stools away. The educarer takes the table, chairs, and food away and the children resume playing.

Over the years many parents have told me that children who never eat bananas at home always eat them at RIE class. This brings to mind a lovely memory. A five-year-old boy who'd attended the classes came back to visit. His mother told me that on the drive to the RIE Center she talked to him about Magda and RIE and he didn't respond. But before he came in the front door, he looked in, pointed, and said, "Bananas!"

Perhaps what stood out in that little boy's mind, and what stands out in all the children's minds who love eating bananas at RIE, is that they are treated with gentle respect. Snack at RIE is a pleasure to watch. It can be surprising to see young children behave in such a cooperative manner. And as the months pass and the children mature, they become even more well mannered. Children sense when they are respected and react in kind.

Keep Mealtimes Slow and Relaxed

As your baby grows, keep mealtimes pressure-free. Don't worry about how much she eats in a day. Looking at what she eats in the course of a week is more realistic. Offer her healthy choices. You can model good eating habits.

Begin meals by telling your child that her food will be ready in a few minutes so she can anticipate the meal. You can show her what you are doing in the kitchen to prepare the meal if she's within viewing distance. When she's older, she can help you prepare the food and set the table.

When the food is ready, sit down near your child on a low stool or a chair, adapting to her environment instead of expecting her to adapt to yours. Have a sponge ready for cleaning the table and a clean, wet washrag for cleaning hands. Tell your child what she will be eating, show her the food, and allow her time to decide to sit down. She should not be allowed to take the food away from the table, but let her get up when she is finished eating. I also do not believe in letting a child walk around with a bottle.

If your child shows interest in holding a spoon, give her a spoon to hold while you feed her with another spoon. Allow her to experiment with feeding herself, as messy as it may be. This is how she will eventually acquire the skill. There is a German saying "Practice makes the master." Learning to eat with a spoon is a long process. Give her time to learn. Patience and encouragement are helpful. You can help her learn the rules by telling her what they are. For example, "The bowl stays on the table" or "The juice stays in the cup. If you pour your juice out, I'll put the cup away."

You can give your beginning eater small pieces of food to pick up and eat with her fingers. I recommend giving your child very small quantities of food at a time rather than placing a large portion in front of her. Let her indicate or ask for more. The goal is for your child to be in control and know when she's hungry or full. Overfeeding destroys the natural feeling of satiation. Offer the food, wait until your child opens her mouth, and stop when she is no longer eager.

Offering a child a large plateful of food not only overwhelms her but also encourages playing with the food instead of eating.

Let her initiate the eating process. Adapt to her eating tempo. Never force her to eat. It's better to feed a little less than to get in that last spoonful. Eating is also a social goal. It should be a no-pressure situation with good feelings attached. Feedings can be fun and a source of quality time. Learn to work together. Let your child enjoy her food while you enjoy her company.

Trying New Foods

If your child rejects a new food, don't force the issue but do reintroduce it at another time. Do you remember a time when you were dining out and a foreign or exotic dish was placed in front of you? Did you ever taste it gingerly or push it away? Each new food is exotic to a child. Some people are more open to novelty than others. Your child needs time to accept the new food into her eating repertoire.

Reintroduce the new food so many times that by the thirtieth time, it no longer feels new to her. Three or four times isn't enough. A few months later you may be surprised to see that the new dish is your child's favorite. Never push. Offer new foods when a child is hungry or thirsty. Then she may be more willing to try something new.

Introduce each new food by itself for two weeks. If several new things are introduced at once, a child doesn't develop the habit of knowing, for instance, that if it's orange, it's carrots, and if it's green, it's spinach. Predictability is important for young children.

You can offer juice, milk, or water in a cup. Very mild chamomile tea, cooled, is soothing. It's helpful to pour the liquid into the cup using a small plastic pitcher. This way your child can see the process and learn how to do this later by herself. Pour only a tiny amount of beverage into the cup, as spills are inevitable. Help your child as she learns how to hold the cup and drink from it. Drinking from a cup—grasping it with the lips, consuming the liquid, and swallowing—are new skills that require practice. In time she will learn to hold the cup by herself. She may become playful and turn the cup over to watch the liquid spill, so leave only small portions of beverage in the cup.

When to End the Meal

When your child shows disinterest in eating by stopping, pushing the food away, or getting up from the table, it's time to end the meal. When a child starts to throw food or turn over the cup, she is showing more of an interest in playing. Playing with food should not be allowed. You can say in a neutral voice, "You turned over your cup. It looks like you're not thirsty anymore. I don't want you to play with the cup. I'm going to take it away." If she enjoys the activity, get her a basin of water and a cup to play with outside, or a little wading pool to splash in. Most children love water. Let her enjoy leisurely baths with plastic bottles and pails to pour and dump. She may be less likely to want to turn over her cup.

When your child is finished eating, remove the food and drink from the table and tell her it's time to clean up. Encourage her to help wipe the table off with the sponge and help wipe her hands and face with the towel. When she is done, let her get up from the table.

Refusing to Eat

Don't worry if your child goes through periods when she loses her appetite or refuses to eat. Except in cases of illness or emotional disturbance, no child who has food available starves. All children go through periods when their appetites lessen, typically in the second year of life when as they begin to walk and talk, they are busy exploring their world. It is also about this time that their rate of growth slows down and they might require less food.

The minute your child refuses food, I would refrain from offering more. This is hard on parents. But have you ever been not hungry? Would you like it if people around you forced you to eat? When your child doesn't have an appetite, assume she's not hungry and put the food away. One should eat only when one is hungry and not for other reasons, especially not to please one's parent.

At the Emmi Pikler Institute in Hungary, children love to eat. But they are never pushed to eat even an additional spoonful if they turn away or show disinterest. Ideally, food should be eaten when a person wants it. Respect your child's internal guide to her appetite and satiation.

Sleeping Issues at This Stage

Sleeping habits change as children pass through different stages of physiological, emotional, and social development. Here are some ways your child's sleep may change, and some suggestions for responding.

Night Wakings

Night wakings are common. A child learning to walk may have a sense that she can physically leave her parents. This may make her fearful and cause night wakings. A child experiencing separation anxiety may awaken and cry for her parent. A child may have a nightmare and cry. As she passes through these different learning periods and stages of development, your child may need you more than usual both during the day and at night.

Be careful not to reinforce new and undesirable nighttime habits. A crying child can easily get into the habit of being rocked to sleep if a parent does this each time she awakens. The longer an undesirable behavior is reinforced, the harder it is to change. Children often cry out at night. Sometimes if you wait a moment, they go back to sleep. Even if your child screams for you in the middle of the night, remain calm and don't add to her fear. As always, start with the minimum.

Go in calmly and do less. If your child awakens, talk to her. If she needs more comfort, stroke her or put your arms around her. Try sitting on the floor next to her crib and talk to her a little more. If she's still upset, you might pick her up and hold her until she calms down. Then put her back in her bed. By your doing less, your child will learn to calm herself, perhaps choosing a stuffed animal for comfort, rocking, or sucking her fingers.

Changes in Naps

Nap times change and usually lengthen as your child settles into her daily routine. If she has been in the habit of experiencing sleep time as a happy time and has been placed in her bed awake, nap times should remain peaceful. During the first year a child typically has a morning and an afternoon nap. After the first year the morning nap is usually dropped, though there are variations depending on each child.

Reinforcing a good bed and nap routine makes your life easier because each day has a predictable rhythm. Follow the same sequence of events. Putting her to sleep in the same place at about the same time each day helps. Respect your child by reinforcing healthy sleep habits that will give her a good start in life.

Go Slowly and with Patience

Why do we hurry? Where do we hurry to? Do we enjoy rushing, pushing ourselves? Our society's attitude seems to be "more, more, faster, faster." Can we really have it all, do it all, be it all? And when will that time be? How about slowing down and enjoying what we have now?

This hurry-up attitude, noted by David Elkind in *The Hurried Child,* is harmful for children and adds unnecessary stress to their lives. In order to flourish, children need a slow, predictable life. As parents and as their models, we must remind ourselves of this.

Children don't react as quickly as adults because their minds and thought processes are still grasping the relationships between things and their meanings. If you tell your child you want to put on her shoes to go outside, give her time to follow through with your expectations. Be patient as the message "goes through gray matter" and she gets it. Allow her this important transition time as you shift gears. Remember, your child is eager to please you. If she is struggling to grasp a toy or pull on her sweater, let her go through her own process, even if it's hard or frustrating to watch knowing it would be faster and easier to do it yourself. This is how to support her.

Developmental phases may inhibit your child's desire to cooperate. A child in pain from teething may not want to put on her shoes or feel like doing anything. This is difficult to deal with if you are in a hurry or are having a rough day. Keep in mind the goal of patience.

Diane says,

> I learned to go slow with my children, to pay attention to them and watch them as opposed to getting them on my

time frame. I learned to adjust to their wavelength rather than forcing them onto mine. It took some practice. I've learned to back off, to let my children do things by themselves, struggle, fail, get frustrated,. and try. I remember learning, when Jennifer was a baby, that if she was on her stomach before she was crawling, and became frustrated in trying to reach a toy, to let her alone. I learned to hang back and watch as she rolled and pulled herself, inch by quarter-inch, and eventually get the toy if she wanted it. To watch her reach for it and see how proud she was when she got it was something I don't think I would have experienced. I would have just handed her the toy. I learned to not interfere with my children and that it didn't matter if things were done the "right" way—like if my daughter wanted to go sideways or backwards down a slide. I was raised being shown how to do everything. It was my instinct to do the same with both my children, but I don't believe it would have been the best thing for them.

Respect your child by adjusting to her pace as she grows and learns. Give her the opportunity and the time to be competent. A child who is allowed freedom and choices learns to make many wise decisions. Trust that she will.

III

As Your Child Grows

Toddlerhood and Its Challenges

8

Your Budding Toddler

When a child learns to walk, he becomes a young toddler, taking the familiar short, tottering steps on his journey from babyhood to childhood. If securely attached to his parents, he has hopefully learned to trust that they are available to him. He comes to see the world (which the parent represents) as a friendly place where he can function effectively and get his needs met. He can then use his energies to explore and learn rather than seek security.

The development of a child's confidence is a slow process established in infancy and childhood, based on security and mastery. In the toddler stage, task mastery evolves as children perform more complex tasks, such as filling buckets with sand and dressing dolls. Time and opportunity for achieving success in completing tasks during play are important for a child's developing sense of self.

As mentioned previously, a child's sense of secure attachment is enhanced by honesty in communication. When you go out, tell your child you are leaving and when you will be back, especially when he's at the peak of separation anxiety. If you do this, he learns that good-bye is just a part of the separating process and that he can trust you. Letting go becomes easier. Remember that knowing what to expect and knowing what will happen next also promote a child's feeling secure.

During toddlerhood, a little person emerges who has his own notions about things. Toddlers are exuberant about the world but haven't developed the judgment they need. The budding toddler may at times feel big and powerful, yet he clings to infancy. Your child may insist on dressing himself yet run to you when he's frightened. Toddlers feel powerful, yet can be afraid of their power. They need our guidance.

Your child is making an important transition, while discovering his strengths and vulnerabilities. The most important thing to understand about your young toddler is that all his behavior is part of his learning process. Endearing and complicated, toddlers are discovering their identities. We can help them by being patient and understanding.

Separation Is a Difficult but Healthy Part of Growing Up

The time when a child learns to walk and climb, run and speak, moving from infancy to childhood, is a wonderful yet demanding time for parents. It's exciting to watch your child face life's difficulties and challenge his fears, yet it's hard to watch him struggle. Toddlers develop so quickly it seems as if they're doing something new every day, playing with endless energy. At this stage, the child is learning to separate from his parents and eventually achieves independence. While learning to separate, a child wants to do things "his way." His will often exceeds his ability, which causes him frustration and anger.

In his book *Identity and the Life Cycle,* Erik Erikson describes how a child develops either a sense of autonomy or doubt during the second and third years of life. If parents recognize the child's need to do what he can do on his own at his own pace, his sense of autonomy is strengthened and doubt diminished.

The role of the child is to separate—to discover his own identity. He disagrees, gets upset or angry, and fights. This is important for him to do. You, the parent, have the tough role of trying to help and yet allow freedom. It's an almost impossible task. As parents, you are in the precarious position of trying to figure out whether to help your child solve a problem and if so, how much help to offer, knowing your help may be met with resistance.

For instance, if you see your child trying to put a shirtsleeve on his foot and getting angry that it doesn't fit, what should you do? Wait. Perhaps even go out of the room. Ask yourself whether your child knows what he's doing won't work. If your child asks for help, say, "How can we do this? Is this for your hand or your foot?" Whenever possible, allow your child to figure out what to do. You can give a minimal amount of help, the smallest facilitating step, enough for him to figure it out. Throw the ball back into his court. Give him confidence. Don't take over the problem and solve it even though it may be faster and easier to do it yourself. If you do, you may convey the message, "I can solve everything but you can't."

Continuing to Build Basic Trust

It's a challenge to prepare your child for the difficulties of life while helping him develop basic trust. It's impossible to raise a child with the promise of happiness forever. You can, however, raise a child who can say, "Yes, I know it's not easy now but I will figure something out." Having basic trust in oneself is important for all ages.

Respect your child by helping him build trust in himself. It develops when you are available for your child to depend on. He learns to trust you and depend on you. You, in turn, see your child as competent and support his competence. Eventually, your child develops confidence and feels comfortable about separation. Establishing basic trust makes separating easier because trust is the foundation for independence. Eventually, a secure child parts from his parents and embraces life's experiences rather than fearing them.

It is important for parents to be consistent with their child. A no is always a no. A child who can easily manipulate his parents may lose his base of security. If a child cries, whines, or screams, and a parent consistently gives in to make peace, a situation may be created where the child feels in charge, while not truly wanting nor benefiting from the responsibility. Too much power (having a feeling of control over his parents) may be unhealthy and scary for a child. When he feels too powerful, he may feel guilty, and guilt can lower self-confidence.

William says,

> I learned to trust Juliana, who's twenty months old. Yesterday we were walking on the boardwalk at the beach. She ran toward the edge, which is about a two-foot drop into the sand. I let her go because I knew she'd get to the edge, look over, and realize that she could get hurt if she fell. I

> learned to trust that she could make a judgment call. To establish this trust, I allowed Juliana to do things on her own. Rather than me teaching her to roll over, sit, walk, and talk, she learned these skills, which every human being eventually learns, on her own. I felt if I showed her how to walk before she was ready, she'd only get frustrated and possibly feel sad that she couldn't do what I was trying to get her to do. I allowed her the opportunity to experiment. Observing her helped me understand her and trust her. There'll be plenty of time for me to teach her—when she's in school.

Liz says this:

> Ezra's learned to work out a lot of his own problems. He's able to deal with other kids and is confident. He's friendly and interested in people. I think these qualities developed from my noninterference in his play with other children. I let him cry, fall down, and bump into things, waiting for his response instead of imposing my own. I let him experience his feelings and tell him that they're valid.

Trust is an important part of the letting-go process, for parents and for children.

Desires: I Want, I Want

Young toddlers have many demands and desires as they discover their bodies, minds, and emotions. Your child may start giving you verbal commands: Go, sit, out, up, get, read, and no. These may later be followed by his taking your hand or pushing you in the direction of something he wants. It is a good sign if a child expresses demands and desires because it shows that he is secure. Insecure children are afraid to demand.

As your child becomes more aware of the world and wants to encounter it, he expresses desires. He becomes aware of his ability to affect those around him. For example, he knows if he tugs on Mommy's pant leg, he will get her attention.

Acknowledge Your Child's Desires

I remember a mother's asking my advice on how to deal with a situation concerning her daughter, Christina. The mother told me how Christina wanted her mommy to "get" everything for her: lightbulbs, planes in the sky, and the moon. The mother said her way of responding was to try to logically explain why she couldn't get those things for Christina—lightbulbs were too hot, a plane too heavy, and the moon too far away. She wondered whether she was responding to her daughter in the most respectful and productive way. She was, after all, being honest.

"Support her desires," I told the mother. "Never negate them. Say to Christina, 'You want to get the moon. Where is that moon? How can you get it?' Maybe one day she will be a poet and touch the moon. There are no 'bad' desires, only bad acts. If you desire that angels fly into your room and stay with you for the night, why shouldn't they come? A desire has wings. That's the beautiful thing. A child could also have the most hideous desire—he might say he wants to kill all the people in the world—and that's still okay. You can say, 'Oh, you want to kill all the people in the world?' Actions are not always okay." The mother told me after that that she had responded to Christina's expressions of desire in a positive and encouraging way, rather than telling her what she couldn't have or hope to get.

By acknowledging a child's desire, you also accept his feelings, the desire's source. For example, if he feels angry, he may want to hit his playmate. By letting him express his desire, his feelings are acknowledged instead of buried. You can respond by saying, "You want to hit Lance, but I won't let you. That will hurt him." Handle this type of intervention with your toddler in a stronger manner, different from telling your exploring baby, "Gentle, easy."

Allow Your Child to Express His Feelings

Encouraging the expression of feelings is healthy. It helps eliminate guilt and promotes honesty. If, by contrast, your child is told, "Don't say that. That's not nice," he won't feel comfortable about expressing himself. Rather, he may feel guilty about his feelings because his parent thinks they're "not nice." Don't manipulate your child's feelings by saying, "Why are you so grumpy? Smile for Mommy." Give him permission to feel the way he does. People go to therapy because they were not allowed to express what they felt as children. Somebody in their past said, "That's not all right."

In studying 119 families, John Gottman, professor of psychology at the University of Seattle, Washington, found that parents were naturally divided into two groups—those who provided guidance about emotions and those who didn't. The children whose parents acknowledged emotions were better able to speak up for themselves and were more successful in and out of school. Gottman believes that this ability to accept and help children label their emotions yet set limits on their behavior creates for children a healthy emotional life and better relations with other people, which carries through all the way to adulthood. Further, he contends that "social and emotional intelligence" can help children withstand the effects of divorce and fortify young people against depression (*Los Angeles Times,* February 2, 1997).

Carol, mother of Clay, nine, and Lily, ten, says,

> Acknowledging my children's feelings is important because it has created a dialogue as they've gotten older and become more verbal. This was a natural progression from the communication we started during diapering, which has continued to build. I feel confident my children and I will continue to have a good relationship as they grow.

Diane says,

> Jennifer, who is six, is very connected to her feelings. She expresses her feelings freely to me and knows how she feels most of the time.
>
> My parents visited us recently. Jennifer was very excited about them coming. Because they were arriving on Valentine's Day, we had ordered a special cake from the bakery. When the bakery delivered the wrong cake, Jennifer fell apart, crying. I took her into the other room to talk. "Grandma and Grandpa come here once a year to visit. It's

hard to believe that they just arrived and you're crying about the cake."

She said, "Mom, I'm not crying about the cake. I'm just overexcited. It's a really bad feeling. It feels so bad all over my body."

Jennifer doesn't hide how she's feeling. The other day she was eating breakfast, sitting under the kitchen table. When I asked her what she was doing, she said, "I can't stand to look at my brother's face right now but I want to eat my breakfast." I love that she feels free enough to tell me something like that. I learned from RIE that whatever a person feels is fine although the behavior may not always be fine.

When a child falls down and cries, you contradict his feelings by saying, "You're not hurt. You're okay." Thus, he learns to distrust his feelings because he hurts, but is told he's all right by the person he trusts. He is also given the message that it's not acceptable to be unhappy. And finally, if a child continually hears she can't get the moon, maybe she'll stop trying.

Our children look to us as guideposts for their feelings, incorporating our attitudes into their psyches. They are sensitive to our reactions. We should always respect their feelings. If the child's ensuing action is undesirable (as when your angry child wants to kick you), acknowledge his feelings, set limits, and give him the opportunity to figure out what to do. "You seem angry. I won't let you kick me. What else can you do?"

Allowing a child to express his feelings, positive and negative, is a healthy way to prepare him for life. If you accept your child's feelings, you will help him accept them, too. Acceptance sets up good communication because he will always feel free to talk to you.

Curiosity Is Part of Creativity

Curiosity is a natural trait in children. It is the doorway to creativity, and should be appreciated and nurtured. Let your child's natural curiosity develop by letting him explore on his own rather than guiding him. Natural curiosity leads to the joy of discovery, as when a child figures out how to unscrew a lid or fit pieces of a puzzle together. Life is, after all, looking at situations and seeing what fits, or is appropriate to do, like figuring out how to assemble a puzzle.

Children find creative solutions to problems if we allow it. They create answers, sometimes the wrong answers. Grown-ups are typically success-oriented so we need to step back and see that with children, the result is not the issue. Learning how to do it is. If we do things for children or criticize them, we make the process harder for them. They then start with a negative feeling. Offer supportive feedback, "You tried." The issue is not the performance but the trial, the ingenuity, that your child attempted. Effort is a positive step in the learning process.

I remember a father's telling me about when his son was learning to pick up food and eat with his hands. A banana slice became a challenge for the child, as it always got stuck to the table. After many tries with his fingers, the child put his mouth to the table and picked it up that way, using this technique when his hunger overrode his tolerance for learning the new skill. The same father told me when his son was learning to eat with a spoon, he was better able to pick up pieces of food by spearing them with the spoon handle rather than scooping the food into the spoon—a creative solution. I was happy to hear that the father allowed his son the freedom to experiment. (By the way, he tells me that now his son, who is three, eats beautifully with a fork and spoon.)

By finding out about the relations between things, and by discovering their similarities and differences, your child learns about the world. He learns about the different properties of sand and water by pouring each into and out of a bucket. Most children understand the meaning of the word "hot" very quickly. Balls, which roll and bounce, are an excellent source of information and useful play objects for a child. Children at all developmental levels can use their budding skills to chase a rolling ball.

Children's play has an important purpose. By understanding the properties of things, children gain knowledge and grow to understand the world. They gain mastery through repetition and enjoy the struggle involved. This is why an environment rich in learning opportunities is invaluable.

Lynne A. Bond, editor of *Facilitating Infant and Early Childhood Development* (University Press of New England, 1982), notes that many effective programs "shared an environment responsive to children, one in which their behaviors had consequences. Thus the children learned that they could have some control of and impact on their environment."

Do I Need to Teach My Toddler?

Young toddlers have no use for learning ABC's or reading, or learning to count or work on a computer. Their primary focus is on separating from their parents while finding out about the world. Children learn to read in school at the appropriate time. A toddler's time is better spent developing a fertile mind, which sows the seeds for future learning.

Children always learn. Every day they are a little different. If you are observant, you will notice the changes. You might note that yesterday your child wasn't the least interested in the set of blocks you left in his room, but today he's picking them up. Children learn only what they are ready for. Imagine the changes that take place in the first three years of life. During that time a newborn baby who only cries evolves into a walking, talking person. In an average environment where there is normal conversation, a child learns shapes, colors, and names of objects without being taught. What is the point of teaching a child something he will learn on his own?

What good comes from forcing a child to read when he isn't ready? Young children let us know they're not ready when they are resistant to what we are trying to teach them. Children aren't born hating to learn. They do learn, all the time. Often we encourage them to learn about what they cannot comprehend rather than what interests them. This detracts from learning. For example, if I started talking to you in Hungarian, you wouldn't be happy because you wouldn't understand it. And maybe you wouldn't want to anyway.

Every average, healthy human being has an innate desire to find out, discover, and learn. Why do adults read the newspaper? Knowing what goes on in the world makes you feel like a participant. The ideal situation for a child would be one in which his parents respect what he is interested in, where he isn't forced to learn something totally out of his realm of understanding and interest. Does it ever come up later in one's life whether a person learned to read at four, five, or six? Learning academic skills should be saved for school-age children. Before that, let your child learn and follow his own rhythm. If you push, he loses his appetite for learning. And it's that appetite that makes him interested and want to learn.

We all have memories of teachers we loved and those who bored us. This shows that it's not necessarily the subject matter. Good teachers awaken and inspire in us the gusto for learning, as in the lovely book by Jean-Jacques Rousseau called *Émile*. Émile was a child who went into the forest with his tutor. They learned about mushrooms, flowers, trees, and the sky—whatever Émile was interested in.

A young child may be able to remember the numbers or colors on a flash card. A monkey can do the same without having a real understanding of what the information means. This kind of learned information is useless until a child has the mental capacity to comprehend its meaning.

In the September 1988 issue of *Young Children,* David A. Caruso cites evidence to support this. He shows that a young child's learning process is better supported in an environment where spontaneous play is allowed, in which a child can come to understand the world on his own terms rather than in adult-structured situations where he is taught by remembering.

Respect your child by letting his interest lead the way.

Safety Issues at This Stage

I continually emphasize safety in your child's environment, whether in the home, the yard, or his safeproofed playroom. Toddlers learn new skills every day. They climb, jump, and pull. Everything is a fair target—shelves, furniture, and blind cords, which, left dangling, are dangerous. I've heard so many parents say, "But my child *never* goes *there.*" You can only honestly say, "Not until now." We should all be more safety-conscious.

A mother told me about a time when her daughter (unexpectedly) learned how to unfasten the safety gate and she found her daughter in the kitchen, handling a knife left on the counter. Children seem to learn things when parents leave the room. Expect the unexpected. Be prepared for what your child might do next before it happens.

Remove potentially dangerous objects or pieces of furniture. If your child constantly climbs on a glass-topped table in your den, remove it. This is safer and less aggravating than spending weeks taking him down from the table, telling him not to climb on it, and fretting. You can start telling him what the "house rules" are and put the table back when he's a little older and has learned to control his impulse to climb on it. Remove floor lamps and any other objects that may be a danger.

Active children need a safe environment and supervision. Having that one hundred percent safeproofed room or play area is a great help.

The Play Environment for Your Young Toddler

When setting up your child's play environment, age-appropriate space and play objects are important considerations. It is best to provide an optimal learning environment according to your child's stage of development. If toys are too simple, your child will not be challenged. Toys that are too complicated or broken can be frustrating for your child. However, allowing some frustration is beneficial because it encourages problem-solving.

Just as new babies need small, cozy spaces to promote security and older babies need more space and play objects, young toddlers have specific requirements, too. Toddlers are scientists and experimenters with tremendous curiosity. They need a rich play area. They need space to walk and run, carry and dump, and climb and explore, where a parent or carer can supervise their play.

An optimal play environment allows for indoor and outdoor play, preferably with the ability to go in and out (a door to a connecting yard). Different floor and ground surfaces, such as wood, cement, sand, and grass, are good for exploration. A hard surface is needed for wheel toys. A sense of nature's presence (sky, trees, and flowers) is desirable, as is the availability of sun and shade. Outdoor play is important because we are the only animals who don't live outside. Outdoors is real life.

Besides providing fresh air and openness, the outdoors gives your child many opportunities for creating his own play. Children love to pick up leaves and sticks, and watch ants, bugs, and birds. They love to roll in grass and play in sand. Having sand and water in the play area is a good idea. Children also sleep better with the natural stimulation the outdoors provides.

Play Objects for Toddlers

Once your child becomes a toddler, you can introduce many new play objects: wheel toys that your child can push or ride, and tricycles. Young children love to push things. Introduce objects from the kitchen such as lightweight pots and pans. Children of this age love to imitate Mommy and Daddy. You can also add hats, wallets, eyeglass cases, purses, scarves, dress-up clothes, and hand puppets so your child can role-play. Books with simple pictures or photos are a good idea. Toddlers like to look at pictures of other people, children, or animals.

Large lifelike clothed dolls that can be dressed and undressed are useful as toddlers like to practice their burgeoning skills on anyone or anything that will cooperate. In addition, dolls can help your child work out conflicts and anxieties, such as dealing with a new sibling. I remember a little boy in RIE class who had a new brother. One day he picked up one of the big cloth dolls and kept slamming it against the floor, saying, "The boy, the boy." I wondered whether he might have been working out the anger or jealousy he felt toward his new sibling. Looking at doll faces may also help your child work out stranger anxiety.

Climbing equipment—wooden platforms, steps, boxes, low slides, and climbing structures, even wooden ladders laid on the ground—is useful for young toddlers. Toddlers will find things to climb on, so it's a good idea to have appropriate equipment available.

Make play objects available to your child by placing them in containers, such as stacking cartons, baskets, or drawers, or on low shelves. Toys should be stacked and arranged neatly so your child knows where to find them.

During play, it may look as if young toddlers run from one toy to the next, with seemingly short attention spans. If you look closer, you will see that they are actually involved in their own learning projects. They carry, dump, spill, pick up, and pull the lids on and off things all day. These activities are typical of this age and part of motor development. Ample space should be allotted for this. Not until about the third year do they become involved in more specific activities.

Show interest when watching your child play. It isn't necessary to react or comment on everything he does, but be fully with him. Share in his joy. In this way he will feel that what he is doing is worthwhile and will be encouraged. A parent's smile is precious. Be generous.

Keep the Television Off

Television is part of most homes. Almost everybody watches it at one time or another. Because television's influence is unavoidable in our culture, I reiterate my feeling that it's best to postpone a child's television viewing, even if it's an "educational" program. I recommend not having a television in your child's play area, and not turning it on while your child is up. I am against young children's watching television. The later they start with it the better.

Television may create desensitization. If your child watches violent programs, and violence of some sort is in many programs, he may become numb to it. Violence can be frequently found in cartoons, where the characters push, hit, and hurt each other, then hit back or simply get up and walk away. This creates a skewed picture in which the repercussions of the hurtful acts are not shown. Cartoon characters do not bruise or bleed.

Besides being desensitizing, it has other dangers. Television is a visual medium. It doesn't require use of a child's thought processes or other senses, creating the opposite experience from what RIE supports. Rather than becoming an active participant, a child becomes a passive observer and a TV addict. Addicted to being entertained instead of creating his own entertainment, a TV-addicted child easily becomes bored and may develop a high need for stimulation. Further, young toddlers who understand language pick up on messages conveyed during commercials, setting them up as targets for advertising gimmicks.

Television is so accepted in our culture that we have lost sight of how strong an influence it has. Studies have shown that violence on TV can cause violent behavior in children who aren't yet mature enough to separate fantasy from reality. Videos and popular educational programs may be a better choice, but any form of television viewing supports passivity. Parents may be tempted to use television as a baby-sitter, but it's not in a child's best interest. You can respect your child by encouraging him to be an active explorer rather than a passively entertained onlooker.

Unfortunately, television can also become an unhealthy bargaining tool. A parent might say, "If you eat your dinner, then you may watch a certain program." And the more it becomes a bargaining chip, the more your child will want it. If you let your older child watch television, be matter-of-fact. Set a special time for viewing by saying, "You want to watch a certain program. Tomorrow we'll eat dinner earlier and you may watch it." Set limits on TV viewing. Some families permit one video a week or a day, or television only on weekends.

Books and Music Nurture the Soul

Books and music are beneficial in a child's life. They involve the mind and the senses and nurture the soul.

Music is the international language. It lifts you up, makes you feel good. And when you read a book or somebody reads you a book, your fantasy creates the story. You hear the words but you see the action in your mind. You actively participate.

Active participation is RIE's goal for children. Involvement and initiative, rather than passivity, will help your child flourish. Nurture these qualities in him by letting him hear beautiful music to stir his imagination. A common reaction usually occurs when children hear music—they move and sway with the flow. Most children love music.

Let your child look at simple, age-appropriate, illustrated books. You can also read to him. Toddlers enjoy seeing pictures or illustrations of children in action. They like to point out what they recognize from their lives. They love looking at pictures of animals and simple, identifiable objects. This is part of the learning process. Rather than teach your toddler ABC's, let him look at picture books that relate to his life.

The creation of a work of art requires that you allow your unconscious to "bubble up," which is what happens when we let children explore and play freely. They continually tap into their resources to figure out situations and solve problems. You can respect your child by nurturing his creative skills in a rich sensory environment. However, it's a good idea not to play music continuously. Quiet is also good for your child.

Are Fairy Tales Harmful?

The benefit versus the harm of reading fairy tales to children has been disputed. Some people feel that they are too scary or violent for young children. Remember *Hansel and Gretel,* and the witch who wanted to eat them? Is it good programming for children to hear that everything always turns out "happily ever after," and that the girl always meets the prince?

In deciding whether to read fairy tales to your child, of course, you have to use your own judgment. I don't find them objectionable because fairy tales have symbolic meaning. They take us into another world, which is also part of our world. Fairy tales are scary, but they release the fears children have inside them so they don't feel so lonely in their fears. Fears usually carry with them thoughts like "I have this horrible idea," "Nobody is as bad as I am," or "Nobody else has these secret desires or thoughts or feelings." In fairy tales, the reader identifies with Hansel and Gretel or Cinderella. The identification process makes misery more bearable. And in the end, you get the prince. Fairy tales aren't real life. However, fantasy can give us pleasure our real life cannot.

Fantasy is part of children's play. It serves as a release for their dreams and desires. In this respect fairy tales are beneficial, enhancing fantasy. You can incorporate fairy tales in your child's library with a variety of other books. Of course, observe your child's reaction to a particular fairy tale. If he is too frightened by it, it might be better to put the book aside. Observation will give you the answer.

Your Toddler's Play

A surprising thing parents may discover is that children at play have marvelous concentration and follow-through when involved in situations that interest them. If we allow and encourage them to be competent explorers, they grow to be strong and agile, possessing good judgment.

If we allow them to move naturally and without restriction, children become confident of their bodies and its abilities, learning on their own about their strengths and limitations. Children who are not taught motor skills are more in harmony with their bodies. At parks and playgrounds, I have often observed well-meaning parents putting their children on tops of slides and climbing structures. The child then begins to cry because he is fearful of getting down. To learn *how* to climb down, your child must first have learned how to climb up.

Through my many years of observing children, I've seen that children who are allowed to progress through various stages of physical development with little interference have fewer accidents. Since a child raised this way wouldn't be placed in a chair until he could climb up himself, he learns the safe and successful way to navigate the chair. He learns to get up and down in his own style, in his own time. His confidence grows in the process, as he figures it out himself, building a history of hits and misses. If you want your child to learn how to go up and down stairs, let him practice on one, then two or more at a time. He may choose to go down face first, bottom first, or on his belly. If you let him figure out how to do it on his own, he'll learn the easiest and safest way for him.

The key to dealing with an obstacle or problem your child encounters during his play is to observe, wait, and then decide what to do. It's a question of judgment. You need to be sensitive as to what can and cannot be resolved by your child.

You may wonder what to do if your child is scaling a climbing structure and gets stuck. Should you help him up or down? It depends. Give him support. Respond by first observing your child. Does he need you to help him down, or maybe just for you to give him the supportive bridge he needs to get where he wants to go?

Is he scared? Sometimes when we are very scared, we are not good problem solvers. Children are the same. Ask your child, "Do you want me to help you down?" If he does, help him. Sometimes the endeavor becomes so scary that a child loses his motivation to go on. However, he will also have less chance of getting hurt if he has scaled the equipment on his own.

Pretend Play

At the toddler stage, many children begin to pretend. You may notice your child pretend to drink from a container or feed his doll. Some parents are concerned when their child begins to pretend, fearing that he can't separate fantasy from reality. Pretend is actually an important element in children's play. Pretend play springs from creativity, which grows in an environment that fosters free exploration. Pretend play usually accompanies a child's learning to speak. Children may also pretend before this. I've seen preverbal children get down on their hands and knees and bark to imitate a dog they hear. As a child becomes familiar with objects in his environment and their uses, he starts to experiment or pretend.

Pretending is wonderful. It allows our fantasies to fly. Why do we adults read books and go to movies? Why do we cry at a movie? It's not reality, yet we cry because we identify with the situation and are touched. It's an outlet to fantasy. Fantasy has always existed.

Pretend play, including pretend "friends," is healthy for children because it is their way of working out conflicts that are difficult to deal with in real life. A little girl who hits her doll may be working out her anger at a parent or sibling, whom she knows she wouldn't be allowed to hit. A child who offers a cup to a doll may be learning to share her belongings.

Pretend play grows more complex as a child develops, and he starts to role-play, becoming the doctor, "Mommy," or "Daddy." Appreciate your child's use of imagination and creativity through his pretend play. Try not to intrude on his pretend world by asking him too many questions about it. This may take some of the magic out of it for him. You may find you get as much joy from listening to and observing your child.

Playing with Other Children

As children grow into toddlerhood, they interact more during playtime. At times children cooperate and play peacefully. However, at this stage disputes over toys escalate as the feeling "I want" becomes stronger. You can help by letting the children solve their own conflicts as long as nobody gets hurt. Children will not be able to solve all their own conflicts nor should we expect them to, but we should let them participate in the process. This will set the stage for their becoming good problem solvers for life. Both problem solving and cooperation can be learned through practice.

Let's see how Luis and Ryan handle a conflict on their own:

> Ryan and Luis both want to ride a tricycle in the play area at their child care center. Each child begins to pull on the tricycle's seat, saying, "Mine, mine." A moment later they both start to cry. Their carer, observing this, moves close to the children. She bends down on one knee and says, "You both want the tricycle." The children continue to struggle. Luis falls against the tricycle and makes it move forward a few inches. Ryan stops crying when he sees the tricycle move. Both children start to giggle and begin pushing the tricycle together.

Tom, Casey, and Jill work things out their own way, too:

> Jill and Casey are pulling on the same plastic bowl. Casey's mother kneels down and says, "You both want that bowl. Casey, can you find another bowl?" Involved in the struggle, neither child will let go of it. They both begin to say, "My bowl. Mine, mine." Tom, playing nearby, picks up another bowl and offers it to Jill. Jill takes the offered bowl and gives up her struggle. All three resume playing peacefully.

Children can and will work situations out if allowed the time, more often than we think. If the adults in the above situations had gotten involved, the result might have been more anger and negative energy generated than was necessary. Give your child the opportunity to resolve conflicts with his friends.

Greg says, "I learned to watch my daughter play with other children and not feel like I need to interfere with what they're doing. I need to make sure nobody gets hurt, but I don't feel I have to assist in their play, augment it, or prod them into playing."

Peter adds, "I learned to allow conflict between the kids. When we go to the classes and there is a conflict, the RIE instructor is willing to allow it to occur unless the kids are hurting each other. Whereas I would be prone to jump in and try to correct the situation or offer a moral judgment, she's willing to let the kids work it out. I've learned to be more hands-off."

Sharing Takes Time to Learn

Sharing is difficult for every toddler because a young child doesn't understand the concept. I've heard so many parents say, "This is just a ball. Can't you share your ball?" If the truth be told, does a woman want to share her favorite dress, or a man his best suit? Young children don't like to share. They don't understand why they should. They fight over a toy as if they're fighting for their lives. It's not a power struggle; rather, it's "What I see, I want. What I want is mine." Then both of them eventually leave the toy on the floor. I would say to two fighting children, "You want it and she wants it, too." See how the children work it out by themselves. If the struggle becomes intense, point out other available toys. They may or may not be interested in them.

Don't, however, let children hurt each other. To lessen the chances of a child's being constantly overpowered or hurt, arrange your child's play with other children of a similar developmental level. For example, don't put your young toddler in a play group where there is an older preschooler, or your crawling baby in a group with children who can walk.

Parents often ask me, "How will my child learn to share?" I tell them, "*You* share and your child will eventually learn to share. Parents who share are modeling generosity. When you see your child share, positively reinforce the behavior by saying, for example, 'That was kind of you to give your truck to Susan. She likes playing with it, too.' "

I've heard parents say, "Give it to her. She had it first," or "You need to take turns." Applying adult logic never works. Forcing children to share makes them feel angry rather than loving. Besides, teaching sharing doesn't make the children *want* to do it, which is the goal. Parents may feel pressured to "make" their child share because that's what is commonly done at play groups. Try to find a group where children aren't forced to share or take turns, or ask if the other parents would mind waiting to see what happens before intervening.

You may worry that your child's difficulty sharing means he will become selfish or that it is a negative reflection on your parenting skills. Remember that a toddler's possessiveness with belongings is a normal phase that will pass.

I remember a RIE class where sharing toys was the topic of the day. The children, between twenty months and two years of age, spent the class time running indoors and out, chasing each other, dumping toys out of buckets, and tossing them back in. They threw balls and hugged each other. At times, a pair of children held on tightly to a toy, neither willing to give it up. In one such incident, Sara and Chad held on to a red plastic basket. Chad remained calm, his fingers locked around the basket. Sara struggled to pull it away from Chad and started crying when she wasn't able to. Neither let go of the basket. I looked at the parents and said, "This is normal life."

"This hard for me to watch," said Chad's mother. "I'm a very sharing person."

"Do you remember how you became a sharing person?" I asked her.

The mother thought a moment and said, "I watched my mother share. My Mom and Dad shared." She looked back at her son. "Chad's older sister takes things away from him so now he's doing it."

"Yes," I said, "but they will take toys from each other even if they don't have an older sister. They don't know the rules of the world. They think, 'Everything I see is mine.' It's very complicated to learn, 'If my mother paid for it, it's mine, and if she didn't, it isn't.' "

After a few minutes, Sara let go of the basket and went to her mother for comfort. A moment later she was busy undressing a doll. Chad dropped the basket and began sorting through a container of jar lids. The basket lay on the floor, forgotten by both children. I continued, "This is typical behavior. The important learning experience is to resolve your problem. Yet, when we see children trying to solve problems, we don't let them. We feel they are suffering."

Another mother shared a story. "My daughter, Jennifer, was having a problem in preschool. There was this one girl who always took whatever toy Jennifer was holding. And my daughter always let it go. One day she finally looked at the girl and said, 'No!' and held on to it. After that she was able to hold on to toys she wanted, and now the two kids are friends."

Self-learned lessons, whether sharing or the will to hold on, stick with us longer.

Iris adds, "When Angelica is in her play group, I sometimes feel pressure from the other parents to make Angelica share, though I don't force her to. Children her age (eighteen months) can't put themselves into another person's shoes so the concept of sharing is alien to them. I'm confident she'll learn it."

Trust that your child will eventually learn to share. Give it time to happen.

Helping Your Child Deal with Aggressive Feelings

Aggression, in the form of yelling, pushing, or hitting, is perfectly normal behavior for toddlers. It's a good sign that your child is actively and openly dealing with his feelings and experiencing his conflicts. As parents, we need to steer our children in the right direction, showing them appropriate ways to express themselves.

Some people, children included, are more aggressive than others. Usually anger or aggression brings with it a certain amount of excitement or energy a person wants to let go of. If your child engages in an undesirable act of aggression, such as shoving or hitting, a simple acknowledgment of his feelings may help. You can ask him, "Are you angry? Do you want to hit?" or you may tell him, "You sure look angry." Be careful not to project by telling him he *is* angry.

It's important to separate desires from actions. If we punished people for thinking bad thoughts, everybody would be in jail. Thoughts and feelings should be free. As far as actions go, society has its rules. In order to socialize, a child must learn the rules, accept them, and obey them. The earlier a child learns the rules, the more natural they feel. How do adults learn not to cheat or lie or steal? At some point they must be self-motivated to follow the rules.

Iris says,

> Angelica goes to child care three days a week, once weekly to a play group, and once a week to RIE. In contrast to the

other groups, RIE is a much more peaceful place. The parents in the play group intervene between the kids more than I feel is needed. They try to socialize the kids by forcing them to share and get along. At eighteen months, the children can't understand the concept. At Angelica's child care the caregivers hover over the kids and try to regiment their behavior. At RIE the kids are allowed to work out their own conflicts and deal with their aggression as much as they can on their own so Angelica has the experience of doing this. I think this will help her in the long run.

When you see your child acting aggressively, allow him to express his feelings while making clear that you will not allow him to hurt another child. This is better than making him feel guilty about his feelings or trying to have him contain them. They may resurface later in undesirable ways. When he learns to speak, you can begin to talk about his feelings. Ask a toddler specific questions like "Are you mad because she took the toy from you?" Simply asking *why* may be too open-ended for him to respond to. Learning to deal with one's aggressive feelings, as everything else, is a long learning process.

Assisting Your Toddler When He's Struggling with Another Child

This scenario is typical and predictable for toddlers: two children are holding on to the same toy, neither willing to let it go. Emotions are running high. One or both children may start to cry or indicate that they might hit one another. Many people would pull the children apart and tell them to be nice. Others might make them take turns with the toy. Another solution could be to take the toy away.

I believe in letting children struggle over a toy as long as neither one gets hurt or hasn't reached a point where he is past his limit of coping with the situation. Struggle is part of life, all aspects of life. There is a famous Hungarian stage play called *The Tragedy of Man*. In one scene God looks down and speaks to Adam and Eve, saying, "Struggle and keep hoping." In any case, struggling or fighting doesn't necessarily lead to a child's getting

hurt. There are social ways of fighting in life. Applicants competing for the same job are in essence fighting, but in a civilized way.

How far you can let a situation between two struggling children escalate? It depends on your familiarity with the children and their frustration levels. This is where observation is important. If you have observed your child (and hopefully his playmates) over time, you will be familiar with how much he can handle on his own. How far you can let a situation escalate also depends on your own level of tolerance. There is no "only way" to handle this type of conflict.

Remain on the children's level with your hands ready to block or intercept the hand of a child who makes a hitting motion. If the children are struggling but seem to be handling it, leave them alone but stay near. You can reflect what's happening. If either child's emotions reach the boiling point and his behavior falls apart, or either child is intent on engaging in aggressively hurtful behavior like hitting or biting, you may decide to separate them. You can say, "I don't want either of you to get hurt and it looks like one of you might. I'm going to separate you now."

You have to use your own judgment in situations like these. It's obviously easier to separate two struggling children at the outset of a conflict. However, I feel that the earlier children learn to struggle, negotiate, and get along with others, the better off they'll be. You may wonder how letting children struggle over a toy teaches them to get along with others. Struggle is a normal part of human relations.

What is the harm in letting your child struggle? Try to see how it ends as long as nobody gets hurt, with you nearby. This requires trust on your part that your child will eventually learn to hold on and let go when it's appropriate for him.

When Children Want to Hit

Most children hit at one time or another, some more often than others. Sometimes this happens during a struggle over a toy. Hitting is normal and is a predictable part of development.

I would never preach to a child who wants to hit. It doesn't work. I remember a mother who always said to her child, "It's not nice to . . ." I identified with the child and wanted to say, "So what? Who wants to be nice?" The parent represents conscience. Children have to learn how to be decent human beings. This happens as they internalize or take on their parents' attitudes and behaviors, not by listening to sermons.

How does your child find out what is good or fair to do unless he tries? Some people never learn it. Before redirecting and overdoing our role, I like to let a child figure out what to do. It takes time for him to know the difference between a person and a doll, or an object and a human being.

Should a parent or carer separate children who start to hit? I tell parents to start by saying, "Uh-uh, I won't let you hit each other." *Wait* before separating them. Underplaying situations is better than overplaying them. The more you make a big deal of it, the less children listen. The more you let children figure things out with guidance, the more capable they become.

If your child is on the verge of hitting, you may block his hand with yours and gently hold him back. Say, "I won't let you. What else can you do?" He may choose to contain his aggressive feelings or find another way to express them. Learning to control aggression and release it into socially acceptable channels is a long process.

As your toddler grows, he is starting to understand the effects of his actions. If one child hits or hurts another during play, ask the aggressor to look at the other child's face so he can see the effect of his actions. Keep your voice neutral, without inflicting guilt. "Look at Zachary. He's crying. When you hit him, it hurt him. It hurt his arm." Simple awareness does more than forced "I'm sorry's" or a time-out. Aggressive children are basically fearful children who act before they are acted upon. They need empathy and firm limits.

Acknowledge the child's feelings who was hit by saying, "Mackenzie hit you. Yes, it looked like it hurt." Reflect rather than offer sympathy. In this way he won't seek to gain attention or find solace by becoming a victim.

During play, toddlers touch and chase each other. Children, like adults, have various sensitivities to being touched. If your child is disturbed by another child's touching, before intervening you may say, "Lani's touching you and it looks like you don't like it. You can tell Lani you don't like that." This acknowledges your child's feelings while encouraging him to talk it out. He may not have the words now, but he will later. Give him a chance to respond to the other child, either by word or by action. He may utter a simple, "No!" or push the child away, and will draw comfort from the fact that you are available to intervene if needed. If he becomes too disturbed, you can ask the other child to stop. As a last resort, separate the children. If the children you saw can talk, ask them what happened. Reflect to them what you saw and why you separated them.

Save speaking in a loud or upset voice for serious or dangerous situations. Your child will sense the urgency involved. A parent who constantly speaks in a raised voice or yells will eventually be ignored. The child may feel, "My mom makes a big deal out of everything."

Setting Limits at Play

Setting limits is a parent's role. Children need to understand that certain behaviors, such as hitting or biting, won't be tolerated. Knowing that you will make him stop an undesirable behavior before he hurts someone else or gets hurt himself helps your child feel secure. This is an ongoing process that takes time to learn. Children need to first understand their parents' expectations. A child who lives with many yeses can also be told no. Persistence is crucial in maintaining limits.

Limits are learned during play, as are important social lessons. Children learn appropriate versus hurtful behavior, how to stand up for their rights, and sometimes even compassion. I am often touched in classes when one child's tears causes another child to cry, too. Children, even young ones, can surprise us with their depth of feeling.

Young children learn from each other, imitating words and behaviors. They learn from their own experiences and from modeling parental behavior. All these things are their "teachers." Life is their teacher.

If Your Child Bites

Why and how does a child develop the habit of biting other children? Biting is a complex issue. Freud talks about the oral stage of children's development, when they experience everything through their mouths. They eat every crumb or piece of lint they find on the ground. Biting is one of the oral activities. It is also connected to teething. Children test out biting on other children. Biting may sometimes be reinforced by the response from the other child or from the adult. Some children seek attention, even negative attention, by biting.

What should you do if your child develops this habit? First, tell your child, "I don't want you to bite another child," so he knows your expectation of his behavior. If he is teething, give him teething biscuits or something to teethe on. If he's not, give him a replacement object to bite, what I call a "bitie." Let him choose which bitie he wants to use when he feels the urge. This can be a designated plastic toy or a teething ring. You need to monitor the situation closely. Your child needs to learn the rules of social interaction, which he *will* learn in time. Some child care centers assign a person to "shadow" a child who bites to prevent it from happening.

If you see your child is about to bite another child and there is no time to give him a bitie, gently hold him back and say, "I won't let you bite your friend."

Say to the child who was bitten, "Laura bit you. Did it hurt?" Comfort her if she requests it. With biting, as with hitting, don't overdo the comforting or you risk making being a victim desirable. It can become negative attention-getting behavior.

This reminds me of a story. During the DIP program in Palo Alto, we had a child who bit. I tried to teach the child that if he needed to bite, he should run to the basket of plastic doughnuts and bite one of them. On one occasion I saw the child run across the room to the doughnuts. Unfortunately, another child collided with him and he bit the other child. I felt sorry for the biter, because he tried. I didn't blame him.

"You really tried," I told him. "You know what we'll do? We'll hang a plastic doughnut around your neck with this string. Now you can bite as much as you want to," which he did.

The child he had bitten saw this and wanted a doughnut, too. Then all the other children wanted doughnuts. They had, what I call, a biting orgy. They made those funny, scrunched-up faces. It was really lovely. We put the name of each child on the doughnuts, hung them on hooks, and said, "We'll keep your doughnuts here until next week." The next week the children were no longer interested in the doughnuts. Biting stopped. They all got it out of their systems.

Tell your child not to bite people, but don't tell your child not to bite at all. He needs to bite. Redirect his biting. The behavior will pass in time.

Gearing Your Intervention to Your Toddler's Behavior

As your toddler's desire and will grow, he encounters frustration. His will often exceeds his ability, so he reacts with impatience. He may want to put on his shoes but not be able to pull the shoe on, so he becomes upset. His verbal skills are developing, but he may still not be able to clearly express his wishes or his frustration to you. Hence, he may become irritable, stubborn, or whiny.

Reflection based on observation offers solace to your struggling child: "I see you're trying to put on your shoe. You're having a hard time." If you think your child needs help, you can say, "I'll help you put your toe in. Let's see if you can pull it on now." If you think your child can do it, you can encourage him by saying, "Can you pull it on yourself?" If you have spent many months carefully observing your child, you now understand much about your child's individual personality and tolerance for frustration. It's common, however, for children to become impatient while learning tasks. Your patience and calm presence will help him. Agitation only breeds agitation.

You can also help build your child's tolerance by allowing and encouraging him to master his own problems. How much should you let him do on his own? Anything that's not dangerous. Try to create the limits for your child *and* for yourself. During mealtime, food will undoubtedly go on the floor. Try not to feed your child on a rug you don't want to mess. This is the big issue: how much freedom and how much control should you allow? If children have too much freedom, they may not know what to do with it. It's the right amount of control that gives freedom. Living in a society, we need rules.

If your child is doing something that frustrates him, like trying to unzip a zipper or stack blocks that keep falling, don't intervene until he asks or looks to you for help. Help if he asks, but start with minimal help. Move to his side and reflect what he's doing. He'll gain confidence from your presence and may be able to complete the task. If he still wants help, take the smallest step to facilitate his project—ask him if he can stack one block. Less help is better, whereas more can't be undone.

Dealing with Regressive Behavior

Children engage in regressive behavior at different times in their development. Dr. T. Berry Brazelton notes in *Touchpoints* (Addison-Wesley, 1992) that before children push through to the next stage of development they may regress, holding on to a known behavior because they don't feel comfortable taking on the new one. A walking child might go back to crawling while he tests out his new-found skill. A new sibling may prompt a child to want to act like the baby, vying for his parent's attention.

And don't we adults indulge in regressive behavior ourselves when we snuggle into our beds or chew on our fingers? All of us want to be babies some of the time and go back to a comfortable time when we were taken care of.

Allow regressive or "incorrect" behavior. Don't force your child to do things the "right" way. Life is not made up of right or wrong, black or white. Unless another person is suffering as a result of your child's actions, it's perfectly fine to allow this. If your child wants to experiment, let him. It's his creativity coming out.

If your walking child wants to crawl, don't belittle him by saying, "Don't crawl. You're not a baby anymore." If a child who's been weaned wants a bottle on a whim, it's all right. If your child wants to read a book upside-down, rather than say, "Turn the book over. That's not the right way to look at it," let him. Respect your child by allowing him to experiment and do what feels comfortable. He may have a unique view of the world upside-down.

When Your Child Tests Your Limits

Toddlers constantly test. This is how they research and discover limits: their own, their parents', and the world's. For example, your child may dump a container of toys on the carpet to see the effect. He may also want to see what happens if he dumps that same container on his playmate, or on the wooden floor. Your child may run in the street, which he has been told not to do, to see what reaction he gets from you. He may also dump his dinner on his head to see how it feels and how you react.

Be careful not to negatively reinforce behaviors you don't want to see continue. If you overreact when the food goes on the floor or when your child throws toys, the behavior may continue. It's better to calmly say what you don't like. If, however, your child runs in the street, or engages in any dangerous behavior, you need to take action first by removing the child from the situation while saying firmly, "*Never*, ever run in the street. It's dangerous."

Reinforce behaviors you want your child to continue by praising them. It's encouraging for a child to hear, "It's good to see how gently you're touching Benjamin," or "Thank you for helping me pick up your toys," or "I appreciate your being so patient and playing quietly while I was on the phone." A child responds to his parents' reactions. React kindly to his positive deeds rather than reacting only to his negative behavior.

No! No! No!

Children at this stage often say the word "no." They say it to themselves, their parents, and the world, as they discover their physical and emotional boundaries and want to preserve them.

I remember one hot summer day, watching a mother and young daughter leaving an ice cream parlor. While licking a cone, the mother asked her child if she wanted a bite. The child reached for the cone and said, "No!"

It's best to ignore the word "no" most of the time. It's a verbal discovery that will pass in time. It is important, however, to differentiate between when your child is truly opposed to something and when he is enjoying himself by saying no. Saying no is a part of the separation process. "No" is just a word. Children have all the time and energy in the world to argue. We have limited time and energy. Save your energy for important things.

When Your Child Refuses to Cooperate

Toddlers may begin to refuse to do things, and seem uncooperative. As your child begins to realize that he is a separate person from his parents, he wants to make decisions on his own. All children refuse. No child always wants to do what his parent wants.

How do you handle a situation where, for example, your child refuses to put on his shoes to go out? First, understand that this behavior is totally normal. Then you have two options. If you don't need to keep an appointment or catch a plane and can stay home, say, "If you don't want to put your shoes on, you stay home." Then do it. This teaches your child the consequences of his actions and he learns a valuable lesson. If he doesn't put on his shoes, he doesn't get to leave the house. He will eventually figure this out and be less resistant. (More on cause/consequence is covered later in this chapter.)

If you don't have time to wait, say, "We need to get your shoes on to go out. Do you want to put them on yourself or do you want me to help you?" The question "Do you want to do it by yourself or do you want me to help you?" is helpful in many situations where you want to elicit your toddler's cooperation. By saying this, you throw the ball back into his court. Often when given this choice a toddler will opt to "do it myself."

If he still resists putting on his shoes, tell him, "I understand you don't want to wear your shoes, but we need to put them on to go." Then pick him up, and as difficult as it may be if he's struggling, put the shoes on him. This is called reality testing. Your child is trying to figure out how far he can go. Be aware of your own tolerance level so you don't get to the point of blowing up at your child. If you suspect your child might resist, start earlier and give yourselves a little more time.

Remember, too, that a child's sense of timing is different from an adult's. Adults have limited time, while children feel they have all the time in the world. They can decide not to put on their shoes for a week. You may find that waiting is the best choice. Your child may not want to put on his shoes right when you ask him to, but a few minutes later he may pick them up and decide to do it. With toddlers, you can choose to make every issue a battleground or an opportunity for growth. Respect your child by telling him what you expect, observing his response, even if it's not your request, and giving him time to do what you want.

Remember that your child *needs* to disagree. It's part of growing. The better the parent, the more the child dares to disagree. I often tell parents, "Choose your battles." If it's not that big an issue, it's okay to give in to your child now and then.

Above all, be patient. Your agitation or anger will only escalate his. Remember to model the behavior you want to reinforce. Talk in simple sentences and avoid preaching. You are your child's role model.

Toddlers may get louder as they get older, and some enjoy yelling or screaming. Their will shows itself through their voices as they loudly proclaim their desires and dislikes. Try to ignore the behavior, since a strong reaction from you only reinforces it. If you are out, at a restaurant or at the market, ask him to use a soft voice. You may have to cut your trip short. However, my basic advice is not to take a child of this age to a restaurant and then expect him to act like an adult. Better yet, hire a baby-sitter and go without your child.

Geralynn says, "Instead of constantly saying no, we say to Delanie, 'I don't want you to . . .' At times I get frustrated, but if I take a moment to think about what's going on, I'm able to step back. I can then let Delanie deal with the situation in her own way or tell her, 'I won't let you do that. We need to do this now.' She's fairly accepting of my requests."

Using Bad Language

I remember one day in class a father posed a question: "Michael's been saying bad words lately, which he hears from the older kids. What should we do?"

I told him, "Ignore bad words. The less upset you become, the better. Your becoming upset can be enticing because Michael then feels he has power over you. This is the time children are figuring out their power and testing it. If he can upset you by saying something, this gives him a lot of power."

Words come and go. At this stage, it's better to look the other way. When your child is older and he understands, you can discuss it with him. If you model appropriate language and refrain from using bad words, he will follow your lead.

A Typical Evening in a "RIE Home"

To demonstrate how all the different facets of the RIE philosophy work together for toddlers, let's view a typical evening with a RIE family, Geralynn and Greg, and their daughter, Delanie, two, who has a friend, Taylor, also two, over to play and eat dinner.

As Taylor enters their house, Delanie hugs Geralynn, and Geralynn kisses her.

Geralynn: "You are so happy to have Taylor here. Oops, I got lipstick on your arm."

Delanie: "Nana."

Geralynn: (laughs) "Nana always does that. You saw her a month ago and you still remember."

Taylor looks up the stairs.

Geralynn: "The noise you hear upstairs is Delanie's daddy. He's working up there."

Taylor starts to climb over the safety gate at the bottom of the stairs.

Geralynn: "We're going to stay downstairs now. Maybe we'll go upstairs later, but now we're going to stay down here."

Taylor climbs down from the gate. Delanie throws a baby doll over another safety gate into the kitchen.

Geralynn: "When you throw something to the other side of the gate, it's going to stay there.

Taylor looks at the wooden rocking horse sitting in the corner.

Taylor: "Want to rock." He climbs up on the horse. Delanie starts to climb up, too.

Geralynn: "Delanie, Taylor's up there right now. I want you to get off. It's not safe for both of you to be up there. The seat is made for one person."

Delanie gets down and sits at its base, her feet under the rocking horse.

Geralynn: "Do you want to put your feet under there? He's going to rock."

Delanie gets up and tries to climb back up on the horse.

Geralynn: "Taylor's up there now. I want you to wait till he gets down. Only one person can ride at a time. I don't want any-body falling off."

Delanie brings Geralynn a book. Greg comes downstairs.

Greg: (to Taylor) "Hi."

Geralynn: (to Taylor) "This is Greg, Delanie's daddy."

Delanie takes off her pants, then starts to remove her diaper.

Greg: "Delanie, your diaper needs to stay on. I don't want you to take it off."

Delanie picks up a basket and dumps out the dress-up clothes inside. She offers Taylor a purse.

Geralynn: "You want Taylor to have the purse. I don't think he wants it, Delanie. You can put it down and if he wants it, he can pick it up." (To Taylor): "That's Delanie's purse and she would like you to use it."

Geralynn: (going into the kitchen, behind the gate) "I'm going to get dinner ready."

Delanie: (standing at the gate) "Um, um!"

Geralynn: "I know you want some. As soon as the microwave beeps, we'll be ready." A moment later, Geralynn enters the dining area with a platter of food and utensils. She pulls two small chairs up to the child-size table. "Delanie, which bib do you want—red or blue?"

Delanie chooses the red bib. Taylor takes the blue.

Geralynn: "Here are some spoons for you. Taylor, which cup would you like?"

Geralynn serves the food. Taylor takes a handful of pasta from Delanie's plate.

Geralynn: "This pasta is Delanie's. You have more on your plate. You can eat from your plate."

Taylor: (eats pasta from his own plate) "Want more apple juice."

Geralynn pours juice. Taylor stands up.

Geralynn: "Taylor, I want you to put the cup on the table if you're going to get up."

Taylor sits and sets the cup down.

Delanie stands with a fistful of raisins.

Geralynn: "Delanie, the raisins need to stay on the table."

Delanie sits back down and eats. Dinner continues. Both children start to play with their food.

Geralynn: "That tells me you're finished. I don't want you to dump your food. I'm going to take the plates away now." (To Taylor): "Let's take off your bib if you want to go play. I'm going to wipe your hands and face."

Geralynn wipes his face and removes his bib, then tells Delanie what she's going to do and removes Delanie's bib. The children get up to play.

Taylor sits in Delanie's chair. Delanie protests.

Geralynn: "Taylor's sitting there now. You got up and he sat down."

Delanie pushes Taylor.

Geralynn: "Delanie, I don't want you to push him off."

Delanie quickly pushes Taylor off the chair and stands over it, checking for Geralynn's reaction. Taylor starts to cry.

Geralynn: (To Taylor, sympathetically): "She pushed you off the chair." (To Delanie, firmly): "It's not okay for you to push him off the chair."

Taylor: (upset) "Want to sit chair."

Geralynn: "You can sit down, Taylor. I'm not going to let Delanie sit down. Delanie, if he gets up, then you can sit here. I'm not going to let you push him off or hurt him."

Delanie steps away from the chair and Taylor sits in it. After a few minutes, Taylor gets up from the chair.

Geralynn: "Taylor got up. Now you can sit here." A moment later, Taylor and Delanie both pull on the same book.

Greg: "You both want that book. One of us can read it to you both."

Geralynn and Greg used calm, slow voices as they stated their expectations and reflected what the children were doing or might be feeling. Geralynn offered them choices and engaged them in creating solutions to their problems rather than overdirecting their play. These are all things that blend together to create an optimal learning, nurturing environment for your toddler.

Tantrums: The Antaeus Story

I've dealt with many tantrums in my work with children with special needs. Of course, most children have tantrums on occasion. A tantrum is an outlet, an "overflow valve," when a child's emotions seem to burst at the seams. He cries and thrashes about, and usually ends up on the floor. A tantrum is a release of energy for all the changes going on in a young child's mind and body. He is growing, learning, struggling, and dealing with a confusing and challenging world. Tantrums are part of normal childhood behavior—a passing phase that occurs when a child cannot yet verbalize his feelings.

A tantrum can be frightening for you, the parent, because your child becomes totally swept away in his feelings. Understanding the reasons for tantrums and knowing that they are normal, though not all children have them, makes handling them a little easier.

I am reminded of the Antaeus story in Greek mythology. Antaeus was the son of Mother Earth. He was very strong but could also be conquered. When Antaeus had a fight with a stronger opponent, the stronger opponent threw Antaeus onto Mother Earth. There, Antaeus drew strength from his mother, the Earth, and was able to get up again. This is wonderful symbolism. Mythology has so much ancient wisdom. When a child gets totally desperate and doesn't know what else to do, he throws himself on the ground. When I see children do this, I say, "That's the Antaeus story."

Anything can trigger tantrums. A child may wake up from a nap and have a tantrum, be upset because he can't have something he wants, or be overtired. The cause is usually a combination of tiredness, low frustration tolerance, and a sense of helplessness. Haven't you ever felt like you'd like to throw a tantrum? Everybody feels this way at times, though as adults we seldom throw ourselves on the floor and start kicking and yelling. Maybe the world would be a better place if we did! Maybe fewer people would commit awful crimes if they had nice, healthy tantrums.

Remain calm during your child's tantrum. You cannot stop a tantrum, nor should you try. They run their own course and must run "through" your child. Each tantrum has its own beginning, peak, and end. Whether you are at home or in a public place, it is best to wait calmly until your child finishes. Anything you do will only prolong it. It will be over quicker if you don't intervene. Try to ignore comments or looks from strangers. If it becomes terribly embarrassing, pick your child up and take him to a more private spot, another room, or your car.

To avoid having to deal with a tantrum in a public place, try to do errands or shop when your spouse, relative, or carer can watch your child so you won't put yourself in this position. This will be easier on both you and your child. Or at least limit your errands. Children are not happy in department stores.

It's not a good idea to give in to whatever your child wants, whether it's an extra cookie or a new toy, hoping to avoid a tantrum or stop one in progress. Your child will soon discover that he can use tantrums to push your limits.

Whether you are at home or out, I recommend that you stay in the room with your child during a tantrum. Don't tell your child you will be back when he is in control of himself. While some experts recommend holding a child tightly during a tantrum, I believe it is better to allow your child to do what he will as long as he doesn't hurt himself or you. Sit quietly and be with him. You don't need to do or say anything.

A tantrum may involve hysterical crying and thrashing around. When it's over, your child comes out of it peacefully and serenely, like a sunset after a storm. Don't we all feel better after a good, hard cry? Wouldn't it sometimes feel good, after a trying day, to lie on the floor and scream?

When the tantrum is finished, don't preach about the tantrum or ask your child why he had it. He probably can't tell you. Allow your child to go through his tantrum, knowing that you will be there to comfort him when he's done. Afterward, if he wants, you can hold him. Be there and available to him.

Remember my mantra: this, too, shall pass. Children typically outgrow tantrums after toddlerhood.

Headbanging, Rocking, and Repetitive Behaviors

Some children feel a need to bang their heads on a crib or wall, rock themselves, or engage in other repetitive behaviors. Perhaps they need the stimulation or are trying to self-calm. You can keep bumpers on the crib, but a child who wants to bang his head will find a hard place on which to do it. You might be able to prevent your child from engaging in the activity while you are with him, but you cannot be with him twenty-four hours a day. This obsessive behavior may comfort the child. Telling him to stop won't stop him. This behavior can be disturbing to parents, but it is something children outgrow. Children, like adults, do many things to relieve tension and stress.

Lasting Discipline Comes from Within

Webster's Dictionary describes discipline as "training that corrects, molds, or perfects." I believe the best and most long-lasting training comes from within. Discipline is first learned externally, based on parental, and then societal expectations. In time your child internalizes or "owns" these behaviors. Your child needs rules to make him feel secure and become a mature, responsible person. Not to discipline him is to neglect his needs.

Discipline means learning you cannot always do what you want to do. You obey the laws. Sigmund Freud explains it with his theories of the id, the ego, and the superego. (The id represents the libido, or unconscious mind. The ego represents the conscious mind. The superego represents the conscience.) The superego tells you, "Uh-uh. It's not good to do that." The id says, "Do it! Do it!" The ego negotiates between the two. Some people call it your angel and your devil.

How to Discipline

How do you discipline? Set limits for your child and consistently enforce them. A child learns discipline by having expectations laid out for him and followed through in a consistent manner by his parents. Setting up an appropriate and safe environment automatically sets limits. For instance, a child knows a gated kitchen is off-limits.

Discipline is the process through which a parent helps his child gain control over his impulses and become a cooperative member of his family, and then, society. Maintaining limits with consistency develops habits that become lifelong patterns. If a child knows that his food will be taken away when he throws it, he learns not to throw it. If a child knows that his bedtime follows a bath and a story, he anticipates and expects to sleep. Children find comfort in rules and routines.

At bedtime, going through the same ritual each night helps reinforce discipline. Sameness is reassuring for children. They learn to accept the routine. I call it "sequencing." Before you put your child to bed, you do two other things connected with bedtime. These things are always done in the same sequence. Tell your child, for example, "You'll eat dinner, then you'll get undressed, then it's time for bed." This makes the future predictable. Routines help predictability, and predictability makes a child more accepting of discipline. Sameness creates security. A young child's life should be unexciting. Too much excitement causes a child to become overstimulated.

Discipline includes modeling. To preach or to say, "Do what I say, not what I do," is unfair. Don't eat a candy bar in front of your child and then say, "Don't eat that. Chocolate's not good for you." If it's not good for you, don't have it in the house. If something is acceptable only as a special treat, have it yourself only on special occasions.

A child raised with respect eventually learns discipline because the rules are clearly spelled out and routinely enforced. He learns to discipline himself.

Raised voices, angry scolding, and punishment in the traditional sense are inappropriate and counterproductive in disciplining children. If you are angry with your child, you can express your anger while acknowledging that it is *your* own anger, which should not seep into the intended disciplinary action. If, for example, your child hits you with a toy and hurts you, you may say to your child, "That hurt me. I'm angry you hit me." Children are quick to sense parental reactions and may repeat an action if a strong response is elicited (the parent yells). However, when you say no to your child, really mean it. Let your face and your body language reflect this. Children tend to nag or whine when they sense ambivalence in a parent.

Testing the Limits

Your toddler will constantly test your limits by noting your reactions to the things he does. It's how he finds out about the world. This is normal, healthy behavior and expect it. Also use patience and consistent responses to deal with it.

Consider this example:

> Toshi rides his tricycle into a planter, flattening the flowers. His mother, watering a nearby flowerbed, looks up and sees this.

Mother: (firmly) "Toshi, please take your tricycle out of the planter. It's crushing my flowers."

Toshi: looks at his mother and smiles.

Mother: (waits a moment) "It looks like you're not moving it. Do you want to move it or do you want me to help you?"

Toshi: sits on the tricycle, on top of the plants. "No!"

Mother: "You're crushing my flowers. I don't want them crushed. I'm going to help you move."

Toshi: steps off the tricycle and moves it away. "I do it."

Mother: (smiles) "Thank you for cooperating."

Toshi: rolls the tricycle back onto the planter.

Mother: "I'm angry. You're not listening to me. I'll help you move the tricycle." (She goes to Toshi and rolls him and the tricycle off the planter.) "If you ride onto the flowers again, I'm going to put the tricycle in the garage."

Toshi: rides the tricycle into the backyard.

The mother tells Toshi what behavior she expects. By soliciting her son's help, she allows him to be an active partner in solving the problem while, at the same time, expressing her own feelings. Toshi senses that his mother will follow through with the consequence, so he complies after testing her limits. This is normal behavior. If his mother were less firm, Toshi might have pushed her even farther.

Give your child the opportunity to develop self-discipline by setting limits while being patient and consistent.

Respecting Your Needs

It's important to set *your* own limits. This is a part of discipline and helps your child build structure into his life. You are also teaching him to respect you and your needs. However, first you must be in tune with what your needs and limits are.

If you are tired, it's all right to tell your child you need some time or space alone. (This is where the safeproofed playroom is invaluable.) It's okay to tell your child you don't feel like reading a book or taking a walk, if you don't. Do this without guilt. Be honest with your child. This teaches him the realities of life, that you are, at times, more or less available to him.

To illustrate this discussion of limits I use the "red light," "yellow light," and "green light." The red light refers to a situation where your child is in danger: for example, he is about to run into the street after a ball. You stop him immediately.

The yellow light is a situation that is negotiable. You decide, for instance, whether you'd rather finish looking at a magazine you've picked up or give in to your child's request to go for a walk. This is where you weigh the situation and decide whose needs take precedence at the moment. Perhaps you can ask your child to wait a few minutes until you've finished. Compromise can be arranged. This teaches your child that he cannot always have what he wants at the moment he wants it, a good lesson for life. Put your response in a positive frame. Rather than saying, "I can't read a book to you now," say, "Yes, I will read a book to you when I finish reading the newspaper."

Sometimes you may give in to your child's requests. At others, your needs may take precedence. When you are clear about what you want, do communicate your wishes to your child in a clear way. You may avoid feeling anger stemming from self-sacrifice.

The green light is a situation in which your child has a choice of things to do such as go for a walk or play in the sandbox, and you are ready and willing to do what he wants. Make time for these important "green light" times, when you are fully available to your child. Green light times give your child the focused attention that allows him to feel content and happy.

How often should you be fully available to your child? It's not a particular number of times per day or week, rather a balance that you work out over time that includes your child's needs as well as yours. This also depends upon individual preference and how often a parent wants to be fully available to his child. Some parents may enjoy spending an hour reading to their child; some may find it difficult getting through one book. Respect your limits.

Iris says,

> I've heard you say so often, "Parents have their needs, too." I don't feel bad saying no to Angelica because it's important that I set *my* boundaries. For instance, I usually eat when Angelica's finished. She'll want to climb up on my lap and eat off my plate. I'll tell her, "No. This is Mama's food." I don't feel guilty not giving her more food even though she's asking for it. My family would never have denied her more food. It's clear to me now when Angelica's needs are met.

There is give and take, of course, on the issue of meeting needs. If your child is sick, tired, or is in a sensitive phase, give more. Taking is okay, too. Take care of yourself so you can take better care of your child.

Is Punishment a Good Way to Discipline?

I don't like the word "punishment." It sounds harsh. I don't think, however, that a child has ever been raised anywhere in the world without being punished. Sometimes the event is the punishment, where a child falls down or gets hurt. Life is full of situational punishments. I know most people punish their children. I did. And I was punished as a child. In the school I attended, if a child did something "bad," he had to stand in the corner. If he did something worse, he was made to kneel in the corner. If he was in big trouble, he had to kneel on kernels of corn in the corner.

What kind of discipline works? Talk to your child about what he did, even if he can't yet respond. Let him know what you don't like: "I don't want you to run away from me at the park" or "I don't want you to keep throwing your ball in the street." If needed, provide consequences (covered later in this chapter). However, let your child know that in any situation safety issues are not negotiable.

Your goal is to keep your child from repeating the undesirable behavior. You want your child, if possible, to be an ally who wants to avoid the not-so-good situation. But in your child's defense, can a normal human being never deviate from the law? It's impossible for an average, healthy child. How does a child discover where the limits are? Children are constantly stretching limits, not doing what they are told, taking risks. There would be no new discoveries if people didn't try to push the limits. People constantly test themselves throughout their lifetimes, wondering "How far can I go?"

Punishment in the traditional sense has no relation to, or is out of proportion to, what the child has done. It is damaging to a young child's confidence because it creates a sense of blame or shame. A young child may not fully understand why he's being punished. Punishment is rarely an effective deterrent.

Your child may, for example, scribble crayon drawings on the wall. For a long time children don't know why one thing is good or accepted and another isn't. If a child draws on paper, everybody says, "How nice!" but doing it on a wall isn't okay. It takes children time to understand what is and what is not acceptable behavior.

A parent once asked me what I would do with a child who has drawn on the wall, and whether I would punish him. I answered, "I would punish the parents." A child young enough to want to draw on walls needs supervision. If he's playing in his safeproofed room, remove the crayons. Setting and enforcing appropriate limits help avoid the use of punishment.

What about Time-out?

Many parents believe in using time-out. When I hear this expression I always wonder: time out from what? Life? Isn't it better to stay "in" life and figure out how to do better the next time?

Time-out is a form of disconnected punishment where the punishment has no relation to the unacceptable act. I don't believe in using them. This is how they work: when a child does something a parent or carer doesn't like, he is assigned to a time-out chair, and must sit there for a length of time usually determined by the child's age. (According to a 1987 California law, time-out is illegal for children under two in child care.) Children experience this as punishment.

I remember a little boy I observed in a play group who played for a few minutes, then, on his own, sat in the time-out chair for a few minutes. He then went back and played, and continued to go back and forth for the entire play time. He may have been carrying around guilty feelings, as he appeared to be inflicting periodical punishment on himself.

Stacy says,

> I worked with kindergarten kids before Christopher was born. I found that when I got angry I separated fighting children, put them in time-out, and told them, "This is where you're going to sit." I now realize the difference between separating children and talking to them, telling them why I'm unhappy with their behavior and what the alternatives are. This has saved me many times from getting angry and using my big person/adult status to punish children. I don't hide my feelings or my disapproval of something Christopher has done that I don't like. I've learned to bring him in and talk about what he did rather than to shut him out. That's a big change.

Is Spanking Respectful?

Situations arise when children engage in dangerous or unacceptable behaviors—a child climbs on a glass table, puts his hand near an oven burner, runs in the street after being told not to, or hits his infant brother. Many of these situations might be avoided in the first place. The glass table can be removed. The kitchen can be made off-limits by gating. A young child should not be allowed access to run in the street. Finally, he should be supervised more closely when with his baby brother. Gentleness can also be modeled.

Parents may consider slapping a child's hand or bottom, or spanking him in situations as these. I am against hitting or spanking a child, regardless of the circumstance. Spanking is disrespectful and unfair. Unfortunately, it's ingrained in many cultures.

Many parents feel justified in spanking because of the old phrase "Spare the rod and spoil the child." But when you hit a child he thinks hitting is normal and he is more likely to become a hitter. The child feels, "Just wait till I grow up, then I will . . ." Many people who were hit, in turn, hit their children, even if they don't believe in it. Unfortunately, it comes naturally. Hitting comes easily because children make us angry, upset, and tired. We are human, too.

If you think of the difference in size, strength, and capabilities between and child and a grown-up, you can see that hitting a child is unfair. I can understand the impulse. Even the best children get on the saintliest parents' nerves. However, spanking is not the way to discipline.

It may be difficult for you, the parent, to separate all these things in the heat of the situation: your own anger, the desire to discipline your child, and the memory of how your parents disciplined you. Try to slow down and ask yourself, "Would I consider hitting my child if I weren't angry?"

Even if spanking is done in the name of discipline, what kind of lesson are we teaching our children? If nothing else works, use violence? That might makes right? Isn't this the attitude we are trying to overcome in today's world? It is also hypocritical to tell your child not to hit other children if you hit him.

If we hit our children, we are teaching them that when you get bigger and stronger, it's okay to hit. Then they can hardly wait to get bigger and stronger. Shouldn't we be the models of more decent behavior? Remember, too, that your child's hands are his primary means of exploring. What is hitting his hands telling him?

Spanking may have the opposite effect from the one you desire. A child who is spanked may stop the behavior (hitting baby brother) but may become resentful or sneaky. Spanking may set off other undesirable behaviors. A child who is hit may hit other children or hit his baby brother when nobody is watching. I can understand how easily anybody can lose control, but I would never recommend spanking. There are healthier and more successful ways of disciplining children.

Let Your Child See That Actions Cause Consequences

I prefer to use cause/consequence as discipline, where the child's behavior has an effect on the consequence you provide. The consequence should be appropriate to the child's stage of readiness and understanding. Try to provide natural consequences, which relate to what the child did, rather than punitive ones, which are either unrelated or too harsh. An example is saying calmly to your toddler, "You didn't get ready to go to the park. You didn't come when I called you, so today we're not going."

This allows your child to see the effect of his actions. If he tosses his bunny out of his crib, leave the stuffed animal on the floor. If he continues throwing blocks at the window, take the blocks away. If he runs into the street, don't allow him to play in the yard for a time. (Of course, no very young child should play unsupervised in a yard that cannot be gated off.) If he gets too wild or out of control in his play, take your child out of it briefly, for a minute or so, so he can calm down. Sit with him and tell him why: "I want you to sit here for a minute and calm down." Taking him out of his play for a minute is different from a time-out in that it isn't done every time your child does something you don't like *and* it has a relation to what he did.

By using cause/consequence your child learns to be in charge of the consequences of his actions. His confidence is enhanced as he begins to take responsibility. During and after the consequence, let your child know that you are still on his side and still love him. Then forget about it. Don't remind your child of what he did.

A mother told me that her son went through a stage where he enjoyed ripping apart any book she gave him, even the heavy cardboard variety. The mother told her son that because he ripped up his books (the cause), she was taking them away from him (the consequence). She gave her son magazines to rip apart. Toddlers love pulling things apart, and especially enjoy the sound of paper tearing. After this, the mother told me, her child stopped ripping up his books because he wanted them back.

Actions do have consequences. Ideally, you want your child to understand how to behave. But you, the parent, are in charge and must follow through with the consequences when he does not.

Once your child learns your expectations, he begins to internalize the behavior you want, to take on your values and apply them to himself. This takes time to learn. Expectations and predictability support discipline.

Supporting Your Toddler's Language Development

As your child grows, he will become more sophisticated in expressing himself. The "goos" and "gahs" of the infant later become single-syllable words like "da" and "ba." Later, a child names the things he sees, like "dog" and "milk." He then learns to make phrases, such as "pick up" and "go out." Finally, he is able to speak in complete sentences, such as "I want the ball." There are one-word sentences like "out," which means "I want to go out." Parents usually understand these words. It's a joy for a parent to hear his child's language develop. Soon, parent and child carry on conversations, better understanding each other.

Don't worry if your child is not saying as many words as another child. Early language doesn't mean higher IQ. Children learn comprehensive language (understanding words) before expressive language (speaking). They first develop language inside. Einstein, who didn't speak until he was three, is proof that late speakers can be very smart. Learning language happens naturally in a home as a parent says, "Oh, you want to open the door."

It isn't necessary to teach a young child the ABC's or use teaching tools in order to help him speak. You don't need to teach him colors and numbers. Rather, talk to him using simple phrases about what you're doing, or events that are happening. "I'm tired. I'm going to lie down and rest," "I'm cutting up slices of apple for your snack," "Daddy's going outside," and "The baby's crying." In this way you help your child connect the event with the words.

You can also reflect on what your child, or other people, are doing or may be feeling: "The juice is cold," "You're picking up the big, red ball," and "Mommy's upset because she hurt her finger." When you do this, your child's—and other people's—actions are acknowledged and put into words. It also encourages your child to verbalize his feelings.

Why Is It Important for Your Child to Be Able to Talk about His Feelings?

Words give your child power. If he is encouraged to communicate his feelings with words and you are receptive to those feelings, your child may choose to speak up rather than act out with aggressive behavior such as pushing or hitting. He may not have to overuse negative behaviors if his feelings, expressed through words, draw attention. He will also feel better about himself. Doesn't everybody like to feel listened to and understood?

Tune in to your child's words. Each child has his own vocabulary, words he repeats. Repeat them back to him: "Dog. You want to pet the dog," "Truck. You see the truck," or "Juice? Do you want orange juice or apple juice?" Children naturally like to point and use a word to tell about what they see. You can also help him finish a word or phrase: If a child says "up," you can say, "You want me to pick you up," or if a child says "Daddy soo," you can say, "Yes, that's Daddy's shoe."

Ask your child simple questions that offer him choices: "Do you want a slice of apple or pear?" "Do you want your doll or your truck?" He will then have the opportunity to make a choice and verbalize it.

A child's words may seem nonsensical to a parent but have meaning to the child. Children's utterances are beginnings of concepts, feelings, and words. Even so-called gibberish has meaning.

Through listening you will understand your child's growing vocabulary. The examples above happen naturally, as your child's nonverbal communications such as gesturing and crying turn into a dialogue. Rather than teaching your child or expecting him to repeat words of your choice, just talk to him. Remember that children imitate what they hear. Be selective with your words.

Your Child and Fear

Fear is a common human emotion. Learning how to deal with it is crucial. Fear can be debilitating; it can also be overcome. But it cannot be avoided entirely. One of RIE's goals is to help children learn how to handle their fears. Children who are securely attached to their parents, allowed to develop at their own rate, and are given freedom to explore their safe environment have a better chance of dealing with their fears.

Always be open when your child says he is afraid. Never belittle him by saying, "There's nothing to be afraid of." Don't argue about fear. Listen to whatever your child wants to express. You don't always have to share the fear, but always be willing to listen. Refrain from saying, "That's silly. That monster under your bed doesn't exist," because it exists in your child's imagination at the time. You have to become a good listener. Later in life people pay huge amounts of money to therapists who don't do anything but listen. Perhaps you can avoid that by listening to him now.

Respect your child by letting him tell you what frightens him. Always acknowledge his feelings, even if there is no real danger. If your child is frightened by loud noises or a barking dog, you can say, "That dog is barking and it's loud. You seem upset." Hold him if he asks or gestures for you to do so. Sometimes children are more startled than hurt by falls during play. If your child falls and is upset, you can say, "You tripped and fell. Did that scare you?"

At times more intervention is needed. If your child is scared of the dark in his room at night, get him a night-light. If he is playing in the yard and becomes upset by the barking dog next door, take him inside. If he becomes frightened when stuck under a table or on top of a climbing structure he has scaled, offer him enough assistance so he can get himself out of the situation.

Nighttime Fears

What should you do if your child cries each time you say good night and leave his room at bedtime? Many children go through periods when they become fearful at nighttime. Sometimes the fear is about a specific thing like a tiger they saw at the zoo or a character in a book. Your child may be going through a period of separation anxiety, or perhaps a family pet has died. Nighttime fears often bubble up when your child lies in his bed and the lights go off. The darkness can propel his imagination.

Try to understand and accept your child's anxieties. If you can pinpoint what the fear is, talk about it. Explain to him in simple terms what you think he is able to understand. "Tigers live at the zoo. There are no tigers at our house. We have a kitty cat, don't we?" Accept that your child feels anxious or scared. Offer him alternatives like "Would you feel better if your teddy bear sleeps with you, or I put on the night-light, or leave the door open?" Tell him where you'll be. Avoid anxiety-provoking statements that might reinforce his anxieties, like "If you don't listen to Mommy, the devil will come and get you."

What should you do if your child wakes up in the middle of the night and cannot be comforted? When you're afraid, you want to be close to the people who protect you. If your child awakens in the middle of the night, go to his room and stay with him until he feels more secure. After a few minutes you may say, "Now we can all go back to sleep." Say good night and go back to your own bed. I believe that parents should have privacy. You can say, "Every Sunday morning (or whenever is acceptable to you), you can come into bed with us," so cuddling in your bed doesn't become a taboo. I think that the morning is the best time for a child to come into the parents' bed. Everybody's awake, and fears and anxieties are less.

Childhood fears, such as separation and stranger anxiety, are predictable. Some children are more sensitive to sights and sounds and become overstimulated or frightened more easily than others. Through observation you can begin to learn what your child's fears are. By being a patient and understanding listener, you can help your child deal with his fears.

If you are worried that your child's fears are excessive, you may want to seek professional help. Go first without your child to get insight into the problem.

Keep Up Your Bedtime Routine

Naptime and bedtime rituals help your child establish a good daily routine and keep sleep times predictable. This is especially important during the toddler years, when your child may test the bedtime limits, saying he doesn't want to go to bed, or repeatedly asks for another story or glass of water. If bed is at a consistent time and is an expected, predictable event and has been since he was born, your child will be less likely to fight it.

You may want to keep a special stuffed animal or blanket in your child's bed. Continue to create a calm, soothing atmosphere before bedtime. Illness, nighttime fears, and teething may cause night wakings, but these are usually temporary situations. Your child derives security from his routines, and over time, will begin to look forward to them.

When your child has a restless night and needs comfort, try sitting or lying on the floor next to his crib. Your presence may reassure him. Talk to him if you feel it's needed. Stay with him a little while until he's ready to settle down, then get up, say good night, and leave. This way he's in charge of when he lies down and goes back to sleep and may do so before you leave the room. If you remain with him without taking him out of the crib, you help him learn to go back to sleep on his own.

At this age your child may begin to climb out of his crib. When this happens, lower the crib rail so that if your child gets out, he won't hurt himself climbing down. Move any furniture, especially anything sharp-edged, away from the crib.

Your child's room should be completely safe so that if he gets out of his crib at night, he won't hurt himself. You can put a safety gate at your child's door, but this has to be started when he's very young so he gets used to it. You can also close his door. If you don't use a safety gate or close his door, or if he can open his door on his own, your child may start to visit you at night. If he seems all right and is not fearful or upset, gently take him back to his crib.

It may also be time to get him a bed, perhaps a mattress on the floor. Some parents leave the crib in the child's room for a time for security, even after a bed is introduced. Your child may want to go back into his crib on occasion.

Keep in mind that lack of sleep causes irritability in children. Help your toddler get enough sleep. Put him to bed before he gets overtired. An overtired child is more likely to fight sleep.

An Example of a Bedtime Routine

The following scenario shows how bedtime can be a cooperative effort. We revisit Geralynn, Greg, and Delanie:

> Delanie is sitting on the floor, playing with her toys after dinner.

Geralynn: "Delanie, in about five minutes it's going to be time to go upstairs and lie down."

A few minutes later, Delanie is looking at a book. She sets it down.

Geralynn: "Okay, Delanie, it looks like you're finished looking at your book. It's time for bed. Do you want to give Dad a kiss good night?"

After saying good night to Greg, Geralynn and Delanie go into Delanie's bedroom. Her bed is a mattress on the floor.

Geralynn: "I'm going to turn on the light. I can tell you had fun today playing with Taylor. I'm going to take off your dirty diaper. Lift your bottom so I can put the clean diaper underneath. You want to help with your diaper? Okay." (Pause) "You can move your hand now. I'm going to put on your undershirt and your jammies. Do you want me to scratch your back?"

Delanie: "Da!"

Geralynn: "Yes, the dog really likes that, doesn't she? I'm going to scratch your back for one minute, then we'll put your jammies on."

Delanie: "Yeah. Da."

Geralynn: "What? Oh, the lotion. We didn't put any on, did we? Where are you going to put it? On your tummy?"

Delanie laughs.

Geralynn: "And I'll do your back. Some for your arms, and your legs. You're putting lotion on your tummy. Now I'll scratch your back for one minute."

A minute later . . .

Geralynn: "Okay. Now it's time to put on your jammies. Which foot do you want to put in? Now this one. Which arm do you want to put in? (A moment later) "Your jammies are on."

They finish and Geralynn dims the light.

Geralynn: "I'm turning down the light and closing the blinds. It's time for your book now. You want to get *Goodnight Moon*? Where are you going to sit? Do you want to choose a place to sit or do you want me to choose one for you? Is that where you're going to sit? On my toes?"

Delanie: "Yeah."

Geralynn: (laughs) "You're kissing my toes. Now I want you to find a place to sit. Thank you." (She starts to read the book.) "I don't want you to tickle my foot right now. We can play tomorrow. Now it's time for bed."

Delanie: "Poop, poop."

Geralynn: "Do we need to check your diaper?" (Geralynn checks it.) "I think you just had gas. I'm going to finish the story. Where are you going to sit? Does that mean you want to sit on my lap?" (Geralynn finishes the story.)

Delanie: "Ah."

Geralynn: "Okay, I'll read it one more time, then it's time for bed." (Geralynn reads the story again.) "It's time to turn off the light now. Good night, light. Do you want me to hold you for one more minute? Okay." (She holds Delanie and then lays her in bed.) "You may hear noises tonight. They're just night noises. Lie down and rest your head. Goodnight, sweetheart." Geralynn closes the door and leaves the room. A few minutes later, Delanie starts to cry.

Geralynn: (calls upstairs) "I hear you, Delanie. I'll be up in a minute." (She goes back into Delanie's room.) "It's time to go to sleep. Do you want me to hold you for one more minute? Okay." (After a minute . . .) "I'll see you in the morning, sweetheart." (She goes out of the room and closes the door. Delanie goes to sleep.)

Note how Geralynn began by letting Delanie know that bedtime was coming so Delanie could anticipate it and cooperate. Geralynn follows the same routine each night with Delanie, which also encourages this. When Delanie got sidetracked, wanting to tease or play, Geralynn gently brought her back to the task at hand, preparing for bed. When Delanie had trouble settling down to sleep, Geralynn went back in and briefly reassured her and said good night. If Delanie had been going through a fearful period or expressed unusual anxiety, Geralynn would have spent more time with her, figuring out what they could do together to make Delanie feel more comfortable.

Keep your child's bedtime a predictable routine and he will learn to fall asleep.

Toddlers and Crying

By toddlerhood, crying has usually lessened. As children learn to talk, they are able to express their feelings and desires more clearly. A baby's greatest survival mechanism, the cry, is replaced by more sophisticated means of communication. Crying becomes more specific—typically reserved for when a child is hurt, tired, or angry.

Respect your child by responding to his cry. Responding may mean simply making eye contact. With a toddler, as with a young infant, allow your child to cry. Ask him why he's crying, and offer comfort if he wants it. Everybody, children included, benefits from a good, cleansing cry.

Whining Gets Your Attention

Your child can learn to use his cry in the form of a whine if he finds that doing so gets results. Every child goes through whining periods. Whining may take place when your child is uncomfortable about something. It can stem from tiredness, and perhaps frustration or even hunger. Most adults hate listening to whining, so it works as an attention-getter.

The best idea is to observe and listen to your child so that he will not need to get attention by whining. Be sure he is well rested and fed on a regular schedule. When your child does whine at you, the best response is to ignore it. You may ask your child to stop whining but it usually doesn't work. If you want to, you can tell your child how you feel about his whining.

Cynthia says, "I can acknowledge my children's feelings while at the same time being honest about my own by saying, 'I know you're really struggling with this but it's hard for me to listen to you when you're whining.' "

Your Toddler's Changing Eating Habits

Because toddlers go through so many bodily and emotional changes, they are prone to drastic changes in eating habits. A child who once ate heartily may pick at his food or refuse to eat at all. A child who once ate everything may only want certain foods, or want his food prepared in a particular way. He may insist upon having long strips of cheese, for example, and refuse the same kind of cheese cut into little squares, pushing them away and saying, "No!"

This is a normal part of a toddler's struggle for security and independence. Toddlers are learning to assert their wills. They are also becoming more active and may lose interest in eating because it may seem less exciting than exploring their environment. Never force your child to eat, no matter how little he consumes. Your child will eat if he's hungry. If you try to force food, mealtime can turn into a battleground. The goal for meals is not nourishment alone, but also to make eating a pleasurable experience.

As your toddler's eating habits change, you should maintain limits. If your child doesn't eat but throws his food or drink on the floor, you may tell him: "It looks like you're not hungry since you're throwing your food." Then remove the food. It is advisable to serve food on a floor that's easy to clean, as food often finds its way down there. Children always test the rules. If the rules are consistently enforced, your child will eventually learn to obey them.

Respect your child by offering him food and making sure that he eats as much as he wants. If he doesn't want large meals, offer him frequent snacks. If he chooses to eat a big breakfast and a small dinner, that's fine. Teething can also be an appetite suppressant, as sore gums make it difficult to chew.

Eating can become a cooperative effort because toddlers like to help with everything. You can encourage your child to use his spoon or drink from his cup. You can also let him enjoy the preparation process by allowing him to help peel his orange or pour juice into his cup, using a small, plastic pitcher.

It's best to offer your child two choices: juice or milk? Apple or pear? More than two choices can be overwhelming and confusing. Asking a yes or no question (Do you want something to drink?) often results in a "no" answer.

Parents often ask me when a child should sit at the table with the family. I tell them, "When he has table manners." This is about the same time your child fits comfortably into an adult chair, sitting at the "big" table. Until this time, I recommend that you continue to use a child-size table and chair.

Cynthia tells me,

> RIE has given me helpful tools to use at home in regard to eating. The little table and chair worked wonderfully with

> my girls. It was at their level so it was safer for them. I set their food out at mealtimes and they'd sit down. I served small portions so they could ask for more. I knew they were finished when they left the table. I was always clear whether they were hungry or wanted to play. I do the same now at the family table. When they're finished eating, they leave.

I remember a particular day in class when it was snack time. I told a little girl named Juliana she had to sit at the table in order to get her banana. Juliana placed the ball she was holding under her like a chair and sat on it, positioning herself perfectly at the table.

"That's called balancing," I said, smiling, and handed Juliana her piece of banana.

Juliana's mother said, "Juliana's has been testing me lately—running away from me when we go on walks, taking a bite of food and running away from the table."

"And she will do more," I answered. "She feels safe. If she were afraid of you, she wouldn't do it. It means she feels free and secure. She has developed basic trust. Remember, you have to choose your battles. The more she can get to you, the more she will. Is it worth a fight or not?"

"She gets up from the table when I do," said the mother.

"Why not stay seated with her?" I said.

Children learn good eating habits over time, and with parental guidance.

Your Teething Toddler

A child's canine teeth and molars typically come in during the toddler stage. Molars can be more painful than other erupting teeth because they are the largest. A teething child may begin, or continue, to wake at night. He may also lose his appetite. The most pain, judging from a child's reaction, usually comes just before teeth break through the gum. At these times, be available to your child, who may become feverish, cranky, or clingy. Try teething remedies such as massaging his gums or frozen juice pops. Hold your child if that is what he wants.

Ask For and Expect Cooperation in Caregiving Tasks

Caregiving tasks become more challenging during the toddler stage. Children want to dress themselves and help in every aspect of their care, saying "me help" or "want." The solution is to allow and encourage your child to help as much as he can.

If he wants to help with diapering, ask him to lift his bottom or hold the lotion. An effective way to give choices to your child is to ask, "Do you want to walk to the changing table or do you want me to carry you?" or "Do you want to hold the clean diaper or the cream?"

If your child strongly resists diapering, first check for a rash or other physical symptoms. His bottom may be sore and he might need a rash medication. If there is no detectable problem, wait a few minutes. Allow him transition time. If your child isn't forced to comply the moment you want him to do something, he may come around on his own. If you need to go, say, "Sorry, I can't wait any longer. If we had more time I would let you stay, but we have to leave. What shall we do? You have to get diapered." Diaper him as best you can, whether he's lying down, standing, or struggling. You can also say, "Soon you will be able to use the toilet and you won't need a diaper." Make toilet learning a desirable thing.

If your child wants to put on his sweater, give him a little assistance, if needed, to get started. Pull the sleeve over his hand and ask him to pull on the sweater. Let him put on his shoes and help with the lacing. At bath time, let him help by scrubbing himself with the washcloth or toweling himself off.

Remember to allow time. Children are slower than we are and need time to process what is asked of them. Then they can follow it up with an action. The tasks we take for granted, such as opening a door, buttoning a jacket, or picking up toys, are processes a child is learning. In class, I often repeat the magic word: *wait*.

There is another mantra you can use with your toddler, which acknowledges his feelings: "I know you want to . . . , but we are going to . . ."

Learning to Use the Toilet

Your child will eventually show interest in using the toilet. It may happen earlier if he has older siblings. Children want to fit in and do what other family members are doing. Learning to use the toilet should not be forced, nor should a child be pressured about it. All children learn to use the toilet sooner or later. There is no need to rush the process, which is complicated.

Your child must first be physically ready—be able to control the muscles necessary to hold in his bladder and bowel movements. He must be cognitively ready—be aware of what is expected of him. And he must be emotionally ready—be able to hold his urge until he sits on the toilet. The third factor is especially dependent on the personality of the child. Children perceive what comes out of their bodies as part of them, and may have a difficult time letting urine and feces go simply to conform to adult standards. They must also be willing to delay a bodily urge. Learning to use the toilet means learning to hold on and to let go. Abraham Maslow, founder of humanistic psychology in the 1940s, says that all of life is a conflict between holding on and letting go.

Children start showing interest in bodily functions in different ways. They may become curious about the toilet, announce when they have soiled their diapers, or say they need to "go potty."

When your child shows interest in using the toilet, observe him to see when he needs to. Observation is important in toilet learning because when you notice your child's urge, you may offer encouragement. When he presses his thighs together or squats, you can say, "It looks like you could go to the bathroom. Do you want to use your potty chair?" When in the bathroom you can say (about the toilet), "This is the place where Mommy and Daddy go to the bathroom [or whatever you call it]. You can either go here or use your potty chair when you need to."

Make a potty chair available if he wants to use it. Some children prefer sitting on a child-size toilet seat placed on the regular toilet seat. You will need to provide a little stepping stool up to the toilet. Some children prefer to sit on the toilet seat backward, facing the tank so they can grip the lid with their hands. Children may sit on the potty chair or toilet and "practice" for many months before they actually use it.

Encourage your child to use the potty chair or toilet if *he* shows an interest. Never force him. You may find that pressuring him will create greater resistance. If a child senses a parent's anxiety about toilet learning, a power struggle may ensue. You, the parent, can't win because there is no way to "make" your child use the toilet.

Just before your child learns to use the toilet, he may resist it strongly. You can say, "Whenever you are ready, the potty chair (or toilet) is here for you." Working with him when *he* is ready to make the step on his own supports his autonomy.

When you feel your child is ready, you may also offer him the choice of wearing diapers or underpants. This gives him more control of the situation. Remember that "accidents" are part of the process. Sometimes your child may not make it to the bathroom on time, or he may relieve his bladder as soon as he steps inside the bathroom door. Or a child may begin to use the toilet or potty chair and abruptly stop, realizing what he's given up. Be patient.

I recommend a helpful book about using the toilet by Alison Mack, called *Toilet Learning* (Little, Brown, 1978), which includes a picture-book section for your child.

A recent study, the first large-scale survey about toilet learning in the United States in the last thirty years, was recently published in the journal *Pediatrics*. The study's author, Dr. Bruce Taubman, an associate professor of pediatrics at the University of Pennsylvania, noted that children are getting toilet-trained at a later age than several decades ago. Four percent of children in the United States are fully toilet-trained by the time they're two, sixty percent by the time they're three, and eighty-eight percent by three and a half. At age four ninety-eight percent are fully trained. Dr. Taubman also noted that many children learned to urinate in the toilet while having difficulty making bowel movements there. He hypothesized that "kids pick up on the fact that feces are negative in our culture" (*Los Angeles Times*, January 14, 1997). Be careful not to convey a negative message.

Learning to use the toilet is a process that takes time. Rather than push or manipulate your child by giving him treats such as candy or a special reward for something that he will learn on his own, trust that he will learn it when he is ready. Respect is based on trust.

Sibling Rivalry

When there is more than one child in a family, competition between them is natural. A parent who was once the exclusive "property" of one child must now be shared by two or more. An excellent way for adults to understand sibling rivalry from a child's point of view is an example I mentioned in chapter 7 from *Siblings without Rivalry* by Adele Faber and Elaine Mazlish: A beautiful woman shows up at a family's home and announces to the wife that she is there to share the husband. In this case the wife feels like an older sibling. Children don't naturally like to share. It is a slow process, which they learn as they mature.

Sibling rivalry has always existed. It's universal. It's in the Bible—think of Cain and Abel. And younger children are teased by older ones, even if the older children are good and decent. Second children are okay in spite of being picked on. The first child sees the second child as an intruder. A first child frequently wants a sibling as a playmate, but if free to speak, would say, "Enough. Now go back where you came from." But they also love each other.

I recommend that you intervene minimally in disputes between siblings. If the age gap is large or a younger child might get hurt, more supervision is needed. The more they can work out on their own, the better. The family is a microcosm of life and its struggles. Close your eyes. The more you see and critique, the tougher it becomes, because then you make your children feel guilty. Guilt is not a good adviser. Whatever you do, one of the children will think it's unfair.

Sometimes your children need guidance. Don't allow them to hurt each other, but don't become the judge by always saying who was wrong and who was right. A parent should be an ally rather than a judge. If you intervene, say, "What else could you have done?" As much as possible, let them come up with the answers. Try to help your child *want* to do something rather than force him.

In class one day the topic of sibling rivalry came up. Michael's father said, "Our older daughter is jealous of Michael."

I said, "For the older one, it's a feeling of being dethroned. Some older children suffer all their lives from this feeling. The second or third child never had the opportunity of being the only child because he is born into a family."

"And Michael gets picked on," the father added.

"Second children are picked on by their older siblings," I told him. "But they survive. They become a little more prepared for life. You learn all your social skills, good and bad, within the family."

Cynthia says, "I encourage my daughters to talk to each other. I say to Heidi, 'I can see you're angry. If something's bothering you, tell your sister.' I ask them to acknowledge their feelings to each other. They've learned to speak up and say, 'I'm angry' or 'I don't like that.' "

Making a big deal out of your children's disputes can make the situation worse. The less you interfere and the more you accept that it's part of family life, the better. It's normal and predictable that siblings will have disputes.

You Don't Have to Be Perfect

No matter how loving the parent, or how much patience he possesses, mistakes happen. Parenting is a learning process. The road is full of wrong turns. Many parents feel guilty if they don't show enough patience. This often happens when they are tired or on the phone. That's all part of life. It doesn't hurt your child. Rather, it prepares him for life. Human beings, by nature, are flawed. Your occasional missteps are part of being human.

If children are surrounded by love and gentleness, and accepted as they are, they learn resilience. Forgive yourselves for your mistakes; love for your child will outweigh them. Guilt can be harmful.

I'll share with you a Hungarian saying. Babies, before they are born, look down from the clouds and say, "I want these two people to be my parents."

Respect yourself, accept your mistakes, and forgive yourself for not being perfect. This will help you be more forgiving of your child's mistakes. And he may later learn to be more forgiving of his own. When he is old enough to understand, he will appreciate that you accepted him for who he is. After all, "he chose you."

RIE Doesn't End at Two

The RIE philosophy focuses on the relationship between parent and child during the first two years. But RIE's influence doesn't end here. A good beginning sets the stage for how one handles later life situations, for both children and parents. If you begin by learning to accept your child as he is, to communicate with him, and to encourage his cooperation and independence, you will influence him in a positive way. This foundation supports your child's sense of self. It also supports your trust in him.

As your child grows beyond toddlerhood through childhood and adolescence, many new stages unfold. The mutual trust that you and your child have hopefully formed can become the foundation for your child's emerging autonomy. Your growing child will learn new ways of communicating and cooperating with you. Just as you observed your baby to understand him better, so you can continue to be available to your child over the years to come—still observing, still listening, still trusting.

A respectful beginning is an investment in the future of the relationship between your child and you, your child and others, and in your child's exploration of the world. A RIE beginning helps to develop a competent, confident child.

References

Bond, Lynne A., ed. *Facilitating Infant and Early Childhood Development.* Hanover, N.H.: University Press of New England, 1982.

Brazelton, T. Berry. *Touchpoints.* Reading, Mass.: Addison-Wesley, 1992.

Brown, Margaret Wise. *Goodnight Moon.* New York: HarperCollins, 1949.

Elkind, David. *The Hurried Child: Growing Up Too Fast Too Soon.* Reading, Mass.: Addison-Wesley, 1987.

Erikson, Erik H. *Identity and the Life Cycle.* New York: Norton, 1980.

Faber, Adele, and Elaine Mazlish. *Siblings without Rivalry.* New York: Norton, 1987.

Ferber, Richard. *Solve Your Child's Sleep Problems.* New York: Fireside, 1986.

Klein, Josephine. *Our Needs for Others.* London and New York: Tavistock Publications, 1987.

Mack, Alison. *Toilet Learning.* New York: Little, Brown, 1983.

Pikler, Emmi. *Peaceful Babies—Contented Mothers.* Freiberg, Germany: Herder/Verlag, 1992 (translated from the German *Friedliche Babys-zufriedene Mutter,* first published in Hungary in 1940 as *Mit tud mar a baba?*).

Reef, Katherine. *Albert Einstein, Scientist of the Twentieth Century.* Minneapolis, Minn.: Dillon Press, 1991.

Rousseau, Jean-Jacques. *Émile.* New York: E. P. Dutton, 1911.

Sammons, William A. H. *The Self-Calmed Baby.* New York: Little, Brown, 1989.

Wachs, Theodore D. *Early Experience and Human Development.* New York: Plenum Press, 1982.

RIE Materials Available

◐ Back issues of *Educaring*.

◐ "RIE for Parents and Caregivers" audiotape (English/Spanish).

◐ "On Their Own with Our Help," a fourteen-minute videotape in which Magda Gerber demonstrates selective intervention—when to intervene with young children and more important, when not to.

◐ "See How They Move," a half-hour videotape that celebrates natural gross motor development of infants and toddlers.

◐ "Seeing Infants with New Eyes," a half-hour videodocumentary that combines a portrait of Magda Gerber with a presentation of her unique philosophy on raising autonomous infants.

◐ "The Way We See Them," a fourteen-minute videotape in which watching infants interact and learn helps viewers see firsthand the value of careful observation.

For more information about RIE certification training, contact the RIE office at:

Phone: (323) 663-5330   Fax: (323) 663-5586

or write:

Resources for Infant Educarers

1548 Murray Circle

Los Angeles, CA 90026

Website: http//:www.rie.org/baby.htm or http//:www.rie.org

Index

CPSIA information can be obtained at www.ICGtesting.com
Printed in the USA
BVOW02s1422200515

401200BV00025B/414/P

9 781118 158791